The VTK User's Guide
Updated for version 4.0

Edited by: William J. Schroeder.

Contributors:
Lisa S. Avila
Sebastien Barre
Berk Geveci
Amy Henderson
William A. Hoffman
C. Charles Law
Kenneth M. Martin
William J. Schroeder
Ana Wanzelak

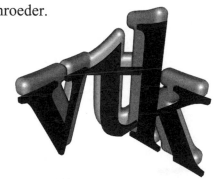

ISBN 1-930934-06-8

Kitware, Inc.
http://www.kitware.com
kitware@kitware.com

Contents

Part II   Learn VTK By Example

Part I

An Introduction to VTK

## Chapter 1

Welcome

Welcome to the *Visualization Toolkit (VTK) User's Guide*. This book has been updated for VTK 4.0 and later versions of the *Visualization Toolkit* software.

VTK is an open-source, object-oriented software system for computer graphics, visualization, and image processing. Although it is large and complex, VTK is designed to be easy to use once you learn about its basic object-oriented design and implementation methodology. The purpose of this *User's Guide* is to help you learn this methodology, plus familiarize you with a variety of important VTK classes.

VTK is a large system. As a result, it is not possible to completely document all VTK objects and their methods in this guide. Instead, this guide will introduce you to important system concepts and lead you up the learning curve as fast and efficiently as possible. Once you master the basics, we suggest that you take advantage of the many resources available from the community of VTK users (see "Additional Resources" on page 4).

The *Visualization Toolkit* is an open-source code system. What this means is that dozens and perhaps hundreds of generous developers and users like you have contributed to the system. If you find VTK a useful tool, we encourage you to contribute bug fixes, algorithms, ideas, and/or applications back to the community. (See "How To Contribute Code" on page 204 for more information.) You can also support commercial firms such as Kitware to develop and add new features and tools.

1.1 Organization

This manual is divided into three parts, each of which is further divided into several stand-alone chapters. Part I is a general introduction to VTK, including—in the next chapter—a description of how to install the *Visualization Toolkit* on your computer. This includes installing pre-compiled libraries and executables, or compiling the software from the source code. Part I also introduces basic system concepts including an overview of the system architecture, and how to build applications in the C++, Tcl, Java, and Python programming languages. In some ways Part II is the heart of *User's Guide*, since dozens of examples are used to illustrate important system features. Part III is for the advanced VTK user. If you are a developer, Part III explains how to create your own classes, extend the system, and interface to various windowing and GUI systems. Chapter 14 contains simplified object diagrams that provide an overview of the relationship of VTK objects, a summary list of filters, and a description of VTK file formats for reading and writing your own data. Chapter 15 describes the contents of the CD-ROM. And finally, the index is a handy tool for random access into the *User's Guide*.

1.2 How To Use VTK

There are two broad categories of users of VTK. First are class developers, who create classes in C++. Second, application developers use the C++ class library to build turn-key applications. Class developers must be proficient in C++, and if you are extending or modifying VTK, you must also be familiar with VTK's internal structures and design (material covered in Part III). Application developers may or may not use C++, since the compiled C++ class library has been "wrapped" with the interpreted languages Tcl, Python, Visual Basic, and Java. However, as an application developer you must know something about the external interface to the VTK objects, and the relationships between them.

The key to using VTK is becoming familiar with its palette of objects and the ways of combining them. If you are a new *Visualization Toolkit* user, begin by installing the software. If you are a class developer, you'll want to install the source code and then compile it. Application developers may only need the precompiled binaries and executables. We recommend that you learn the system by studying the examples (if you are an application developer) and then studying the source code (if you are a class developer). Start by reading Chapters 3, which provides an overview of some of the key concepts in the system, and then review the examples in Part II. You may also wish to run the dozens of examples distributed with the source code found in the directory VTK/Examples. (Please see the file VTK/Examples/README.txt for a description of the examples contained in the various subdirectories.) There are also several hundred tests found in the source distribution; such as those found in VTK/Graphics/Testing/Tcl and VTK/Graphics/Testing/Cxx, most of which are undocumented testing scripts. However, they may be useful to see how classes are used together in VTK.

1.3 Additional Resources

For more information about the *Visualization Toolkit* we recommend the following resources.

- The text *The Visualization Toolkit An Object-Oriented Approach to 3D Graphics (Second Edition)*. This book goes into detail about many of the algorithms, data structures, and system issues found in VTK. The text is published by Prentice Hall and available from `amazon.com`, local book stores such as Barnes & Noble or Border's, or from Prentice Hall directly. ISBN 0-13-954694-4, 646 pages, 40 color pages, hard bound, with CD-ROM.

- The Web pages `http://public.kitware.com/` contain pointers to many other resources such as on-line manual pages, a FAQ, and an archive of the `vtkusers` mailing list (see below). In particular, the Doxygen manual pages are absolutely wonderful. Although they are available on the companion VTK CD, you can also view them on-line at `http://public.kitware.com/VTK/doc/nightly/html`.

- Many other VTK users and developers also maintain Web pages. One recommended site is Sebastien Barre's links to VTK resources `http://www.barre.nom.fr/vtk/links.html`.

- The `vtkusers` mailing list allows users and developers to ask questions and receive answers; post updates, bug fixes, and improvements; and offer suggestions for improving the system. There are instructions at `http://public.kitware.com/mailman/listinfo/vtkusers` describing how to join this list.

- Commercial support and consulting are available from Kitware at `http://www.kitware.com`. Kitware also sells and supports commercial products built with VTK including VolView (volume rendering/image processing), *Acti*Viz for Microsoft Visual Basic/COM/ActiveX support, and the GoFly analysis tool for complex mechanical systems. See the Web pages for terms and pricing.

As a last resort, you can e-mail Kitware at `kitware@kitware.com`. We will answer questions as time and resources permit.

## Chapter 2

Installation

This chapter describes the steps required to install VTK on your computer system. The overall difficulty of this process depends on several factors. If you are developing using the precompiled, interpreted executables and libraries (e.g., Tcl), the installation is painless and fast. On the other hand, if you are compiling the VTK source code and building your own libraries, expect to spend one-half hour on faster, multi-processor systems, and several hours on slower, memory limited systems. Also, the installation depends on how many interpreted languages you wrap around the VTK C++ core, and your system configuration.

You may wish to refer to "System Architecture" on page 19 for an overview of the VTK architecture—this may make the compile process easier to follow. Also, if you run into trouble, you can contact the vtkusers list (see "Additional Resources" on page 4).

2.1 Overview

Installing VTK on your computer can range from the easy to difficult, depending on the specifics of your configuration. A simple PC binary installation might take less than a minute. A full source code compilation can take several hours. For some unfortunate people it has taken many days and considerable frustration. This chapter will help prevent you from falling into this category. Carefully following the instructions in this chapter should result in a successful installation of VTK with a minimal amount of effort.

The chapter is divided into two sections based on the type of operating system that you are installing on: either Windows or UNIX (for Macintosh OSX or Linux, follow the UNIX instructions). You only need to read the appropriate section for your installation. The *Visualization Toolkit* does not run on older versions of Windows such as Windows 3.1. It also does not run on any Macintosh OS older than OSX.

2.2 Installing VTK on Windows 9x/NT/ME/2000/XP

Under Windows there are two types of installations. The first is an binary/executable installation that lets you do development in C++, Java, Tcl, and/or Python by compiling and linking against pre-compiled libraries (C++), or running pre-compiled executables (e.g. Java, Tcl, or Python). The second type is a full source code installation requiring you to compile the VTK source code (to generate C++ libraries) and VTK wrapper code (to generate Java, Tcl, and Python executables). Of the two types of installations, the binary installation is much easier, and is recommended. The source code installation has the advantage that you can monitor, debug, and modify VTK code—which is probably what you want if you are a class developer. Note, however, that even if you choose the binary installation, you can still extend VTK in a variety of ways—creating your own class (see "Writing A VTK Class: An Overview" on page 208), using run-time programmable filters (see "Programmable Filters" on page 292), and replacing VTK classes at run-time with your own versions of the class (see "Object Factories" on page 211).

Binary Installation

To install the VTK libraries and executables, run `setup.exe`, which is located on the included CD ROM. (These instructions assume installation from the CD. Minor differences exist if you download from the web.) There are a few ways to do this. The easiest is to double click on the `My Computer` icon on your windows desktop. A window will appear containing icons for your hard drive, CD, and floppy, among others devices. Double click on the CD icon and you should get a window with a number of file icons in it. Double click on the `setup` or `setup.exe` icon and the VTK installation process will start, bringing up a little installation GUI something like that shown in **Figure 2–1**.

The first thing you'll need to decide is what parts of VTK you want to install. The binary installation process is packaged into five parts, as shown below.

1. `vtk40Core` — This part contains the VTK DLL for Windows 9x/NT/ME/2000/XP.
2. `vtk40Cpp` — This part contains include files and libraries for C++ development under Microsoft Visual C++ (version 6.0).
3. `vtk40Tcl` — This part contains the libraries and DLLs for Tcl.
4. `vtk40Java` — This part contains the libraries and DLLs for Java.

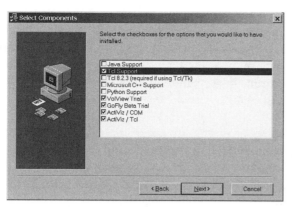

Figure 2–1 The VTK installation wizard for Windows 9x/NT /ME/2000/XP systems. Select the VTK components that you wish installed, and then proceed according to the directions given. You can use the same approach to install nightly or other releases found on the VTK home page http://public.kitware.com/VTK. Note that you also have the choice to install 30-day trial versions of ActiViz and VolView, commercial products available from Kitware.

5. `vtk40Python` — This part contains the libraries and DLLs for Python.

6. `CMake` - This part contains the source and Windows 9x/NT/ME/2000/XP binaries for CMake, a tool used to build VTK from source.

Depending on what you plan on doing with VTK, you'll want to install anywhere from two to five parts (`vtk40Core` should always be installed). For example, if you're doing C++ development, install `vtk40Core` and `vtk40Cpp`. If you're creating Tcl applications, you'll want to install `vtk40Tcl`; similarly for Java and Python. After you choose which parts you wish to install, answer the installation questions that follow (location of installation, etc.). If you are installing onto Windows98 or WindowsME/2000/XP then you should select Windows NT when prompted, not Windows95.

If you have installed Tcl, there should be a `vtk` option under your `Start/Programs` submenu. You can then run the examples in the installation directory, or you can also run the Tcl examples off of the CD ROM. To do this, just navigate to the CD ROM as before using either the Windows Explorer or `My Computer`. On the CD ROM in the VTK folder (`vtk-src-windows`), you will see a folder called `Examples`. Under the `Examples` folder, there are folders such as `GUI`, `MangledMesa` and `Parallel`; each of those folders will have a sub folder called `Tcl` that contains various Tcl examples. In addition to the `Examples` folder, there are library folders like `Graphics`, `Imaging`, and `Filtering`. Each of these folders contains a `Testing/Tcl` sub folder containing the regression tests for VTK. Try running any example by double clicking on the Tcl file. When you double click on a Tcl file (`.tcl` extension) for the first time, a dialog box may appear asking you what to use to open the file. This means that you need to create an association between Tcl files and an executable to run them. If this happens, click the `Other` button on the dialog. A new dialog will appear. Use this dialog to go to the directory where you installed VTK. Normally this is C:\Program Files\vtk (or a similar variation, e.g., vtk40 or even possibly Visualization Toolkit). In there you should see a bin folder which in turn contains a program called vtk. Double click on vtk and then select the Ok button on the original dialog. Your example should then run. In the future, double clicking on any Tcl scripts will automatically begin execution of vtk.

For best results on a PC, make sure the display setting are set to more than 256 colors. This can be done by going to the Start menu, selecting the Settings/Control Panel option. A window will appear with about twenty icons in it. Double click on the Display icon which will bring up another dialog with a Settings tab. Select that tab and then adjust the color palette to some value more than 256 colors. Click on the Ok button and then follow any additional instructions. You might have to restart your machine at this point.

That completes the binary installation process for Windows. In Chapter 3 we'll go into more detail on how to write your own C++, Tcl, Java and Python applications.

Source Code Installation

To develop C++ applications and extend VTK, you will need to do a source code installation. This is more challenging and will tie up your machine for a few hours as it compiles VTK. First you need to make sure your machine is capable of building a VTK source code release. You must be running Windows95, Windows98, Windows ME, Windows NT 4.0, Windows 2000 or Windows XP. You will need a C++ compiler installed on your machine. The instructions in this guide are oriented towards Microsoft Visual C++ Version 6.0 or Microsoft Visual C++ .NET which work well with VTK. We also support (to a lesser degree) the Borland C++ compiler. If you have not installed a C++ compiler, then you should do this first.

The next issue to consider is what additional tools you plan to use. If you plan to do development in Java then you must download and install the Java JDK which is available from Sun Microsystems at http://www.java.sun.com. If you plan on using Tcl/Tk and you are not using Microsoft Visual C++, then you will need to download and build the source code version of Tcl/Tk from http://www.scriptics.com. (Note: download Tcl/Tk version 8.3.2.)

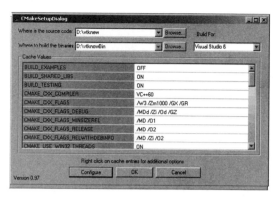

Figure 2–2 CMake is used to generate projects, makefiles, or workspaces for different compilers and operating systems. CMake is cross-platform, and on Windows, runs with a GUI that allows you to easily set compile flags. These flags can be set by left-mouse clicking in the build flag value.

Copying the Source Code. The VTK CD ROM comes with a complete copy of the source code stored in the VTK folder. If you don't plan on modifying the source code or creating your own classes then you can leave the source code on the CD ROM. Otherwise, we suggest that you copy the VTK-src-windows folder from the CD onto your hard disk. This has the added benefit that it will improve your compile time. (Be careful;: using the standard copying tools code on a Windows system from a CD will result in write-protected files. You may wish to use the DOS xcopy command or Unix tools such as Cygwin.)

Installing CMake. To compile VTK, you will first need to install a program called CMake. CMake is an open source, cross platform build tool (http://public.kit-ware.com/CMake). The use of CMake allows VTK to be configured and built on a variety of machines using the same source tree and build files. You can obtain CMake from http://public.kitware.com/CMake/HTML/Download.html. For Microsoft and Borland compilers there is a pre-compiled binary that you can download and install, which is the preferred installation method.

Running CMake. After you have setup your C++ compiler, installed CMake, and installed any additional packages such as Tcl, Java, and Python, you are ready to run CMake. To run CMake, there should be a CMake entry in the Start menu under Pro-grams->CMake->CMakeSetup. The CMakeSetup.exe interface (**Figure 2–2**) is a simple interface that allows you to customize the build to your particular machine and desired options for VTK. First you must tell CMakeSetup where the source tree for VTK is located and where you want to put the VTK binaries (these are generated as a result of compilation of the source code). You can specify those directories with the Browse buttons or by typing in the paths manually. The next step is to choose the build system that you are going to use (Microsoft Visual Studio 6, Microsoft Visual Studio .NET or Borland). Once the source, binary and build system have been selected, you should click on the Configure button. This will fill the CMakeSetup GUI with a list of variables and values found in the CMake cache. When first run, all the variables will be colored red. The red indicates that the cache entry was generated or changed during the previous configure step.

At this point, you can customize your VTK build. For example, if you want to enable the Tcl wrapping feature of VTK, scroll down in the cache values editor to the entry VTK_WRAP_TCL, and click on the value to toggle it from NO to YES. After that, click the Configure button again. This will cause most of the values to change to gray, and any new values to appear in red. If you installed Tcl/Tk from binary, none of the new values should have NOTFOUND as values, if they do, you will have to specify those paths manually with the CMake interface. To set any value in the CMake interface, you click to the right of the variable where the value is displayed. Depending on the type of variable, there may be a file chooser, edit box or pull down that will allow you to edit the value.

These are some important cache values for VTK are:

- BUILD_SHARED_LIBS — If this Boolean value is set to yes, then DLLs or shared libraries will be built. If it is no, then static libraries will be built. The default is static libraries. The static libraries are somewhat easier to work with, since they do not need to be in your path when executables are run. The executables will be self-contained. This is preferred for distribution of VTK based applications.

- VTK_WRAP_TCL — This determines if Tcl wrapping will be built.

- VTK_WRAP_PYTHON — This determines if Python wrapping will be built.

- VTK_WRAP_JAVA — This determines if Java wrapping will be built.

To get on-line help for any variable in CMake, simply click right over the value and select "Help for Cache Entry". Most of the defaults should be correct.

Continue to click on Configure until there are no longer any red values and you are happy with all of the values. At this point, you can click the OK button. This will cause CMake to write out the build files for the build type selected. For Microsoft, a project file will be located in the binary path you selected. Simply load this project file VTK.dsw into Visual Studio, and select the configuration you want to build in the Build->Set Active Configuration menu of Visual Studio. You will have the choice of Debug, Release, MinsizeRel (minimum size release), and RelWithDebInfo (release with debug information). You can select the ALL_BUILD project, and compile it as you would any other

Visual Studio project. For Borland, makefiles are generated, and you have to use the command line make supplied with that compiler. The makefiles are located in the binary directory you specified.

Once VTK has been built all libraries and executables produced will be located in the binary directory you specified to CMake in a sub-folder called bin (unless you changed the EXECUTABLE_OUTPUT_PATH, or LIBRARY_OUTPUT_PATH variables in CMake.

(**Note:** Do not use the MSVC++ "Rebuild All" menu selection to rebuild the source code. This deletes all CMakeLists.txt files which are then automatically regenerated as part of the build process. MSVC will then try reloading them and an error will result. Instead, to rebuild everything, remove your VTK binary directory, rerun CMake, and then rebuild.)

Once VTK has been built, you need to let Windows know where to find the DLLs, if you turned on BUILD_SHARED_LIBS. There are a couple ways to do this. First you can simply copy the resulting DLLs into a directory Windows normally checks such as Windows/ System or Winnt/System. The other choice is to modify your PATH environment variable to include the directories where the libraries are stored. If you decide to copy the DLLs and executables, you will need to copy all the files in the bin/selected con- figuration/ directory (where selected configuration is the build configuration that you chose earlier).

If you choose not to copy the DLLs, then you will need to edit your PATH environment variable. Under Windows95 and Windows98 you can do this using sysedit to add a line to the autoexec.bat file. Four examples are given below that correspond to the four different configurations listed earlier. All four examples assume that you build VTK in C:\vtkbin.

1. PATH=C:\vtkbin\bin\Debug
2. PATH=C:\vtkbin\bin\Release
3. PATH=C:\vtkbin\bin\MisizeRel
4. PATH=C:\vtkbin\bin\RelWithDebInfo

The same idea can be used in Windows NT/ME/2000/XP except that it should be done by right clicking on the My Computer icon. Select the Properties option and a dialog should pop up. Select the Environment tab (it may be found under the Advanced tab). Either modify or add a PATH environment variable with the path as described above. If a

PATH variable already exists, add the VTK paths to the front of it. For example, if the original path was

```
C:\winnt\system;C:\some\other=dir;%PATH%
```

change it to

```
C:\vtkbin\bin\Debug; C:\winnt\system;C:\some\other=dir;%PATH%
```

If you've made it this far, you've successfully built VTK on a PC. It can be a challenging process, partly due to limitations in the current compilers, and partly due to the size and complexity of the software. Please pay careful attention to the instructions given earlier. If you do run into problems, you may wish to join the vtkusers mailing list (see "Additional Resources" on page 4) and ask for help there. Commercial support is also available from Kitware.

2.3 Installing VTK On Unix Systems

There are a wide variety of flavors of Unix systems. As a result you will have to compile the VTK source code to build binaries and executables.

Source Code Installation

This section will walk you through the steps required to build VTK on a UNIX system. Unlike the PC, pre-compiled libraries and executables are not available for most Unix systems, so it's likely that you'll have to compile VTK yourself. (Note: check the vtkusers list and other resources as described in "Additional Resources" on page 4—some users maintain binaries on the Web.) Typically, it is a fairly simple process and it should take about one to four hours depending on the size of your machine. (High-end, large-memory multi-processor machines using parallel builds can build the C++ and Tcl libraries and executables in under 10 minutes!) Most of this time is spent waiting for the computer to compile the source code. Only about 10-30 minutes of your time will be required. The first step is to make sure you have the necessary resources to build VTK. To be safe, you will need about 300 megabytes of disk space. On some systems, such as the SGI, you may need more space, especially if compiling a debug version of VTK. You will also need a C++ compiler since VTK is written in C++. Typically the C++ compiler will be called CC, g++, or ACC. If you are not sure that you have a C++ compiler, check with your support staff.

If you are planning to use VTK with Tcl/Tk, Python, or Java, then you will first need to download and install those packages. The Java JDK is available from Sun Microsystems at `http://www.java.sun.com`. If you plan on using Tcl/Tk then you will need to download and build the source code version of Tcl/Tk from `http://www.scriptics.com`. Do not download the pre-compiled version of Tcl/Tk as the binary files will not work with VTK. Python can be downloaded from `http://www.python.org`. Follow the instructions in these packages to build them.

Next, we recommend that you copy the VTK source code from the CD ROM onto your hard disk. Typically, a UNIX command like

```
/bin/cp -r /Your/CDROM/vtkunix /yourdisk/vtk
```

is used. Now you need to decide if you are doing an in-place build. An in-place build puts the object files into the same directory as the source code. If you do not have gmake (GNU make) installed on your computer, you will need to do an in-place build. If you have gmake and will be building VTK for a few different types of machines, you can choose to do a multiple architecture build. Instructions for the in-place build are provided below, followed by instructions for a multiple architecture build.

Running CMake

For Unix, VTK uses CMake for the build process just like in the windows environment (see "Running CMake" on page 11). However, there are no pre-compiled binaries for CMake. So, to build VTK, you will first have to build and install CMake. In addition, CMake is typically not run from a GUI on UNIX platforms. If you want a GUI for CMake on UNIX, you will need to install FLTK prior to building CMake. To build and install CMake, simply untar the sources into a directory, and then run:

```
./configure
make install
```

If you do not have root privileges, you can skip the install target, and just type make. The command line CMake executable will be located at CMake/Source/cmake.

To run CMake on Unix, you use the command line interface to CMake. If you installed FLTK, there will be a GUI version in CMake/Source/CMakeSetup. However, these instructions are for the command line interface, see the Windows installation for information about the GUI version.

It is a good idea to tell CMake which C++ and C compilers you want to use. On most systems, you can set the information this way:

```
setenv CXX /your/c++/compiler
setenv CC /your/c/compiler
```

or

```
export CXX=/your/c++/compiler
export CC=/your/c/compiler
```

Otherwise CMake will default to the GNU compiler (gcc). Once you've done this, run CMake in the source directory simply as

```
cmake
```

(This is called an in-place build because you are generating object code and binaries in the VTK source directory. To support multiple platforms, or place binaries in a separate directories, see "Building VTK On Multiple Platforms" on page 17

UNIX developers familiar with configure scripts will notice that CMake and configure are similar in their functionality. However, configure takes command line arguments to control the generation of makefiles. CMake is controlled from its CMakeCache.txt file. To modify the operation of CMake, edit this file as necessary, keeping in mind that every time you modify CMakeCache.txt you need to rerun CMake.

Customizing the Build. Once you run CMake, it will create a file call CMake-Cache.txt that will contain all of the information that CMake could figure out about your system. It is a good idea to look at the contents of this file and make sure CMake was able to find important things like your OpenGL library. (Note: the CMake process is iterative. After you run it the first time, you change files in CMakeCache.txt and rerun until no changes are made.) If you want to build one of the wrapped languages like Tcl or Python, you will have to turn on VTK_USE_TCL in the cache file. Then re-run CMake. This will cause your cache to be filled with more values, and you should check the cache to make sure it found the correct Tcl installation you wanted to use. Each time you edit the cache, you should re-run CMake. Note, after the first run, it is no longer necessary to specify a compiler to CMake, and CMake can be run from `make`, with the command: `make rebuild_cache`. When you are done editing the `CMakeCache.txt` file, all your makefiles should be generated and VTK is ready to build.

Compiling the Source Code

Once CMake has completed running, you can type `make` (or `gmake`, if you are using GNU make) and VTK should compile. Some make utilities support parallel builds (e.g., `gmake` with the `-j` option). Use parallel make if possible, even if on a single processor system, because usually the process is IO bound and the processor can handle multiple compiles. If you do run into problems, you may wish to join the `vtkusers` mailing list (see "Additional Resources" on page 4) and ask for help there. Commercial support is also available from Kitware.

Building VTK On Multiple Platforms

If you are planning to build VTK for multiple architectures then you can either make a copy of the entire VTK tree for each architecture and follow the instructions above; or, if you have `gmake`, you can have one copy of the VTK source tree and compile it in a different manner. Instead of running CMake in the VTK source directory, create a new directory where you have some free disk space (not in the VTK tree), such as `vtk-solaris`. Change directory (`cd`) into this directory and then run CMake similar to the following example:

```
cd /yourdisk
ls      (output is: vtk vtk-solaris vtk-sgi)
cd vtk-solaris
cmake ../vtk
```

This will create makefiles and a `CMakeCache.txt` file in the `vtk-solaris` directory. Then you can edit `CMakeCache.txt` and `make rebuild_cache` until the values are correct as you did for the in-place build. Note: It is possible to pre-load the cache for CMake. To do this, you can take some important values that CMake can not figure out on its own, like the path to your Tcl installation, and create a `CMakeCache.txt` file in your build directory before running CMake. CMake will use those values and add more values to the cache file as needed.

Installing VTK

Now that VTK has been built, the executables and libraries will be located in the build directory, in the sub-directory `bin/`. If you plan to share the build with more than one developer on the UNIX system, it is often a good idea to run the make install command. This will install VTK into `/usr/local`, unless you changed the cache value `CMAKE_INSTALL_PREFIX` to another location. Running make install will copy all the files you need to compile and run VTK into a directory that more people can use.

This concludes the build and installation guide for VTK under UNIX. In Chapter 3 more details will be provided on how to run examples and create your own applications.

System Overview

The purpose of this chapter is to provide you with an overview of the *Visualization Toolkit* system, and to show you the basic information you'll need to create applications in C++, Java, Tcl, and Python. We begin by introducing basic system concepts and object model abstractions. We close the chapter by demonstrating these concepts, and describing what you'll need to know to build applications.

3.1 System Architecture

The *Visualization Toolkit* consists of two basic subsystems: a compiled C++ class library, and an "interpreted" wrapper layer that lets you manipulate the compiled classes using the languages Java, Tcl, and Python. See **Figure 3–1**.

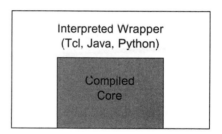

The advantage of this architecture is that you can build efficient (in both CPU and memory) algorithms in the compiled language C++, and retain the rapid code development features of interpreted languages (avoidance of compile/link cycle,

Figure 3–1 The Visualization Toolkit consists of a compiled (C++) core wrapped with various interpreted languages (Java, Tcl, Python).

simple but powerful tools, and access to GUI tools). Of course, for those proficient in C++ and who have the tools to do so, applications can be built entirely in C++.

The *Visualization Toolkit* is an object-oriented system. The key to using VTK effectively is to develop a good understanding of the underlying object models. Doing so will remove much of the mystery surrounding the use of the hundreds of objects in the system. With this understanding in place it's much easier to combine objects to build applications. You'll also need to know something about the capabilities of the many objects in the system; this only comes with reviewing code examples and man pages. In this User's Guide, we've tried to provide you with useful combinations of VTK objects that you can adapt to your own applications.

In the remainder of this section, we will review the two object models that make up the *Visualization Toolkit*: the graphics model and the visualization model. These sections are fairly high-level—we recommend that you augment this reading with a review of the examples, either those in this chapter, in the next chapter, or by executing the hundreds of examples available in the VTK source distribution.

The Graphics Model

The VTK graphics model consists of the following core objects. (Note: this is not an exhaustive list of all objects, just the ones you'll use most often.)

- vtkActor, vtkActor2D, vtkVolume—subclasses of vtkProp and/or vtkProp3D.
- vtkLight
- vtkCamera
- vtkProperty, vtkProperty2D
- vtkMapper, vtkMapper2D—subclasses of vtkAbstractMapper
- vtkTransform
- vtkLookupTable, vtkColorTransferFunction—subclasses of vtkScalarsToColors
- vtkRenderer
- vtkRenderWindow
- vtkRenderWindowInteractor

When we combine these objects together we create a scene. (Refer to the object diagram of **Figure 14–8** to see how these objects are related.)

Props represent the things that we "see" in the scene. Props that are positioned and manipulated in 3D (i.e., have a general 4x4 transformation matrix) are of type vtkProp3D (for example, vtkActor is a concrete subclass of vtkProp3D; or if we are volume rendering, vtkVolume). Props that are positioned and represent 2D data (i.e., image data) are of type vtkActor2D. Props don't directly represent their geometry; instead they refer to mappers, which are responsible for representing data (among other things). Props also refer to a property object. The property object controls the appearance of the prop (e.g., color, diffuse, ambient specular lighting effects, rendering representation: wireframe versus surface, and so on). Actors and volumes (via their superclass vtkProp3D) also have an internal transformation object (vtkTransform). This object encapsulates a 4x4 transformation matrix that in turn controls the prop's position, orientation, and scale.

Lights (vtkLight) are used to represent and manipulate the lighting of the scene. Lights are used only in 3D. In 2D, we do not need lights.

The camera object (vtkCamera) controls how 3D geometry is projected into the 2D image during the rendering process. The camera has several methods for positioning, pointing, and orienting it. In addition, the camera controls perspective projection and stereo viewing (if enabled). Cameras are not needed for 2D imaging data.

The mapper (vtkMapper), in conjunction with a lookup table, (vtkLookupTable), is used to transform and render geometry. The mapper provides the interface between the visualization pipeline (described in the next section) and the graphics model. vtkLookupTable is a subclass of vtkScalarsToColors, as is vtkColorTransferFunction. (Typically vtkColorTransferFunction is used for volume rendering—see "Volume Rendering" on page 136.) Subclasses of vtkScalarsToColors are responsible for mapping data values to color, one of the most important visualization techniques.

Renderers (vtkRenderer) and render windows (vtkRenderWindow) are used to manage the interface between the graphics engine and you computer's windowing system. The render window is the window on your computer that the renderer draws into. More than one renderer may draw into a single render window; and you may create multiple render windows. The region that a renderer draws into is called the viewport, of which several may exist in a rendering window.

Once you draw objects into the render window, chances are that you will interact with the data. The *Visualization Toolkit* has several methods of interaction into the scene. One of them is the object vtkRenderWindowInteractor, which is a simple tool for manipulating the camera, picking objects, invoking user-defined methods, entering/exiting stereo viewing, and changing some of the properties of actors.

Many of the objects described above have subclasses that specialize the object's behavior. For example, vtkAssembly, vtkFollower, and vtkLODActor are all subclasses of vtkActor. vtkAssembly allows hierarchies of actors, properly managing the transformations when the hierarchy is translated, rotated, or scaled. vtkFollower is an actor that always faces a specified camera (useful for billboards or text). vtkLODActor (LOD means level-of-detail) is an actor that changes its geometric representation to maintain interactive frame rates.

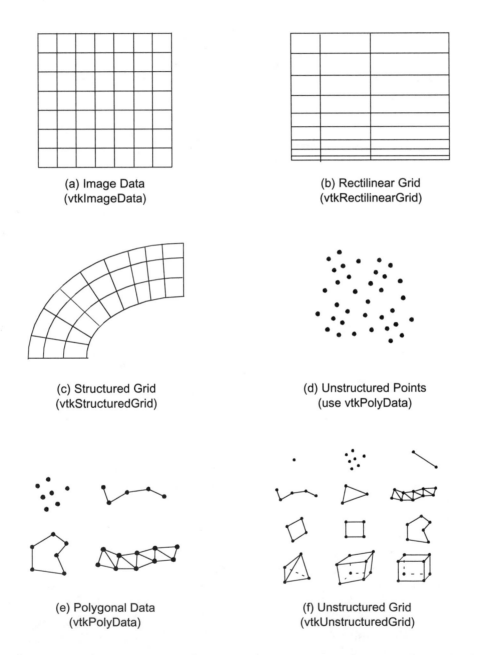

(a) Image Data
(vtkImageData)

(b) Rectilinear Grid
(vtkRectilinearGrid)

(c) Structured Grid
(vtkStructuredGrid)

(d) Unstructured Points
(use vtkPolyData)

(e) Polygonal Data
(vtkPolyData)

(f) Unstructured Grid
(vtkUnstructuredGrid)

Figure 3–2 Dataset types found in **VTK**. Note that unstructured points can be represented by either polygonal data or unstructured grids, so are not explicitly represented in the system.

The Visualization Model

The role of the graphics pipeline is to transform graphical data into pictures. The role of the visualization pipeline is to transform information into graphical data. Another way of looking at this is that the visualization pipeline is responsible for constructing the geometric representation that is then rendered by the graphics pipeline.

The *Visualization Toolkit* uses a data flow approach to transform information into graphical data. There are two basic types of objects involved in this approach.

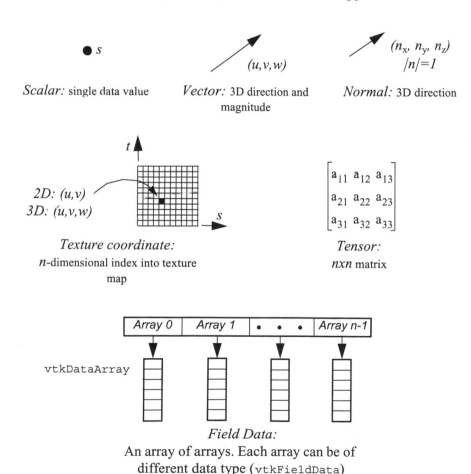

Scalar: single data value *Vector:* 3D direction and magnitude *Normal:* 3D direction

Texture coordinate: n-dimensional index into texture map

Tensor: nxn matrix

Field Data: An array of arrays. Each array can be of different data type (vtkFieldData)

Figure 3–3 Data attributes associated with the points and cells of a dataset.

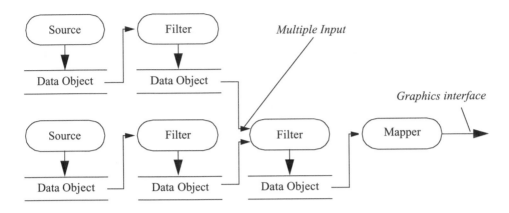

Figure 3–4 Data objects are connected with process objects to create the visualization pipeline. The arrows point in the direction of data flow.

- vtkDataObject
- vtkProcessObject

Data objects represent data of various types. The class vtkDataObject can be viewed as a generic "blob" of data. Data that has a formal structure is referred to as a dataset (class vtkDataSet). **Figure 3–2** shows the dataset objects supported in VTK. Data objects consist of a geometric and topological structure (points and cells) as illustrated by the figure, as well as associated attribute data such as scalars or vectors. The attribute data can be associated with the points or cells of the dataset. Cells are topological organizations of points; cells form the atoms of the dataset and are used to interpolate information between points **Figure 14–15** shows the various cell types supported by VTK. **Figure 3–3** shows the attribute data supported by VTK.

Process objects, also referred to generically as filters, operate on data objects to produce new data objects. Process objects represent the algorithms of the system. Process and data objects are connected together to form visualization pipelines (i.e., data-flow networks). **Figure 3–4** is a depiction of a visualization pipeline.

This figure together with **Figure 3–5** illustrate some important visualization concepts. Source process objects are objects that produce data by reading (reader objects) or constructing one or more data objects (procedural source objects). Filters ingest one or more data objects, and generate one or more data objects on output. Mappers, which we have seen earlier in the graphics model, transform data objects into graphics data, which is then rendered by the graphics engine. Writers are a type of mapper that write data to a file or stream.

There are several important issues regarding the construction of the visualization pipeline that we will briefly introduce here. First, pipeline topology is constructed using variations of the methods

```
aFilter->SetInput( anotherFilter->GetOutput() );
```

which sets the input to the filter aFilter to the output of the filter anotherFilter. (Filters with multiple input and output have similar methods for setting input and output.) Second, we must have a mechanism for controlling the execution of the pipeline. We only want to execute those portions of the pipeline necessary to bring the output up to date. The *Visualization Toolkit* uses a lazy evaluation scheme (executes only when the data is

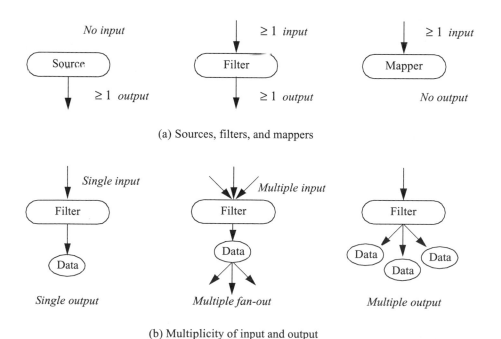

(a) Sources, filters, and mappers

(b) Multiplicity of input and output

Figure 3–5 Different types of process objects. Filters ingest one or more inputs and produce one or more output data objects.

requested) based on an internal modification time of each object. Third, the assembly of the pipeline requires that only those objects compatible with one another can fit together with the SetInput() and GetOutput() methods. In VTK, C++ compile-time type checking enforces this (interpreters such as Tcl report errors at run-time). Finally, we must decide whether to cache, or retain, the data objects once the pipeline has executed. Since visualization datasets are typically quite large, this is important to the successful application of visualization tools. VTK offers methods to turn data caching on and off, use of reference counting to avoid copying data, and methods to stream data in pieces if an entire dataset cannot be held in memory. (We recommend that you review Chapter 4 of The Visualization Toolkit text for more information.)

Please note that there are many varieties of both process and data objects. **Figure 11–2** shows six different data object types supported by the current version of VTK. Process objects vary in the type(s) of input data and output data, and of course the particular algorithm they implement.

Pipeline Execution. In the previous section we discussed the need to control the execution of the visualization pipeline. In this section we will expand our understanding of some key concepts regarding pipeline execution.

As indicated in the previous section, the VTK visualization pipelines only executes when data is required for computation (lazy evaluation). For example, if you instantiate a reader object and ask for the number of points (the language shown here is Tcl):

```
vtkPLOT3DReader reader
    reader SetXYZFileName "$VTK_DATA_ROOT/Data/combxyz.bin
    [reader GetOutput] GetNumberOfPoints
```

the reader object will return "0" from the GetNumberOfPoints() method call, despite the fact that the data file contains thousands of points. However, if you add the Update() method

```
    reader->Update
    [reader GetOutput] GetNumberOfPoints
```

then the reader object will return the correct number. The reason for this is that—in the first example—the GetNumberOfPoints() methods does not require computation, and the object simply returns the current number of points, which is "0". In the second example, the Update() method forces execution of the pipeline, thereby forcing the reader to execute and read the data from the file indicated.

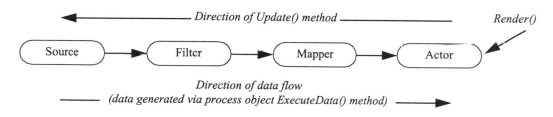

Figure 3–6 Conceptual overview of pipeline execution.

Normally, you do not need to manually invoke Update() because the filters are connected into a visualization pipeline. In this case, when the actor receives a request to render itself, it forwards the method to its mapper, and the Update() method is automatically sent through the visualization pipeline. From a high level, the execution of the pipeline appears shown in **Figure 3–6**. As this figure illustrates, the Render() method often initiates the request for data, which is then delivered down through the pipeline. Depending on which portions of the pipeline are out of date, the filters in the pipeline may re-execute, thereby bringing the data at the end of the pipeline up-to-date, which is then rendered by the actor. (For more information about the execution process, see Chapter 10 "Managing Pipeline Execution" on page 219.)

Image Processing. VTK supports an extensive set of image processing and volume rendering functionality. In VTK, both 2D (image) and 3D (volume) data are referred to as vtkImageData. An image dataset in VTK is one in which the data is arranged in a regular, axis-aligned array. Images, pixmaps, and bitmaps are examples of 2D image datasets; volumes (a stack of 2D images) is a 3D image dataset.

Process objects in the imaging pipeline always input and output image data objects. Because of the regular and simple nature of the data, the imaging pipeline has other important features. Volume rendering is used to visualize 3D vtkImageData (see "Volume Rendering" on page 136), and special image viewers are used to view 2D vtkImageData. Almost all process objects in the imaging pipeline are multithreaded, and are capable of streaming data in pieces (to satisfy a user-specified memory limit). Filters automatically sense the number of processors available on the system and create that number of threads during execution, as well as automatically separating data into pieces that are streamed through the pipeline. (See "Using Streaming" on page 232 for more information.)

This concludes our brief overview of the *Visualization Toolkit* system architecture. We recommend the *Visualization Toolkit* text for more details on many of the algorithms found in VTK. Learning by example is another helpful approach. Chapters 4 through 8 contain many annotated examples demonstrating various capabilities of VTK. Also, since source code is available, and there are hundreds of examples, you may wish to study these as well.

With this abbreviated introduction behind us, let's look at ways to create applications in C++, Tcl, Java, and Python.

3.2 Create An Application

This section covers the basic information you need to develop VTK applications in the four programming languages Tcl, C++, Java, and Python. (Kitware offers commercial products to build VTK applications with Visual Basic or ActiveX/COM. (See "Visual Basic / COM / ActiveX" on page 38) After reading this introduction, you should jump to the subsection(s) that discuss the language(s) you are interested in using. In addition to providing you with instructions on how to create and run a simple application, each section will show you how to take advantage of callbacks in that language.

User Methods, Observers, and Commands

Callbacks (or *user methods*) are implemented in VTK using the Subject/Observer and Command design pattern. This means that every class in VTK (every subclass of vtkObject) has an AddObserver() method that can be used to setup callbacks from VTK. The observer looks at every event invoked on an object, and if it matches one of the events that the observer is watching for, then an associated command is invoked (i.e., the callback). For example, all VTK filters invoke a StartEvent right before they start to execute. If you add an observer that watches for a StartEvent then it will get called every time that filter starts to execute. Consider the following Tcl script that creates an instance of vtkElevationFilter, and adds an observer for the StartEvent to call the procedure PrintStatus.

```
proc PrintStatus {} {
puts "Starting to execute the elevation filter"
}
vtkElevationFilter foo
foo AddObserver StartEvent PrintStatus
```

This type of functionality (i.e., callback) is available to all the languages VTK supports. Each section that follows will show a brief example of how to use it. Further discussion on user methods is provided in "Integrating With The Windowing System" on page 303. (This section also discusses user interface integration issues.)

To create your own application, we suggest starting with one of the examples that come with VTK. They can be found in VTK/Examples in the source distribution, and in subdirectories with the PC executable distribution. In the source distribution the examples are organized first by topic and then by language. Under VTK/Examples you will find directories for different topics and under the directories there will be subdirectories for different languages such as Tcl.

Tcl

Tcl is one of the easiest languages with which to start creating VTK applications. Once you have installed VTK, you should be able to run the Tcl examples that come with the distribution. Under UNIX you have to compile VTK with Tcl support as mentioned in "Installing VTK On Unix Systems" on page 14. Under Windows you can just install the self extracting archive as described in "Installing VTK on Windows 9x/NT/ME/2000/XP" on page 8, and you are ready to go.

Windows. Under Windows, you can run a Tcl script just by double clicking on the file (test1.tcl in this example). If nothing happens you might have an error in your script. To detect this you need to run vtk.exe first. vtk.exe can be found on your start menu under VTK. Once execution begins, a console window should appear with a prompt in it. At this prompt type in a cd command to change directory to where test1.tcl is located. Two examples are given below:

```
% cd "c:/Program Files/Visualization Toolkit/examples"

% cd "c:/VTK/Examples/Tutorial/Tcl"
```

Then you will need to source in the example script using the following command:

```
% source Cone.tcl
```

Then Tcl will try to execute test1.tcl and you will be able to see additional errors or warning messages that would otherwise not show up.

Unix. Under UNIX, Tcl development can be done by running the VTK executable (after you have compiled the source code) that can be found in your binary directory such as `VTK/bin/vtk`, or `VTK-Solaris/bin/vtk`, etc., and then providing the Tcl script as the first argument. For example:

```
unix machine> cd VTK/Examples/Tutorial/Step1/Tcl
unix machine> /home/VTK-Solaris/bin/vtk Cone.tcl
```

User methods can be setup as shown in the introduction of this chapter. An example can be found in `Examples/Tutorial/Step2/Tcl`. The key changes are shown below:

```
proc myCallback {} {
    puts "Starting to render"
}

vtkRenderer ren1
ren1 AddObserver StartEvent myCallback
```

or by simply providing the body of the proc directly to AddObserver() as shown below:

```
vtkRenderer ren1
ren1 AddObserver StartEvent {puts "Starting to render"}
```

C++

Using C++ as your development language will typically result in smaller, faster, and more easily deployed applications than most any other language. C++ development also has the advantage that you do not need to compile any additional support for Tcl, Java, or Python. This section will show you how to create a simple VTK C++ application for the PC with Microsoft Visual C++, and also for UNIX using the appropriate compiler. We will start with a simple example called `Cone.cxx` which can be found in `Examples/Tutorial/Step1/Cxx`. For both windows and UNIX you can use a source code installation of VTK or installed binaries. These examples will work with both.

The first step in building your C++ program is to use CMake to generate a Makefile (Unix) or Microsoft Workspace (Windows MSVC++). The `CMakeList.txt` file that comes with `Cone.cxx` (shown below) makes use of the FindVTK and UseVTK CMake modules. These modules attempt to locate VTK and then setup your include paths and link lines for building C++ programs. If they do not successfully find VTK, you will have to manually specify the appropriate CMake parameters, and rerun CMake as necessary.

```
PROJECT (Step1)

INCLUDE (${CMAKE_ROOT}/Modules/FindVTK.cmake)
IF (USE_VTK_FILE)
  INCLUDE(${USE_VTK_FILE})
ENDIF (USE_VTK_FILE)

LINK_LIBRARIES(
  vtkRendering
  vtkGraphics
  vtkImaging
  vtkFiltering
  vtkCommon
)

ADD_EXECUTABLE(Cone Cone.cxx)
```

Microsoft Visual C++. Once you have run CMake for the Cone example you are ready to start up Microsoft Visual C++ and load the Cone.dsw workspace. You can now select a build type (such as Release or Debug) and build your application. If you want to integrate VTK into an existing project that does not use CMake, you can copy the settings from this simple example into your existing workspaces.

Now consider an example of a true Windows application. The process is very similar to what we did above, except that we create a windows application instead of a console application, as shown in the following. Much of the code is standard Windows code and will be familiar to any Windows developer. This example can be found in Examples/ GUI/Win32/SimpleCxx. Notice that the only significant change to the CMakeLists.txt file was the addition of the WIN32 parameter in the ADD_EXECUTABLE command.

```
#include "vtkConeSource.h"
#include "vtkPolyDataMapper.h"
#include "vtkRenderWindow.h"
#include "vtkRenderWindowInteractor.h"

static HANDLE hinst;
long FAR PASCAL WndProc(HWND, UINT, UINT, LONG);

// define the vtk part as a simple c++ class
```

```
class myVTKApp
{
public:
  myVTKApp(HWND parent);
  ~myVTKApp();
private:
  vtkRenderWindow *renWin;
  vtkRenderer *renderer;
  vtkRenderWindowInteractor *iren;
  vtkConeSource *cone;
  vtkPolyDataMapper *coneMapper;
  vtkActor *coneActor;
};
```

We start by including the required VTK include files. We do not need to include the standard windows header files because the VTK header files include them. Next we have two standard windows prototypes followed by a small class definition called myVTKApp. When developing in C++, you should try to use object-oriented approaches instead of the scripting programming style found in many of the Tcl examples. Here we are encapsulating the VTK components of the application into a small class.

```
myVTKApp::myVTKApp(HWND hwnd)
{
  // Similar to Examples/Tutorial/Step1/Cxx/Cone.cxx
  // We create the basic parts of a pipeline and connect them
  this->renderer = vtkRenderer::New();
  this->renWin = vtkRenderWindow::New();
  this->renWin->AddRenderer(this->renderer);

  // setup the parent window
  this->renWin->SetParentId(hwnd);
  this->iren = vtkRenderWindowInteractor::New();
  this->iren->SetRenderWindow(this->renWin);

  this->cone = vtkConeSource::New();
  this->cone->SetHeight( 3.0 );
  this->cone->SetRadius( 1.0 );
  this->cone->SetResolution( 10 );
  this->coneMapper = vtkPolyDataMapper::New();
  this->coneMapper->SetInput(this->cone->GetOutput());
  this->coneActor = vtkActor::New();
  this->coneActor->SetMapper(this->coneMapper);

  this->renderer->AddActor(this->coneActor);
```

```
   this->renderer->SetBackground(0.2,0.4,0.3);
   this->renWin->SetSize(400,400);

   // Finally we start the interactor so that event will be handled
   this->renWin->Render();
}
```

This is the constructor for myVTKApp. As you can see it allocates the required VTK objects, sets their instance variables, and then connects them to form a visualization pipeline. Most of this is straightforward VTK code except for the vtkRenderWindow. This constructor takes a HWND handle to the parent window that should contain the VTK rendering window. We then use this in the SetParentId() method of vtkRenderWindow so that it will create its window as a child of the window passed to the constructor.

```
myVTKApp::~myVTKApp()
{
   renWin->Delete();
   renderer->Delete();
   iren->Delete();
   cone->Delete();
   coneMapper->Delete();
   coneActor->Delete();
}
```

The destructor simply frees all of the VTK objects that were allocated in the constructor.

```
int PASCAL WinMain (HINSTANCE hInstance, HINSTANCE hPrevInstance,
 LPSTR lpszCmdParam, int nCmdShow)
{
   static char szAppName[] = "Win32Cone";
   HWND hwnd ;
   MSG msg ;
   WNDCLASS wndclass ;

   if (!hPrevInstance)
     {
     wndclass.style = CS_HREDRAW | CS_VREDRAW | CS_OWNDC;
     wndclass.lpfnWndProc = WndProc ;
     wndclass.cbClsExtra = 0 ;
     wndclass.cbWndExtra = 0 ;
     wndclass.hInstance = hInstance;
     wndclass.hIcon = LoadIcon(NULL,IDI_APPLICATION);
     wndclass.hCursor = LoadCursor (NULL, IDC_ARROW);
```

```
   wndclass.lpszMenuName = NULL;
   wndclass.hbrBackground = (HBRUSH)GetStockObject(BLACK_BRUSH);
   wndclass.lpszClassName = szAppName;
   RegisterClass (&wndclass);
   }
hinst = hInstance;

hwnd = CreateWindow ( szAppName,
                      "Draw Window",
                      WS_OVERLAPPEDWINDOW,
                      CW_USEDEFAULT,
                      CW_USEDEFAULT,
                      400,
                      480,
                      NULL,
                      NULL,
                      hInstance,
                      NULL);
ShowWindow (hwnd, nCmdShow);
UpdateWindow (hwnd);
while (GetMessage (&msg, NULL, 0, 0))
   {
   TranslateMessage (&msg);
   DispatchMessage (&msg);
   }
return msg.wParam;
}
```

The WinMain code here is all standard windows code and has no VTK references in it. As you can see the application has control of the event loop. Events are handled by the Wnd-Proc described below.

```
long FAR PASCAL WndProc (HWND hwnd, UINT message,
UINT wParam, LONG lParam)
{
   static HWND ewin;
   static myVTKApp *theVTKApp;
   switch (message)
      {
      case WM_CREATE:
         {
         ewin = CreateWindow("button","Exit",
                             WS_CHILD | WS_VISIBLE | SS_CENTER,
                             0,400,400,60,
                             hwnd,(HMENU)2,
```

```
                        (HINSTANCE)GetWindowLong(hwnd,GWL_HINSTANCE),
                        NULL);
    theVTKApp = new myVTKApp(hwnd);
    return 0;
    }
  case WM_COMMAND:
    switch (wParam)
      {
      case 2:
        PostQuitMessage (0);
        if (theVTKApp)
          {
          delete theVTKApp;
          theVTKApp = NULL;
          }
        break;
      }
    return 0;

  case WM_DESTROY:
    PostQuitMessage (0);
    if (theVTKApp)
      {
      delete theVTKApp;
      theVTKApp = NULL;
      }
    return 0;
  }
  return DefWindowProc (hwnd, message, wParam, lParam);
}
```

This WndProc is a very simple event handler. For a full application it would be significantly more complicated but the key integration issues are the same. At the top of this function we declare a static reference to a myVTKApp instance. When handling the WM_CREATE method we create an Exit button and then construct and instance of myVT-KApp passing in the handle to the current window. The vtkRenderWindowInteractor will handle all of the events for the vtkRenderWindow so that you do not need to handle them here. You probably will want to add code to handle resizing events so that the render window resizes appropriate to your overall user interface. If you do not set the ParentId of the vtkRenderWindow, it will show up as a top-level independent window. Everything else should behave the same as before.

UNIX. Creating a C++ application on UNIX is done by running CMake and then make. CMake creates a Makefile that specified the include paths, link lines, and dependencies. make then uses this makefile to compile the application. This should result in a Cone executable that you can run. If `Cone.cxx` does not compile then check the make errors and correct them. Make sure that the values in the top of `CMakeCache.txt` are valid. If it does compile, but you receive errors when you try running it, you might need to set your `LD_LIBRARY_PATH` as described in Chapter 2.

User Methods in C++. You can add user methods (using the observer/command design pattern) in C++ by creating a subclass of vtkCommand that overrides the Execute() method. Consider the following example taken from `Examples/Tutorial/Step2/Cxx`:

```
myCallback : public vtkCommand {
static myCallback *New() {return new myCallback;}
virtual void Execute(vtkObject *caller, unsigned long, void *callData)
  { cerr << "Starting to Render\n"; }
};
```

While the Execute() method is always passed the calling object (caller) you do not need to use it. If you do use the caller you will typically want to perform a SafeDownCast() to the actual type. For example:

```
virtual void Execute(vtkObject *caller, unsigned long, void *callData)
{
  vtkRenderer *ren = vtkRenderer::SafeDownCast(caller);
  if (ren) { ren->SetBackground(0.2,0.3,0.4); }
}
```

Once you have created your subclass of vtkCommand you are ready to add an observer that will call your command on certain events. This can be done as follows:

```
// Here is where we setup the observer,
//we do a new and ren1 will eventually free the observer
myCallback *mo1 = myCallback::New();
ren1->AddObserver(vtkCommand::StartEvent,mo1);
```

The above code creates an instance of myCallback and then adds an observer on `ren1` for the `StartEvent`. Whenever ren1 starts to render the Execute() method of myCallback will get called. When ren1 is deleted then the callback will be deleted as well.

Java

To create Java applications you must first have a working Java development environment. This section provides instructions for using Sun's JDK 1.3 or later on either Windows or UNIX. Once your JDK has been installed and you have installed VTK, you need to set your CLASSPATH environment variable to include the VTK classes. Under Microsoft Windows this can be set in your autoexec.bat file using the sysedit program or on Windows 2000 by right clicking on the My Computer icon, selecting the properties option, and then selecting the Advanced tab. Then add a CLASSPATH environment variable and set it to include your VTK/java directory. For a Windows executable installation this will be something similar to C:\Program Files\Visualization Toolkit\java\vtk.jar. For a Windows build it will be something like C:\vtkbin\java. Under UNIX you should set your CLASSPATH environment variable to something similar to /yourdisk/vtk/java or /yourdisk/vtk-solaris/java.

The next step is to byte compile your Java program. For starters try byte compiling (with javac) the Cone.java example that comes with VTK under Examples/Tutorial/Step1/Java. Then you should be able to run the resulting application using the java command. It should display a cone which rotates 360 degrees and then exits. The next step is to create your own applications using the examples provided as a starting point.

One note of caution: Java is undergoing some growing pains and you will undoubtedly run into some problems. For example, running VTK applets inside of a web browser can be a difficult process. We recommend that if you use VTK, you plan your development for running within the AppletViewer or as a standard Java program. Callbacks in Java are essentially public void class methods such as:

```
public void myCallback()
{
   System.out.println("Starting a render");
}
```

You setup a callback by passing three arguments. The first is the name of the event you are interested in, the second is an instance of a class, the third is the name of the method you want to invoke. In this example we setup the StartEvent to invoke the myCallback method on me (which is an instance of Cone2). The myCallback method must of course be a valid method of Cone2 to avoid an error.

```
Cone2 me = new Cone2();
ren1.AddObserver("StartEvent",me,"myCallback");
```

Python

Before running Python you will need to set up your PYTHONPATH environment variable. This environment variable is used by Python to find additional modules and libraries. This will typically be something like VTK/Wrapping/Python or vtkbin/bin. Once this is set you should be able to run Examples/Tutorial/Step1/Python/Cone.py as follows

```
python Cone.py
```

Creating your own Python scripts is a simple matter of using some of our example scripts as a starting point. User methods can be setup by defining a function and then passing it as the argument to the AddObserver as shown below.

```
def myCallback(obj,event):
print "Starting to render"
ren1.AddObserver("StartEvent",myCallback)
```

You can look at Examples/Tutorial/Step2/Python/Cone2.py for the source code shown above.

Visual Basic / COM / ActiveX

If you are interested in creating applications in Microsoft Visual Basic or ActiveX/COM, Kitware offers commercial products to support this. These products are known as the ActiViz component library. See Kitware's Web site at http://www.kitware.com/ActiViz.htm for more information.

3.3 Conversion Between Languages

As we have seen, VTK's core is implemented in C++ and then wrapped with the Tcl, Java, and Python programming languages. This means that you have a language choice when developing applications. Your choice will depend on which language you are most comfortable with, the nature of the application, and whether you need access to internal data structures and/or have special performance requirements. C++ offers several advantages over the other languages when you need to access internal data structure or require the highest-performing applications possible. However, using C++ means the extra burden of the compile/link cycle, which often slows the software development process.

You may find yourself developing prototypes in an interpreted language such as Tcl, and then converting them to C++. Or, you may discover example code (in the VTK distribution or from other users) that you wish to convert to your implementation language.

Converting VTK code from one language to another is fairly straightforward. Class names and method names remain the same across languages, what changes are the implementation details and GUI interface, if any. For example, the C++ statement

```
anActor->GetProperty()->SetColor(red,green,blue);
```

in Tcl becomes

```
[anActor GetProperty] SetColor $red $green $blue
```

in Java becomes

```
anActor.GetProperty().SetColor(red,green,blue);
```

and in Python becomes

```
anActor.GetProperty().SetColor(red,green,blue)
```

One major limitation you'll find is that some C++ applications cannot be converted to the other three languages because of pointer manipulation.

Part II

Learn VTK By Example

## Chapter 4

The Basics

The purpose of this chapter is to introduce you to some of VTK's capabilities by way of a selected set of examples. Our focus will be on commonly used methods and objects, and combinations of objects. We will also introduce important concepts and useful applications. By no means are all of VTK's features covered; this chapter is meant to give you a broad overview of what's possible. You'll want to refer to man pages or class .h files to learn about other options each class might have.

Most of the examples included here are implemented in the Tcl programming language. They could just as easily be implemented in C++, Java, and Python—the conversion process between the languages is straightforward (see "Conversion Between Languages" on page 38). C++ does offer some advantages, mainly access and manipulation of data structures and pointers, and some examples reflect this by being implemented in the C++ language.

Each example presented here includes sample code and often a supplemental image. We indicate the name of the source code file (when one exists in the accompanying distribution CD), so you will not have to enter it manually. We recommend that you run and understand the example and then experiment with object methods and parameters. You may also wish to try suggested alternative methods and/or classes. Often, the *Visualization Toolkit* offers several approaches to achieve similar results. Note also that the scripts are often modified from what's found in the source code distribution. This is done to simplify concepts or remove extraneous code.

Learning an object-oriented system like VTK first requires understanding the programming abstraction, and then becoming familiar with the library of objects and their methods. We recommend that you review "System Architecture" on page 19 for information about the programming abstraction. The examples in this chapter will then provide you with a good overview of the many VTK objects.

 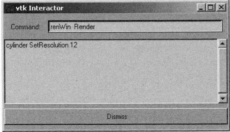

Figure 4–1 Using Tcl and Tk to build an interpreted application.

4.1 Creating Simple Models

The use of the *Visualization Toolkit* typically goes as follows: read/generate some data, filter it, render it, and interact with it. In this section, we'll start by looking at ways to read and generate data.

There are two basic ways to obtain data. The data may exist in a file (or files, streams, etc.) that is read into the system; or, the data may be procedurally generated (via an algorithm or mathematical expression). Recall that objects that initiate the processing of data in the visualization pipeline are called source objects (see **Figure 3–5**). Objects that generate data are called procedural (source) objects, and objects that read data are called reader (source) objects.

Procedural Source Object

We'll start off by rendering a simple cylinder. The example code shown below (VTK/Examples/Rendering/Tcl/Cylinder.tcl) demonstrates many basic concepts in the visualization and graphics systems. Refer to **Figure 4–1** to see the results of running the script.

We begin the script by invoking a Tcl command to load the VTK package (package require vtk) and create a GUI interpreter (package require vtkinteractor) that lets you type commands at run-time. Also, we load vtktesting which defines a set of colors, one of which (tomato) is used later in the script.

Historical note: In previous versions of VTK, the shared VTK libraries were loaded by calling catch {load vtktcl} instead of package require vtk.

```
package require vtk
package require vtkinteraction
package require vtktesting
```

We then create a procedural source object: vtkCylinderSource. This source creates a polygonal representation of a cylinder. The output of the cylinder is set as the input to the vtkPolyDataMapper via the method SetInput(). We create an actor (the object that is rendered) that refers to the mapper as its defining geometry. Notice the way objects are constructed in Tcl: we use the class name followed by the desired instance name:

```
vtkCylinderSource cylinder
    cylinder SetResolution 8
vtkPolyDataMapper cylinderMapper
    cylinderMapper SetInput [cylinder GetOutput]
vtkActor cylinderActor
    cylinderActor SetMapper cylinderMapper
    eval [cylinderActor GetProperty] SetColor $tomato
    cylinderActor RotateX 30.0
    cylinderActor RotateY -45.0
```

(As a reminder of how similar a C++ implementation is to a Tcl (or other interpreted languages) implementation, the same code implemented in C++ is shown below, and can be found in VTK/Examples/Rendering/Cxx/Cylinder.cxx.)

```
vtkCylinderSource *cylinder = vtkCylinderSource::New();
    cylinder->SetResolution(8);
vtkPolyDataMapper *cylinderMapper = vtkPolyDataMapper::New();
    cylinderMapper->SetInput(cylinder->GetOutput());
vtkActor *cylinderActor = vtkActor::New();
    cylinderActor->SetMapper(cylinderMapper);
    cylinderActor->GetProperty()->SetColor(1.0000, 0.3882, 0.2784);
    cylinderActor->RotateX(30.0);
    cylinderActor->RotateY(-45.0);
```

Recall that source objects initiate the visualization pipeline, and mapper objects terminate the pipeline, so in this example we have a pipeline consisting of two process objects (i.e., a source and mapper). The VTK pipeline uses a lazy evaluation scheme, so even though the pipeline is connected, no generation or processing of data has yet occurred (since we have not yet requested the data).

Next we create graphics objects which will allow us to render the actor. The vtkRenderer instance ren1 coordinates the rendering process for a viewport of the render window `renWin`. The render window interactor `iren` is a 3D widget that allows us to manipulate the camera.

```
#Create the graphics stuff
#
vtkRenderer ren1
vtkRenderWindow renWin
    renWin AddRenderer ren1
vtkRenderWindowInteractor iren
    iren SetRenderWindow renWin
```

Notice that we've associated the renderer with the render window via the AddRenderer() method. We must also associate the actor with the renderer using the AddActor() method.

```
# Add the actors to the renderer, set the background and size
ren1 AddActor cylinderActor
ren1 SetBackground 0.1 0.2 0.4
renWin SetSize 200 200
```

The SetBackground() method specifies the background color of the rendering window using RGB (red, green, blue) values between (0,1), and SetSize() specifies the window size in pixels. Finally, we conclude this example by associating the GUI interactor with the render window interactor's user-defined method. (The user-defined method is invoked by pressing the u key when the mouse focus is in the rendering window. See "Using VTK Interactors" on page 48.) The Initialize() method begins the event loop, and the Tcl/Tk command `wm withdraw .` makes sure that the interpreter widget `.Interact` is not visible when the application starts.

```
# Associate the "u" keypress with a UserEvent and start the event loop
#
iren AddObserver UserEvent {wm deiconify .vtkInteract}
iren Initialize

# suppress the tk window
wm withdraw .
```

When the script is run, the visualization pipeline will execute because the rendering process will request data. (The window expose event will force the render window to render itself.) Only after the pipeline executes are the filters up-to-date with respect to the input data. If you desire, you can manually cause execution of the pipeline by invoking `renWin Render`.

After you get this example running, you might try a couple of things. First, use the interactor by mousing in the rendering window. Next, change the resolution of the cylinder object by invoking the `cylinder SetResolution 12`. You can do this by editing the example file and re-executing it, or by pressing u in the rendering window to bring up the interpreter GUI and typing the command there. Remember, if you are using the Tcl interactor popup, the changes you make are visible only after data is requested, so follow changes with a `renWin Render` command, or by mousing in the rendering window.

Reader Source Object

This example is similar to the previous example except that we read a data file rather than procedurally generating the data. A stereo-lithography file is read (suffix `.stl`) that represents polygonal data using the binary STL data format. (Refer to **Figure 4–2** and the Tcl script `VTK/Examples/Rendering/Tcl/CADPart.tcl`.)

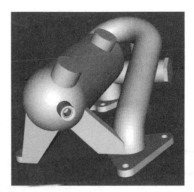

Figure 4–2 Reader source object.

```
vtkSTLReader part
    part SetFileName $VTK.-DATA-ROOT/Data/42400-IDGH.stl
vtkPolyDataMapper    partMapper
    partMapper SetInput [part GetOutput]
vtkLODActor partActor
    partActor SetMapper partMapper
```

Notice the use of the vtkLODActor. This actor changes its representation to maintain interactive performance. Its default behavior is to create a point cloud and wireframe, bounding-box outline to represent the intermediate and low-level representations. (See "Level-Of-Detail Actors" on page 61 for more information.) You may want to try replacing vtkLODActor with an instance of vtkActor to see the difference.

Many of the readers do not sense when the input file(s) change and re-execute. For example, if the file `42400-IDGH.stl` changes, the pipeline will not re-execute. You can manually modify objects by invoking the Modified() method on them. This will cause the filter to re-execute, as well as all filters downstream of it.

The *Visualization Toolkit* has limited, built-in modeling capabilities. If you want to use VTK to edit and manipulate complex models (e.g., those created by a solid modeler or modeling tool), you'll typically use a reader (see "Readers" on page 185) to interface to the data. (Another option is importers, which are used to ingest entire scenes. See "Importers" on page 189 for more information.)

4.2 Using VTK Interactors

Once you've visualized your data, you typically want to interact with it. The *Visualization Toolkit* offers several approaches to do this. The first approach is to use the built in class vtkRenderWindowInteractor. The second approach is to create your own interactor by specifying event bindings. And don't forget (if you are using an interpreted language) that you can type commands at run-time. You may also wish to refer to "Picking" on page 65 to see how to select data from the screen. (Note: Developers can also interface to a windowing system of their choice. See "Integrating With The Windowing System" on page 303.)

vtkRenderWindowInteractor

The simplest way to interact with your data is to instantiate vtkRenderWindowInteractor. This class responds to pre-defined set of events and actions, and provides a way to override the default actions. vtkRenderWindowInteractor allows you to control the camera and actors, as well as offering two interaction styles: position sensitive (i.e., joystick mode); and motion sensitive (i.e., trackball mode). (More about interactor styles shortly.)

vtkRenderWindowInteractor responds to the following events in the render window. (Remember that multiple renderers can draw into a rendering window, and that the renderer draws into a viewport within the render window. Interactors support multiple renderers in a render window.)

*   `Keypress j` / `Keypress t` — toggle between **joystick** (position sensitive) and **trackball** (motion sensitive) **styles**. In joystick style, motion occurs continuously as long as a mouse button is pressed. In trackball style, motion occurs when the mouse button is pressed and the mouse pointer moves.

*   `Keypress c` / `Keypress a` — toggle between **camera** and **actor** (object) **modes**. In camera mode, mouse events affect the camera position and focal point. In object mode, mouse events affect the actor that is under the mouse pointer.

- Button 1 — **rotate** the camera around its focal point (if camera mode) or rotate the actor around its origin (if actor mode). The rotation is in the direction defined from the center of the renderer's viewport towards the mouse position. In joystick mode, the magnitude of the rotation is determined by the distance the mouse is from the center of the render window.

- Button 2 — **pan** the camera (if camera mode) or **translate** the actor (if object mode). In joystick mode, the direction of pan or translation is from the center of the viewport towards the mouse position. In trackball mode, the direction of motion is the direction the mouse moves. (Note: with a 2-button mouse, pan is defined as <Shift>-Button 1.)

- Button 3 — **zoom** the camera (if camera mode) or **scale** the actor (if object mode). Zoom in/increase scale if the mouse position is in the top half of the viewport; zoom out/decrease scale if the mouse position is in the bottom half. In joystick mode, the amount of zoom is controlled by the distance of the mouse pointer from the horizontal centerline of the window.

- Keypress 3 — **toggle** the render window into and out of **stereo mode**. By default, red-blue stereo pairs are created. Some systems support Crystal Eyes LCD stereo glasses; you have to invoke SetStereoTypeToCrystalEyes() on the rendering window.

- Keypress e — **exit** the application.

- Keypress f — **fly-to** the point under the cursor. This sets the focal point and allows rotations around that point.

- Keypress p — perform a **pick** operation. The render window interactor has an internal instance of vtkPropPicker that it uses to pick. See "Picking" on page 65 for more information about picking.

- Keypress r — **reset** the camera view along the current view direction. Centers the actors and moves the camera so that all actors are visible.

- Keypress s — modify the representation of all actors so that they are **surface**s.

- Keypress u — invoke the **user-defined method**. Typically, this keypress will bring up an interactor that you can type commands into.

- Keypress w — modify the representation of all actors so that they are **wireframe**.

The default interaction style is position sensitive (i.e., joystick style)—that is, it manipulates the camera or actor and renders continuously as long as a mouse button is pressed. If you don't like the default behavior, you can change it, or write your own. (See "vtkRenderWindow Interaction Style" on page 303 for information about writing your own style.)

vtkRenderWindowInteractor has other useful features. Invoking LightFollowCameraOn() (the default behavior) causes the light position and focal point to be synchronized with the camera position and focal point (i.e., a "headlight" is created). Of course, this can be turned off with LightFollowCameraOff(). A callback that responds to the "u" keypress can be added with "AddObserver(UserEvent) method. It is also possible to set several pick-related methods. AddObserver(StartPickEvent) defines a method to be called prior to picking, and AddObserver(EndPickEvent) defines a method after the pick has been performed. (Please see "User Methods, Observers, and Commands" on page 28 for more information on defining user methods.) You can also specify an instance of a subclass of vtkAbstractPicker to use via the SetPicker() method (see "Picking" on page 65).

If you are using vtkLODActor, you may wish to set the desired frame rate via SetDesiredUpdateRate() in the interactor. Normally, this is handled automatically (when the mouse buttons are activated, the desired update rate is increased, when the mouse button is released, the desired update rate is set back down). Refer to "Level-Of-Detail Actors" on page 61 for more information.

We've seen how to use vtkRenderWindowInteractor previously, here's a recapitulation.

```
vtkRenderWindowInteractor iren
    iren SetRenderWindow renWin
    iren AddObserver UserEvent {wm deiconify .vtkInteract}
```

Interactor Styles

There are two distinctly different ways to control interaction style in VTK. The first is to use a subclass of vtkInteractorStyle, either one supplied with the system or one that you write. The second method is to manage the event loop directly.

vtkInteractorStyle. The class vtkRenderWindowInteractor can support different interaction styles. When you type "t" or "j" in the interactor (see the previous section) you are changing between trackball and joystick interaction styles. The way this works is that vtkRenderWindowInteractor forwards any events it receives (e.g., mouse button press, mouse motion, keyboard events, etc.) to its style. The style is then responsible for handling the events and performing the correct actions. To set the style, use the vtkRenderWindowInteractor::SetInteractorStyle() method. For example:

```
vtkInteractorStyleFlight flightStyle
vtkRenderWindowInteractor iren
    iren SetInteractorStyle flightStyle
```

(Note: When vtkRenderWindowInteractor is instantiated, a window-system specific render window interactor is actually instantiated. For example, on Unix systems the class vtkXRenderWindowInteractor is actually created, and returned as an instance of vtkRenderWindowInteractor. On Windows, the class vtkWin32RenderWindowInteractor is instantiated.)

Managing The Event Loop. You may wish to create your own event bindings. The bindings can be managed in any language that VTK supports, including C++, Tcl, Python, and Java. (Normally you'll do this in the system with which you're building the GUI. For more information about interfacing VTK to the windowing system, see "Integrating With The Windowing System" on page 303.) One example to look at is Wrapping/Tcl/TkInteractor.tcl, which defines bindings for Tcl/Tk. Here's a portion of that example to give you an idea of what's going on. The bind command is a Tcl/Tk command that associates events in a widget with a callback or function invocation.

```
proc BindTkRenderWidget {widget} {
    bind $widget <Any-ButtonPress> {StartMotion %W %x %y}
    bind $widget <Any-ButtonRelease> {EndMotion %W %x %y}
    bind $widget <B1-Motion> {Rotate %W %x %y}
    bind $widget <B2-Motion> {Pan %W %x %y}
    bind $widget <B3-Motion> {Zoom %W %x %y}
    bind $widget <Shift-B1-Motion> {Pan %W %x %y}
    bind $widget <KeyPress-r> {Reset %W %x %y}
    bind $widget <KeyPress-u> {wm deiconify .vtkInteract}
    bind $widget <KeyPress-w> {Wireframe %W}
    bind $widget <KeyPress-s> {Surface %W}
    bind $widget <KeyPress-p> {PickActor %W %x %y}
    bind $widget <Enter> {Enter %W %x %y}
    bind $widget <Leave> {focus $oldFocus}
    bind $widget <Expose> {Expose %W}
}
```

Notice that the bindings are quite similar to vtkRenderWindowInteractor. These bindings are like the trackball interactor style; that is, the camera does not change unless the mouse is moved.

4.3 Filtering Data

The previous examples consisted of a source and mapper object; the pipeline had no filters. In this section we show how to add a filter into the pipeline.

Filters are connected by using the SetInput() and GetOutput() methods. For example, we can modify the script in "Reader Source Object" on page 46 to shrink the polygons that make up the model. The script is shown below. (Only the pipeline and other pertinent objects are shown.) The complete script can be found at `VTK/Examples/Rendering/Tcl/FilterCADPart.tcl`.

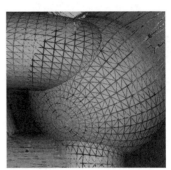

Figure 4–3 Filtering data. Here we use a filter to shrink the polygons forming the model towards their centroid.

```
vtkSTLReader part
    part SetFileName "$VTK_DATA_ROOT/Data/
42400-IDGH.stl"
vtkShrinkPolyData shrink
    shrink SetInput [part GetOutput]
    shrink SetShrinkFactor 0.85
vtkPolyDataMapper partMapper
    partMapper SetInput [shrink GetOutput]
vtkLODActor partActor
    partActor SetMapper partMapper
```

As you can see, creating a visualization pipeline is simple. You need to select the right classes for the task at hand, make sure that the input and output type of connected filters are compatible, and set the necessary instance variables. (Input and output types are compatible when the output dataset type is of the same type as the input will accept, or a subclass of the input type.) Visualization pipelines can contain loops, although the output of a filter cannot be directly connected to its input.

4.4 Controlling The Camera

You may have noticed that in the proceeding scripts no cameras or lights were instantiated. If you're familiar with 3D graphics, you know that lights and cameras are necessary to render objects. In VTK, if lights and cameras are not directly created, the renderer automatically instantiates them.

Instantiating The Camera

The following Tcl script shows how to instantiate and associate a camera with a renderer.

```
vtkCamera cam1
    cam1 SetClippingRange 0.0475572 2.37786
    cam1 SetFocalPoint 0.052665 -0.129454 -0.0573973
    cam1 SetPosition 0.327637 -0.116299 -0.256418
    cam1 ComputeViewPlaneNormal
    cam1 SetViewUp -0.0225386 0.999137 0.034901
ren1 SetActiveCamera cam1
```

Alternatively, if you wish to access a camera that already exists (for example, a camera that the renderer has automatically instantiated), in Tcl you would use

```
set cam1 [ren1 GetActiveCamera]
$cam1 Zoom 1.4
```

Let's review some of the camera methods that we've just introduced. SetClippingPlane() takes two arguments, the distance to the near and far clipping planes along the view plane normal. Recall that all graphics primitives not between these planes are eliminated during rendering, so you need to make sure the objects you want to see lie between the clipping planes. The FocalPoint and Position (in world coordinates) instance variables control the direction and position of the camera. ComputeViewPlaneNormal() resets the normal to the view plane based on the current position and focal point. (If the view plane normal is not perpendicular to the view plane you can get some interesting shearing effects.) Setting the ViewUp controls the "up" direction for the camera. Finally, the Zoom() method magnifies objects by changing the view angle (e.g., SetViewAngle()). You can also use the Dolly() method to move the camera in and out along the view plane normal and either enlarge or shrink the visible actors.

Simple Manipulation Methods

The methods described above are not always the most convenient ones for controlling the camera. If the camera is "looking" the point you want (i.e., the focal point is set), you can use the Azimuth() and Elevation() methods to move the camera about the focal point.

```
cam1 Azimuth 150
cam1 Elevation 60
```

These methods move the camera in a spherical coordinate system centered at the focal point by moving in the longitude direction (azimuth) and the latitude direction (elevation) by the angle (in degrees) given. These methods depend on the view-up vector remaining constant, and do not modify the view-up vector. Note that there are singularities at the north and south pole—the view-up vector becomes parallel with the view plane normal. To avoid this, you can force the view-up vector to be orthogonal to the view vector by using OrthogonalizeViewUp(). However, this changes the camera coordinate system, so if you're flying around an object with a natural horizon or view-up vector (such as terrain), camera manipulation is no longer natural with respect to the data.

Controlling The View Direction

A common function of the camera is to generate a view from a particular direction. You can do this by invoking SetFocalPoint(), SetPosition(), and ComputeViewPlaneNormal() followed by invoking ResetCamera() on the renderer associated with the camera.

```
vtkCamera cam1
   cam1 SetFocalPoint 0 0 0
   cam1 SetPosition 1 1 1
   cam1 ComputeViewPlaneNormal
   cam1 SetViewUp 1 0 0
   cam1 OrthogonalizeViewUp
ren1 SetActiveCamera cam1
ren1 ResetCamera
```

The initial direction (view vector or view plane normal) is computed from the focal point and position of the camera, which, together with ComputeViewPlaneNormal(), defines the initial view vector. Optionally, you can specify an initial view-up vector and orthogonalize it with respect to the view vector. The ResetCamera() method then moves the camera along the view vector so that the renderer's actors are all visible to the camera.

Perspective Versus Orthogonal Views

In the examples shown thus far, we have assumed that the camera is a perspective camera; that is, a view angle controls the projection of the actors onto the view plane during the rendering process. Perspective projection, while generating more natural looking images, introduces distortion that can be undesirable in some applications. Orthogonal (or parallel) projection is an alternative projection method. In orthogonal projection, view rays are parallel, and objects are rendered without distance effects.

To set the camera to use orthogonal projection, use the vtkCamera::ParallelProjectionOn() method. In parallel projection mode, the camera view angle is no longer effective for controlling zoom. Instead, use the SetParallelScale() method to control the magnification of the actors.

Saving/Restoring Camera State

Another common requirement of applications is the capability to save and restore camera state (i.e., recover a view). To save camera state, you'll need to save (at a minimum) the clipping range, the focal point and position, and the view-up vector. You'll also want to compute the view plane normal (as shown in the example in "Instantiating The Camera" on page 53). Then, to recover camera state, simply instantiate a camera with the saved information and assign it to the appropriate renderer (i.e., SetActiveCamera()).

In some cases you may need to store additional information. For example, if the camera view angle (or parallel scale) is set, you'll need to save these. Or, if you are using the camera for stereo viewing, the EyeAngle and Stereo flag are required.

4.5 Controlling Lights

Lights are easier to control than cameras. The most frequently used methods are SetPosition(), SetFocalPoint(), and SetColor(). The position and focal point of the light control the direction in which the light points. The color of the light is expressed as a RGB vector. Also, lights can be turned on and off via the SwitchOn() and SwitchOff() methods, and the brightness of the light can be set with the SetIntensity() method.

By default, instances of vtkLight are directional lights. That is, the position and focal point define a vector parallel to which light rays travel, and the light source is assumed to be located at the infinity point. This means that the lighting on an object does not change if the focal point and position are translated identically.

Lights are associated with renderers as follows.

```
vtkLight light
   light SetColor 1 0 0
```

```
light SetFocalPoint [cam1 GetFocalPoint]
light SetPosition [cam1 GetPosition]

ren1 AddLight light
```

Here we've created a red headlight: a light located at the camera's (cam1's) position and pointing towards the camera's focal point. This is a useful trick, and is used by the interactive renderer to position the light as the camera moves (see "Using VTK Interactors" on page 48).

Positional Lights

It is possible to create positional (i.e., spot lights) by using the PositionalOn() method. This method is used in conjunction with the SetConeAngle() method to control the spread of the spot. A cone angle of 180 degrees indicates that no spot light effects will be applied (i.e., truncated light cone); only the effects of position.

4.6 Controlling 3D Props

Objects in VTK that are to be drawn in the render window are generically known as "props." (The word prop comes from the vocabulary of theatre—a prop is something that appears on stage.) There are several different types of props including vtkProp3D and vtkActor. vtkProp3D is an abstract superclass for those types of props existing in 3D space. (vtkProp3D has a 4x4 transformation matrix that supports scaling, translating, rotating, and geometric projection in 3D space.) The class vtkActor is a type of vtkProp3D whose geometry is defined by analytic primitives such as polygons and lines. We will examine vtkActor and other types of vtkProp3D's later in this section.

Specifying the Position of a vtkProp3D

We have already seen how to use cameras to move around an object; alternatively, we can also hold the camera steady and transform the props. The following methods can be used to define the position of a vtkProp3D (and its subclasses).

- SetPosition(x,y,z) — Specify the position of the vtkProp3D in world coordinates.

- `AddPosition(deltaX,deltaY,deltaZ)` — Translate the prop by the specified amount along each of the x, y, and z axes.

- `RotateX(theta), RotateY(theta), RotateZ(theta)` — Rotate the prop by theta degrees around the x, y, z coordinate axes, respectively.

- `SetOrientation(x,y,z)` — Set the orientation of the prop by rotating about the z axis, them about the x axis, and then about the y axis.

- `AddOrientation(a1,a2,a3)` — Add to the current orientation of the prop.

- `RotateWXYZ(theta,x,y,z)` — Rotate the prop by theta degress around the x-y-z vector defined.

- `Scale(sx,sy,sz)` — Scale the prop in the x, y, z axes coordinate directions.

- `SetOrigin(x,y,z)` — Specify the origin of the prop. The origin is the point around which rotations and scaling occurs.

These methods work together in complex ways to control the resulting transformation matrix. The most important thing to remember is that the operations listed above are applied in a particular order, and the order of applications dramatically affects the resulting actor position. The order used in VTK to apply these transformations is as follows:

Shift to Origin → *Scale* → *Rotate Y* → *Rotate X* → *Rotate Z* →
Shift from Origin → *Translate*

The shift to and from the origin is a negative and positive translation of the Origin value, respectively. The net translation is given by the Position value of the vtkProp3D. The most confusing part of these transformations are the rotations. For example, performing an x rotation followed by a y rotation gives very different results than the operations applied in reverse order (see **Figure 4–4**). For more information about actor transformation, please refer to page 74 of the *Visualization Toolkit* text.

In the next section we describe a variety of vtkProp3D's—of which the most widely used class in VTK is called vtkActor. Later on (see "Controlling vtkActor2D" on page 70) we will examine 2D props (i.e., vtkActor2D) which tend to be used for annotation and other 2D operations.

Figure 4–4 The effects of applying rotation in different order. On the left, first a *x* rotation followed by a *y* rotation; on the right, first a *y* rotation followed by a *x* rotation.

Actors

An actor is the most common type of vtkProp3D. Like other concrete subclasses of vtkProp3D, vtkActor serves to group rendering attributes such as surface properties (e.g., ambient, diffuse, specular color), representation (e.g., surface or wireframe), texture maps, and/or a geometric definition (a mapper).

Defining Geometry. As we have seen in previous examples, the geometry of an actor is specified with the SetMapper() method:

```
vtkPolyDataMapper mapper
    mapper SetInput [aFilter GetOutput]
vtkActor anActor
    anActor SetMapper mapper
```

In this case `mapper` is of type vtkPolyDataMapper, which renders geometry using analytic primitives such as points, lines, polygons, and triangle strips. The mapper terminates the visualization pipeline, and serves as the bridge between the visualization subsystem and the graphics subsystem.

Actor Properties. Actors refer to an instance of vtkProperty, which in turn controls the appearance of the actor. Probably the most used property is actor color, which we will describe in the next section. Other important features of the property are its representation (points, wireframe, or surface), its shading method (either flat or Gouraud shaded), the actor's opacity (relative transparency), and the ambient, diffuse, and specular color and related coefficients. The following script shows how to set some of these instance variables.

```
vtkActor anActor
    anActor SetMapper mapper
    [anActor GetProperty] SetOpacity 0.25
    [anActor GetProperty] SetAmbient 0.5
    [anActor GetProperty] SetDiffuse 0.6
    [anActor GetProperty] SetSpecular 1.0
    [anActor GetProperty] SetSpecularPower 10.0
```

Notice how we dereference the actor's property via the GetProperty() method. Alternatively, we can create a property and assign it to the actor:

```
vtkProperty prop
    prop SetOpacity 0.25
    prop SetAmbient 0.5
    prop SetDiffuse 0.6
    prop SetSpecular 1.0
    prop SetSpecularPower 10.0
vtkActor anActor
    anActor SetMapper mapper
    anActor SetProperty prop
```

The advantage of the latter method is that we control the properties of several actors by assigning each the same property.

Actor Color. Color is perhaps the most important property applied to an actor. The simplest procedure is to use the SetColor() method to set the red, green, and blue (RGB) values of the actor. Each value ranges from zero to one.

```
    anActor SetColor 0.1 0.2 0.4
```

Alternatively, you can set the ambient, diffuse, and specular colors separately.

```
vtkActor anActor
    anActor SetMapper mapper
    [anActor GetProperty] SetAmbientColor .1 .1 .1
    [anActor GetProperty] SetDiffuseColor .1 .2 .4
    [anActor GetProperty] SetSpecularColor 1 1 1
```

In this example we've set the ambient color to a dark gray, the diffuse color to a shade of blue, and the specular color to white. (Note: The SetColor() method sets the ambient, diffuse, and specular colors to the color specified.)

Important: The color set in the actor's property only takes effect if there is no scalar data available to the actor's mapper. By default, the mapper's input scalar data colors the actor, and the actor's color is ignored. To ignore the scalar data, use the method ScalarVisibility-Off() as shown in the Tcl script below.

```
vtkPolyDataMapper planeMapper
    planeMapper SetInput [CompPlane GetOutput]
    planeMapper ScalarVisibilityOff
vtkActor planeActor
    planeActor SetMapper planeMapper
    [planeActor GetProperty] SetRepresentationToWireframe
    [planeActor GetProperty] SetColor 0 0 0
```

Actor Transparency. Many times it is useful to adjust transparency (or opacity) of an actor. For example, if you wish to show internal organs surrounded by the skin of a patient, adjusting the transparency of the skin allows the user to see the organs in relation to the skin. Use the vtkProperty::SetOpacity() method as follows:

```
vtkActor popActor
    popActor SetMapper popMapper
    [popActor GetProperty] SetOpacity 0.3
    [popActor GetProperty] SetColor .9 .9 .9
```

(Please note that transparency is implemented in the rendering library using an α-blending process. This process requires that polygons are rendered in the correct order. In practice, this is very difficult to achieve, especially if you have multiple transparent actors. To order polygons, you should add transparent actors to the end of renderer's list of actors (i.e., add them last). Also, you can use the filter vtkDepthSortPolyData to sort polygons along the view vector. Please see VTK/Examples/VisualizationAlgorithms/Tcl/ DepthSort.tcl for an example using this filter.)

Miscellaneous Features. Actors have several other important features. You can control whether an actor is visible with the VisibilityOn() and VisibilityOff() methods. If you don't want to pick an actor during a picking operation, use the PickableOff() method (see "Picking" on page 65 for more information about picking). Actors also have a pick event that can be invoked when they are picked. You can also get the axis-aligned bounding box of actor with the GetBounds() method.

Level-Of-Detail Actors

One major problem with graphics systems is that they often become too slow for interactive use. To handle this problem, VTK uses level-of-detail actors to achieve acceptable rendering performance at the cost of lower-resolution representations.

In "Reader Source Object" on page 47 we saw how to use a vtkLODActor. Basically, the simplest way to use vtkLODActor is to replace instances of vtkActor with instances of vtkLODActor. In addition, you can control the representation of the levels of detail. The default behavior of vtkLODActor is to create two additional, lower-resolution models from the original mapper. The first is a point cloud, sampled from the points defining the mapper's input. You can control the number of points in the cloud as follows. (The default is 150 points.)

```
vtkLODActor dotActor
   dotActor SetMapper dotMapper
   dotActor SetNumberOfCloudPoints 1000
```

The lowest resolution model is a bounding box of the actor. Additional levels of detail can be added using the AddLODMapper() method. They do not have to be added in order of complexity.

To control the level-of-detail selected by the actor during rendering, you can set the desired frame rate in the rendering window:

```
vtkRenderWindow renWin
   renWin SetDesiredUpdateRate 5.0
```

which translates into five frames per second. The vtkLODActor will automatically select the appropriate level-of-detail to yield the requested rate. (Note: The interactor widgets such as vtkRenderWindowInteractor automatically control the desired update rate. They typically set the frame rate very low when a mouse button is released, and increase the rate when a mouse button is pressed. This gives the pleasing effect of low-resolution/high frame rate models with camera motion, and high-resolution/low frame rate when the camera stops. If you would like more control over the levels-of-detail, see "vtkLODProp3D" on page 64. vtkLODProp3D allow you to specifically set each level.)

Assemblies

Actors are often grouped in hierarchal assemblies so that the motion of one actor affects the position of other actors. For example, a robot arm might consist of an upper arm, forearm, wrist, and end effector, all connected via joints. When the upper arm rotates around the shoulder joint, we expect the rest of the arm to move with it. This behavior is implemented using assemblies, which are a type of (subclass of) vtkActor. The following script shows how it's done (from VTK/Examples/Rendering/Tcl/assembly.tcl).

```
# create four parts: a top level assembly and three primitives
vtkSphereSource sphere
vtkPolyDataMapper sphereMapper
    sphereMapper SetInput [sphere GetOutput]
vtkActor sphereActor
    sphereActor SetMapper sphereMapper
    sphereActor SetOrigin 2 1 3
    sphereActor RotateY 6
    sphereActor SetPosition 2.25 0 0
    [sphereActor GetProperty] SetColor 1 0 1

vtkCubeSource cube
vtkPolyDataMapper cubeMapper
    cubeMapper SetInput [cube GetOutput]
vtkActor cubeActor
    cubeActor SetMapper cubeMapper
    cubeActor SetPosition 0.0 .25 0
    [cubeActor GetProperty] SetColor 0 0 1

vtkConeSource cone
vtkPolyDataMapper coneMapper
    coneMapper SetInput [cone GetOutput]
vtkActor coneActor
    coneActor SetMapper coneMapper
    coneActor SetPosition 0 0 .25
    [coneActor GetProperty] SetColor 0 1 0

vtkCylinderSource cylinder
vtkPolyDataMapper cylinderMapper
    CylinderMapper SetInput [cylinder GetOutput]
vtkActor cylinderActor
    cylinderActor SetMapper cylinderMapper
    [cylinderActor GetProperty] SetColor 1 0 0
```

```
vtkAssembly assembly
    assembly AddPart cylinderActor
    assembly AddPart sphereActor
    assembly AddPart cubeActor
    assembly AddPart coneActor
    assembly SetOrigin 5 10 15
    assembly AddPosition 5 0 0
    assembly RotateX 15

# Add the actors to the renderer, set the background and size
ren1 AddActor assembly
ren1 AddActor coneActor
```

Notice how we use vtkAssembly's AddPart() method to build the hierarchies. Assemblies can be nested arbitrarily deeply as long as there are not any self-referencing cycles. Note that vtkAssembly is a subclass of vtkProp3D, so it has no notion of properties or of an associated mapper. Therefore, the leaf nodes of the vtkAssembly hierarchy must carry information about material properties (color, etc.) and any associated geometry. Actors may also be used by more than one assembly (notice how coneActor is used in the assembly and as an actor). Also, the renderer's AddActor() method is used to associate the top level of the assembly with the renderer; those actors at lower levels in the assembly hierarchy do not need to be added to the renderer since they are recursively rendered.

You may be wondering how to distinguish the use of an actor relative to its context if an actor is used in more than one assembly, or is mixed with an assembly as in the example above. (This is particularly important in activities like picking, where the user may need to know which vtkProp was picked as well as the context in which it was picked.) We address this issue along with the introduction of the class vtkAssemblyPath, which is an ordered list of vtkProps with associated transformation matrices (if any), in detail in "Picking" on page 65.

Volumes

The class vtkVolume is used for volume rendering. It is analogous to the class vtkActor. Like vtkActor, vtkVolume inherits methods from vtkProp3D to position and orient the volume. vtkVolume has an associated property object, in this case a vtkVolumeProperty. Please see "Volume Rendering" on page 136 for a thorough description of the use of vtkVolume and a description of volume rendering.

vtkLODProp3D

The vtkLODProp3D class is similar to vtkLODActor (see "Level-Of-Detail Actors" on page 61) in that it uses different representations of itself in order to achieve interactive frame rates. Unlike vtkLODActor, vtkLODProp3D supports both volume rendering and surface rendering. This means that you can use vtkLODProp3D in volume rendering applications to achieve interactive frame rates. The following example shows how to use the class.

```
vtkLODProp3D lod
   set level1 [lod AddLOD volumeMapper volumeProperty2 0.0]
   set level2 [lod AddLOD volumeMapper volumeProperty 0.0]
   set level3 [lod AddLOD probeMapper_hres probeProperty 0.0]
   set level4 [lod AddLOD probeMapper_lres probeProperty 0.0]
   set level5 [lod AddLOD outlineMapper outlineProperty 0.0]
```

Basically, you create different mappers each corresponding to a different rendering complexity, and add the mappers to the vtkLODProp3D. The AddLOD() method accepts either volume or geometric mappers, and optionally a texture map and property object. (There are different signatures for this method depending on what information you wish to provide.) The last value in the field is an estimated time to render. Typically you set it to zero to indicate that there is no initial estimate. The method returns an integer id that can be used to access the appropriate LOD (i.e., to select a level or delete it).

vtkLODProp3D measures the time it takes to render each LOD and sorts them appropriately. Then, depending on the render window's desired update rate, vtkLODProp3D selects the appropriate level to render. See "Using a vtkLODProp3D to Improve Performance" on page 162 for more information.

4.7 Using Texture

Texture mapping is a powerful graphics tool for creating realistic and compelling visualizations. The basic idea behind 2D texture mapping is that images can be "pasted" onto a surface during the rendering process, thereby creating richer and more detailed images. Texture mapping requires two pieces of information: a texture map, which in VTK is a vtkImageData dataset (i.e., a 2D image); and texture coordinates, which control the positioning of the texture on a surface. (Note: 3D textures are also possible, but not yet widely supported by most rendering hardware.)

The following example (**Figure 4–5**) demonstrates the use of texture mapping (see VTK/Examples/Rendering/Tcl/TPlane.tcl). Notice that the texture map (of class vtkTexture) is associated with the actor, and the texture coordinates come from the plane (the texture coordinates are generated by vtkPlaneSource when the plane is created).

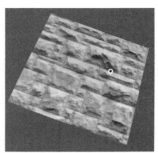

```
# load in the texture map
vtkBMPReader bmpReader
    bmpReader SetFileName "$VTK_DATA_ROOT/Data/
masonry.bmp"
vtkTexture atext
    atext SetInput [bmpReader GetOutput]
    atext InterpolateOn

# create a plane source and actor
vtkPlaneSource plane
vtkPolyDataMapper  planeMapper
    planeMapper SetInput [plane GetOutput]
vtkActor planeActor
    planeActor SetMapper planeMapper
    planeActor SetTexture atext
```

Figure 4–5 Texture map on plane

Often times texture coordinates are not available, usually because they are not generated in the pipeline. If you need to generate texture coordinates, refer to "Generate Texture Coordinates" on page 112. Also, you should note that while system graphics hardware/ libraries (e.g., OpenGL) only accept texture maps that are powers of two in dimensions (e.g., 128 x 256 and so on), in VTK non-power of two textures are automatically resampled onto a power of two, which may impact performance in some applications.

4.8 Picking

Picking is a common visualization task. Picking is used to select data and actors, or interrogate underlying data values. A pick is made when a display position (i.e., pixel coordinate) is selected and used to invoke vtkAbstractPicker's Pick() method. Depending on the type of picking class, the information returned from the pick may be as simple as an x-y-z global coordinate, or may include cell ids, point ids, cell parametric coordinates, the instance of vtkProp that was picked, and/or assembly paths. The syntax of the pick method is as follows.

```
Pick(selectionX, selectionY, selectionZ, Renderer)
```

Notice that the pick method requires a renderer. The actors associated with the renderer are the candidates for pick selection. Also, `selectionZ` is typically set to 0.0—it relates to depth in the *z*-buffer. (In typical usage, this method is not invoked directly. Rather the user interacts with the class vtkRenderWindowInteractor which manages the pick. In this case, the user would control the picking process by assigning an instance of a picking class to the vtkRenderWindowInteractor, as we will see in the example following later.)

The *Visualization Toolkit* supports several types of pickers of varying functionality and performance. (Please see **Figure 14–12** which is an illustration of the picking class hierarchy.) The class vtkAbstractPicker serves as the base class for all pickers. It defines a minimal API which allows the user to retrieve the pick position (in global coordinates) using the GetPickPosition() method.

Three direct subclasses of vtkAbstractPicker exist. The first, vtkWorldPointPicker, is a fast (usually in hardware) picking class that uses the *z*-buffer to return the *x-y-z* global pick position. However, no other information (about the vtkProp that was picked, etc.) is returned. The class vtkAbstractPropPicker is another direct subclass of vtkAbstractPicker. It defines an API for pickers that can pick an instance of vtkProp. There are several convenience methods in this class to allow query for the return type of a pick. The functionality of these methods can be obtained by calling GetPath() on the picker and using the IsA() method to determine the type.

- `GetProp()` — Return the instance of vtkProp that was picked. If anything at all was picked, then this method will return a pointer to the instance of vtkProp, otherwise `NULL` is returned.

- `GetProp3D()` — If an instance of vtkProp3D was picked, return a pointer to the instance of vtkProp3D.

- `GetActor2D()` — If an instance of vtkActor2D was picked, return a pointer to the instance of vtkActor2D.

- `GetActor()` — If an instance of vtkActor was picked, return a pointer to the instance of vtkActor.

- `GetVolume()` — If an instance of vtkVolume was picked, return a pointer to the instance of vtkVolume.

- `GetAssembly()` — If an instance of vtkAssembly was picked, return a pointer to the instance of vtkAssembly.

- `GetPropAssembly()` — If an instance of vtkPropAssembly was picked, return a pointer to the instance of vtkPropAssembly.

A word of caution about these methods. The class (and its subclass) return information about the *top level of the assembly path* that was picked. So if you have an assembly whose top level is of type vtkAssembly, and whose leaf node is of type vtkActor, the method GetAssembly() will return a pointer to the instance of vtkAssembly, while the GetActor() method will return a NULL pointer (i.e., no vtkActor). If you have a complex scene that includes assemblies, actors, and other types of props, the safest course to take is to use the GetProp() method to determine whether anything at all was picked, and then use GetPath().

There is one direct subclass of vtkAbstractPropPicker. vtkPropPicker uses hardware picking to determine the instance of vtkProp that was picked, as well as the pick position (in global coordinates). It is generally faster than vtkPicker and its subclasses, but cannot return information about what cell was picked, etc. Warning: In some graphics hardware (especially lower-cost PC boards) the pick operation is not implemented properly. In this case, you will have to use a software version of vtkAbstractPicker (one of the three classes described next.)

The third subclass of vtkAbstractPicker is vtkPicker, a software-based picker that selects vtkProp's based on their bounding box. Its pick method fires a ray from the camera position through the selection point and intersects the bounding box of each prop 3D; of course, more than one prop 3D may be picked. The "closest" prop 3D in terms of its bounding box intersection point along the ray is returned. (The GetProp3Ds() method can be used to get all prop 3D's whose bounding box was intersected.) vtkPicker is fairly fast but cannot generate a single unique pick.

vtkPicker has two subclasses that can be used to retrieve more detailed information about what was picked (e.g., point ids, cell ids, etc.) vtkPointPicker selects a point and returns the point id and coordinates. It operates by firing a ray from the camera position through the selection point, and projecting those points that lie within Tolerance onto the ray. The projected point closest to the camera position is selected, along with its associated actor. (Note: The instance variable Tolerance is expressed as a fraction of the renderer window's diagonal length.) vtkPointPicker is slower than vtkPicker but faster than vtkCellPicker. It cannot always return a unique pick because of the tolerances involved.

vtkCellPicker selects a cell and returns information about the intersection point (cell id, global coordinates, and parametric cell coordinates). It operates by firing a ray and intersecting all cells in each actor's underlying geometry, determining if each intersects this ray, within a certain specified tolerance. The cell closest to the camera position along the specified ray is selected, along with its associated actor. (Note: The instance variable Tolerance is used during intersection calculation, and you may need to experiment with its value to get satisfactory behavior.) vtkCellPicker is the slowest of all the pickers, but provides the most information. It will generate a unique pick within the tolerance specified.

Several events are defined to interact with the pick operation. The picker invokes Start-PickEvent prior to executing the pick operation. EndPickEvent is invoked after the pick operation is complete. The PickEvent and the actor's PickEvent are invoked each time an actor is picked.

vtkAssemblyPath

An understanding of the class vtkAssemblyPath is essential if you are to perform picking in a scene with different types of vtkProp's, especially if the scene contains instances of vtkAssembly. vtkAssemblyPath is simply an ordered list of vtkAssemblyNode's, where each node contains a pointer to a vtkProp, as well as an optional vtkMatrix4x4. The order of the list is important: the start of the list represents the root, or top level node in an assembly hierarchy, while the end of the list represents a leaf node in an assembly hierarchy. The ordering of the nodes also affects the associated matrix. Each matrix is a concatenation of the node's vtkProp's matrix with the previous matrix in the list. Thus, for a given vtkAssemblyNode, the associated vtkMatrix4x4 represents the position and orientation of the vtkProp (assuming that the vtkProp is initially untransformed).

Example

Typically, picking is automatically managed by vtkRenderWindowInteractor ("Using VTK Interactors" on page 48 for more information about interactors). For example, when pressing the p key, vtkRenderWindowInteractor invokes a pick with its internal instance of vtkPropPicker. You can then ask the vtkRenderWindowInteractor for its picker, and gather the information you need. You can also specify a particular vtkAbstractPicker instance for vtkRenderWindowInteractor to use, as the following script illustrates. The results on a sample data set are shown in **Figure 4–6**. The script for this example can be found in VTK/Examples/Annotation/Tcl/annotatePick.tcl.

```
vtkCellPicker picker
   picker AddObserver EndPickEvent annotatePick
vtkTextMapper textMapper
   textMapper SetFontFamilyToArial
   textMapper SetFontSize 10
   textMapper BoldOn
   textMapper ShadowOn
vtkActor2D textActor
   textActor VisibilityOff
   textActor SetMapper textMapper
   [textActor GetProperty] SetColor 1 0 0
vtkRenderWindowInteractor iren
   iren SetRenderWindow renWin
   iren SetPicker picker

proc annotatePick {} {
    if { [picker GetCellId] < 0 } {
       textActor VisibilityOff
    } else {
       set selPt [picker GetSelectionPoint]
       set x [lindex $selPt 0]
       set y [lindex $selPt 1]
       set pickPos [picker GetPickPosition]
       set xp [lindex $pickPos 0]
       set yp [lindex $pickPos 1]
       set zp [lindex $pickPos 2]
       textMapper SetInput "($xp, $yp, $zp)"
       textActor SetPosition $x $y
       textActor VisibilityOn
    }
    renWin Render
}
picker Pick 85 126 0 ren1
```

Figure 4–6 Annotating a pick operation.

This example uses a vtkTextMapper to draw the world coordinate of the pick on the screen (see "Annotation" on page 71 for more information). Notice that we register the EndPick-Event to perform setup after the pick occurs. The method is configured to invoke the annotatePick() procedure when picking is complete.

4.9 vtkCoordinate and Coordinate Systems

The *Visualization Toolkit* supports several different coordinate systems, and the class vtk-Coordinate manages transformations between them. The supported coordinate systems are as follows.

- DISPLAY — *x-y* pixel values in the (rendering) window. (Note that vtkRenderWindow is a subclass of vtkWindow). The origin is the lower-left corner (which is true for all 2D coordinate systems described below).

- NORMALIZED DISPLAY — *x-y* (0,1) normalized values in the window.

- VIEWPORT — *x-y* pixel values in the viewport (or renderer — a subclass of vtkViewport)

- NORMALIZED VIEWPORT — *x-y* (0,1) normalized values in viewport

- VIEW — *x-y-z* (-1,1) values in camera coordinates (*z* is depth)

- WORLD — *x-y-z* global coordinate value

- USERDEFINED - *x-y-z* in user-defined space. The user must provide a transformation method for user defined coordinate systems. See vtkCoordinate for more information.

The class vtkCoordinate can be used to transform between coordinate systems, and linked together to form "relative" or "offset" coordinate values. Refer to the next section for an example of using vtkCoordinate in an application.

4.10 Controlling vtkActor2D

vtkActor2D is analogous to vtkActor, except that it draws on the overlay plane, and does not have a 4x4 transformation matrix associated with it. Like vtkActor, vtkActor2D refers to a mapper (vtkMapper2D) and a property object (vtkProperty2D). The most difficult part when working with vtkActor2D is positioning it. To do that, the class vtkCoordinate is used (See previous section, "vtkCoordinate and Coordinate Systems"). The following script shows how to use the vtkCoordinate object.

```
vtkActor2D bannerActor
    bannerActor SetMapper banner
    [bannerActor GetProperty] SetColor 0 1 0
    [bannerActor GetPositionCoordinate]
```

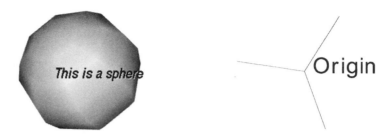

Figure 4–7 2D (left) and 3D (right) annotation.

```
                    SetCoordinateSystemToNormalizedDisplay
[bannerActor GetPositionCoordinate] SetValue 0.5 0.5
```

What's done in this script is to access the coordinate object and define it's coordinate system. Then the appropriate value is set for that coordinate system. In this script a normalized display coordinate system is used, so display coordinates range from zero to one, and the values (0.5,0.5) are set to position the vtkActor2D in the middle of the rendering window. vtkActor2D also provides a convenience method, SetDisplayPosition(), that sets the coordinate system to DISPLAY, and accepts the values as pixel offsets in the render window. The example in the following section shows how the method is used.

4.11 Annotation

The *Visualization Toolkit* offers two ways to annotate images. First, text (and graphics) can be rendered on top of the underlying 3D graphics window (often referred to as the overlay plane). Second, text can be created as 3D polygonal data, and transformed and displayed as any other 3D graphics object. We refer to this as 2D and 3D annotation, respectively. See **Figure 4–7** to see the difference.

2D Annotation

To use 2D annotation, we employ 2D actors (vtkActor2D and its subclasses such as vtkScaledTextActor) and mappers (vtkMapper2D and subclasses such as vtkTextMapper). 2D actors and mappers are similar to their 3D counterparts, except that they render in the overlay plane on top of underlying graphics or images. Here's an example Tcl script found in `VTK/Examples/Annotation/Tcl/TestText.tcl`; the results are shown on the left side of **Figure 4–7**.

```
vtkSphereSource sphere
vtkPolyDataMapper    sphereMapper
    sphereMapper SetInput [sphere GetOutput]
    sphereMapper GlobalImmediateModeRenderingOn
vtkLODActor sphereActor
    sphereActor SetMapper sphereMapper

vtkTextMapper textMapper
    textMapper SetInput "This is a sphere"
    textMapper SetFontSize 18
    textMapper SetFontFamilyToArial
    textMapper BoldOn
    textMapper ItalicOn
    textMapper ShadowOn
vtkScaledTextActor text
    text SetMapper textMapper
    text SetDisplayPosition 90 50
    [text GetProperty] SetColor 0 0 1

# Create the RenderWindow, Renderer and both Actors
vtkRenderer ren1
vtkRenderWindow renWin
    renWin AddRenderer ren1
vtkRenderWindowInteractor iren
    iren SetRenderWindow renWin

# Add the actors to the renderer, set the background and size
ren1 AddActor2D text
ren1 AddActor sphereActor
```

Instances of the class vtkTextMapper allow you to control font family (Arial, Courier, or Times), turn bolding and italics on and off, and support font shadowing (shadowing is used to make the font more readable when placed on top of complex background images). The position and color of the text is controlled by the associated vtkActor2D (in this example, the position is set using display or pixel coordinates). Notice how the AddActor2D() method is used to associate 2D actors with the renderer.

vtkTextMapper also supports justification (vertical and horizontal) and multi-line text. Use the methods SetJustificationToLeft(), SetJustificationToCentered(), and SetJustifica-

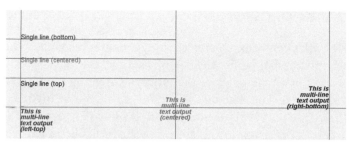

Figure 4–8 Justification and use of multi-line text. Use the \n character embedded in the text string to generate line breaks. Both vertical and horizontal justification is supported.

tionToRight() to control the horizontal justification. Use the methods SetVerticalJustification-ToBottom(), SetVerticalJustificationToCentered(), and SetVerticalJustificationTo-Top() to control vertical justification. By default, text is left-bottom justified. To insert multi-line text, use the \n character embedded in the text. The example in **Figure 4–8** demonstrates justification and multi-line text (taken from VTK/Examples/Annota-tion/Tcl/multiLineText.tcl)

The essence of the example is shown below.

```
vtkTextMapper textMapperL
    textMapperL SetInput "This is\nmulti-line\n
                            text output\n(left-top)"
    textMapperL SetFontSize 14
    textMapperL SetFontFamilyToArial
    textMapperL BoldOn
    textMapperL ItalicOn
    textMapperL ShadowOn
    textMapperL SetJustificationToLeft
    textMapperL SetVerticalJustificationToTop
    textMapperL SetLineSpacing 0.8
vtkActor2D textActorL
    textActorL SetMapper textMapperL
    [textActorL GetPositionCoordinate]
                    SetCoordinateSystemToNormalizedDisplay
    [textActorL GetPositionCoordinate] SetValue 0.05 0.5
    [textActorL GetProperty] SetColor 1 0 0
```

Note the use of the vtkCoordinate object (obtained by invoking the GetPositionCoordi-nate() method) to control the position of the actor in the normalized display coordinate system. See the previous section "vtkCoordinate and Coordinate Systems" on page 70 for more information about placing annotation.

3D Annotation and vtkFollower

3D annotation is implemented using vtkVectorText to create a polygonal representation of a text string, and then appropriately positioned in the scene. One useful class for positioning 3D text is vtkFollower. This class is a type of actor that always faces the renderer's active camera, thereby insuring that the text is readable. This Tcl script found in VTK/ Examples/Annotation/Tcl/textOrigin.tcl shows how to do this (**Figure 4–7**). The example creates an axes and labels the origin using an instance of vtkVectorText in combination with a vtkFollower.

```
vtkAxes axes
    axes SetOrigin 0 0 0
vtkPolyDataMapper axesMapper
    axesMapper SetInput [axes GetOutput]
vtkActor axesActor
    axesActor SetMapper axesMapper

vtkVectorText atext
    atext SetText "Origin"
vtkPolyDataMapper textMapper
    textMapper SetInput [atext GetOutput]
vtkFollower textActor
    textActor SetMapper textMapper
    textActor SetScale 0.2 0.2 0.2
    textActor AddPosition 0 -0.1 0
...etc...after rendering...
textActor SetCamera [ren1 GetActiveCamera]
```

As the camera moves around the axes, the follower will orient itself to face the camera. (Try this by mousing in the rendering window to move the camera.)

4.12 Special Plotting Classes

The *Visualization Toolkit* provides several composite classes that perform supplemental plotting operations. These include the ability to plot scalar bars, perform simple x-y plotting, and place flying axes for 3D spatial context.

Scalar Bar

The class vtkScalarBar is used to create a color-coded key that relates color values to numerical data values as shown in **Figure 4–9**. There are three parts to the scalar bar: a rectangular bar with colored segments, labels, and a title. To use vtkScalarBar, you must reference an instance of vtkLookup-Table (defines colors and the range of data values), position and orient the scalar bar on the overlay plane, and optionally specify attributes such as color, number of labels, and text string for the title. The following example shows typical usage.

Figure 4–9 vtkScalarBarActor used to create color legends.

```
vtkScalarBarActor scalarBar
   scalarBar SetLookupTable [mapper
GetLookupTable]
     scalarBar SetTitle "Temperature"
     [scalarBar GetPositionCoordinate] \
               SetCoordinateSystemToNormalizedViewport
     [scalarBar GetPositionCoordinate] SetValue 0.1 0.01
     scalarBar SetOrientationToHorizontal
     scalarBar SetWidth 0.8
     scalarBar SetHeight 0.17
```

The orientation of the scalar bar is controlled by the methods SetOrientationToVertical() and vtkSetOrientationToHorizontal(). To control the position of the scalar bar (i.e., its lower-left corner), set the position coordinate (in whatever coordinate system you desire—see "vtkCoordinate and Coordinate Systems" on page 70), and then specify the width and height using normalized viewport values (or alternatively, specify the Position2 instance variable to set the upper-right corner).

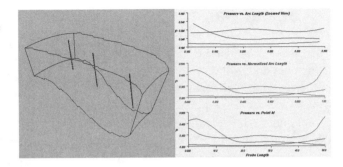

Figure 4–10 Example of using the vtkXYPlotActor2D class to display three probe lines using three different techniques (see Hybrid/Testing/Tcl/xyPlot.tcl).

X-Y Plots

The class vtkXYPlotActor generates *x-y* plots from one or more input datasets, as shown in **Figure 4–10**. This class is particularly useful for showing the variation of data across a sequence of points such as a line probe or a boundary edge.

To use vtkXYPlotActor2D, you must specify one or more input datasets, axes, and the plot title and position the composite actor on the overlay plane. The PositionCoordinate instance variable defines the lower-left location of the x-y plot (specified in normalized viewport coordinates) and the Position2Coordinate instance variable defines the upper-right corner. (Note: The Position2Coordinate is relative to PositionCoordinate, so you can move the vtkXYPlotActor around the viewport by setting just the PositionCoordinate.) The combination of the two position coordinates specifies a rectangle in which the plot will lie. The following example (from `VTK/Examples/Annotation/Tcl/xyPlot.tcl`) shows how the class is used.

```
vtkXYPlotActor xyplot
    xyplot AddInput [probe GetOutput]
    xyplot AddInput [probe2 GetOutput]
    xyplot AddInput [probe3 GetOutput]
    [xyplot GetPositionCoordinate] SetValue 0.0 0.67 0
    [xyplot GetPosition2Coordinate] SetValue 1.0 0.33 0
    xyplot SetXValuesToArcLength
    xyplot SetNumberOfXLabels 6
    xyplot SetTitle "Pressure vs. Arc Length (Zoomed View)"
    xyplot SetXTitle ""
    xyplot SetYTitle "P"
    xyplot SetXRange .1 .35
    xyplot SetYRange .2 .4
    [xyplot GetProperty] SetColor 0 0 0
```

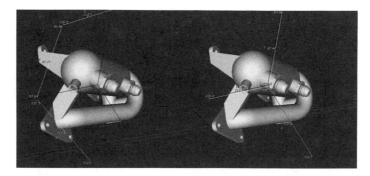

Figure 4–11 Use of vtkCubeAxisActor2D. On the left, outer edges of the cube are used to draw the axes. On the right, the closest vertex to the camera is used.

Note the *x* axis definition. By default, the *x* coordinate is set as the point index in the input datasets. Alternatively, you can use arc length and normalized arc length of lines used as input to vtkXYPlotActor to generate the *x* values.

Bounding Box Axes (vtkCubeAxesActor2D)

Another composite actor class is vtkCubeAxesActor2D. This class can be used to indicate the position in space that the camera is viewing, as shown in **Figure 4–11**. The class draws axes around the bounding box of the input dataset labeled with *x-y-z* coordinate values. As the camera zooms in, the axes are scaled to fit within the cameras viewport, and the label values are updated. The user can control various font attributes as well as the relative font size (The font size is selected automatically—the method SetFontFactor() can be used to affect the size of the selected font.) The following script demonstrates how to use the class (taken from VTK/Examples/Annotation/Tcl/cubeAxes.tcl).

```
vtkCubeAxesActor2D axes
    axes SetInput [normals GetOutput]
    axes SetCamera [ren1 GetActiveCamera]
    axes SetLabelFormat "%6.4g"
    axes ShadowOn
    axes SetFlyModeToOuterEdges
    axes SetFontFactor 0.8
    [axes GetProperty] SetColor 1 1 1
```

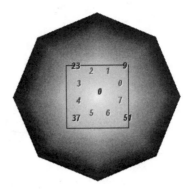

Figure 4–12 Labelling point and cell ids on a sphere within a window.

Note that there are two ways that the axes can be drawn. By default, the outer edges of the bounding box are used (SetFlyModeToOuterEdges()). You can also place the axes at the vertex closest to the camera position (SetFlyModeToClosestTriad())

Labeling Data

In some applications, you may wish to display numerical values from an underlying data set. The class vtkLabeledDataMapper allows you to label the data associated with the points of a dataset. This includes scalars, vectors, tensors, normals, texture coordinates, and field data, as well as the point ids of the dataset. The text labels are placed on the overlay plane of the rendered image as shown in **Figure 4–12**. The figure was generated from the Tcl script VTK/Examples/Annotation/Tcl/labeledMesh.tcl and included in part below. The script uses three new classes, vtkCellCenters (to generate points at the parametric centers of cells), vtkIdFilter (to generate ids as scalar or field data from dataset ids), and vtkSelectVisiblePoints (to select those points currently visible), to label the cell and point ids of the sphere. In addition, vtkSelectVisiblePoints has the ability to define a "window" in display (pixel) coordinates in which it operates—all points outside of the window are discarded.

```
# Create a sphere
vtkSphereSource sphere
vtkPolyDataMapper    sphereMapper
    sphereMapper SetInput [sphere GetOutput]
    sphereMapper GlobalImmediateModeRenderingOn
vtkActor sphereActor
    sphereActor SetMapper sphereMapper
```

```
# Generate ids for labeling
vtkIdFilter ids
    ids SetInput [sphere GetOutput]
    ids PointIdsOn
    ids CellIdsOn
    ids FieldDataOn

# Create labels for points
vtkSelectVisiblePoints visPts
    visPts SetInput [ids GetOutput]
    visPts SetRenderer ren1
    visPts SelectionWindowOn
    visPts SetSelection $xmin [expr $xmin + $xLength] \
    $ymin [expr $ymin + $yLength]
vtkLabeledDataMapper ldm
    ldm SetInput [visPts GetOutput]
    ldm SetLabelFormat "%g"
    ldm SetLabelModeToLabelFieldData
vtkActor2D pointLabels
    pointLabels SetMapper ldm

# Create labels for cells
vtkCellCenters cc
    cc SetInput [ids GetOutput]
vtkSelectVisiblePoints visCells
    visCells SetInput [cc GetOutput]
    visCells SetRenderer ren1
    visCells SelectionWindowOn
    visCells SetSelection $xmin [expr $xmin + $xLength] \
    $ymin [expr $ymin + $yLength]
vtkLabeledDataMapper cellMapper
    cellMapper SetInput [visCells GetOutput]
    cellMapper SetLabelFormat "%g"
    cellMapper SetLabelModeToLabelFieldData
vtkActor2D cellLabels
    cellLabels SetMapper cellMapper
    [cellLabels GetProperty] SetColor 0 1 0

# Add the actors to the renderer, set the background and size
ren1 AddActor sphereActor
ren1 AddActor2D pointLabels
ren1 AddActor2D cellLabels
```

4.13 Transforming Data

As we saw in the section "Specifying the Position of a vtkProp3D" on page 56, it is possible to position and orient vtkProp3D's in world space. However, in many applications we wish to transform the data prior to using it in the visualization pipeline. For example, to use a plane to cut ("Cutting" on page 96) or clip ("Clip Data" on page 111) an object, the plane must be positioned within the pipeline, not via the actor transformation matrix. Some objects (especially procedural source objects) can be created at a specific position and orientation in space. For example, vtkSphereSource has a Center and Radius instance variable, and vtkPlaneSource has Origin, Point1, and Point2 instance variables that allow you to position the plane using three points. However, many classes do not provide this capability, without moving data into a new position. In this case, you must transform the data using vtkTransformFilter or vtkTransformPolyDataFilter.

vtkTransformFilter is a filter that takes vtkPointSet dataset objects as input. Datasets that are subclasses of the abstract class vtkPointSet represent points explicitly, that is, an instance of vtkPoints is used to store coordinate information. vtkTransformFilter applies a transformation matrix to the points and create a transformed points array; the rest of the dataset structure (i.e., cell topology) and attribute data (e.g., scalars, vectors, etc.) remains unchanged. vtkTransformPolyData-Filter does the same thing as vtkTransformFilter except that it is more convenient to use in a visualization pipeline containing polygonal data.

Figure 4–13 Transforming data within the pipeline.

The following example (taken from VTK/Examples/DataManipulation/Tcl/ marching.tcl with results shown in **Figure 4–13**) uses a vtkTransformPolyDataFilter to reposition a 3D text string (See "3D Annotation and vtkFollower" on page 74) for more information about 3D text)

```
#define the text for the labels
vtkVectorText caseLabel
  caseLabel SetText "Case 12c - 11000101"
vtkTransform aLabelTransform
  aLabelTransform Identity
  aLabelTransform Translate  -.2 0 1.25
  aLabelTransform Scale .05 .05 .05
vtkTransformPolyDataFilter labelTransform
```

```
labelTransform SetTransform aLabelTransform
labelTransform SetInput [caseLabel GetOutput]
vtkPolyDataMapper labelMapper
labelMapper SetInput [labelTransform GetOutput];
vtkActor labelActor
labelActor SetMapper labelMapper
```

Notice that vtkTransformPolyDataFilter requires that you supply it with an instance of vtkTransform. Recall that vtkTransform is used by actors to control their position and orientation in space. Instances of vtkTransform supports many methods, some of the most commonly used are shown here.

*   RotateX(angle) — apply rotation (angle in degrees) around the *x* axis

*   RotateY(angle) — apply rotation around the *y* axis

*   RotateZ(angle) — apply rotation around the *z* axis

*   RotateWXYZ(angle,x,y,z) — apply rotation around a vector defined by *x-y-z* components

*   Scale(x,y,z) — apply scale in the *x*, *y*, and *z* directions

*   Translate(x,y,z) — apply translation

*   Inverse() — invert the transformation matrix

*   SetMatrix(m) — specify the 4x4 transformation matrix directly

*   GetMatrix(m) — get the 4x4 transformation matrix

*   PostMultiply() — control the order of multiplication of transformation matrices. If PostMultiply() is invoked, matrix operations are applied on the right hand side of the current matrix.

*   PreMultiply() — matrix multiplications are applied on the left hand side of the current transformation matrix

The last two methods described above remind us that the order in which transformations are applied dramatically affects the resulting transformation matrix (see "Specifying the Position of a vtkProp3D" on page 56). We recommend that you spend some time experimenting with these methods, and the order of application, to fully understand vtkTransform.

Advanced Transformation

Advanced users may wish to use VTK's extensive transformation hierarchy. (Much of this work was done by David Gobbi.) The hierarchy, of which the class hierarchy is shown in **Figure 14–13**, supports a variety of linear and non-linear transformations.

A wonderful feature of the VTK transformation hierarchy is that different types of transformation can be used in a filter to give very different results. For example, the vtkTransformPolyDataFilter accepts any transform of type vtkAbstractTransform (or a subclass). This includes transformation types ranging from the linear, affine vtkTransform (represented by a 4x4 matrix) to the non-linear, warp vtkThinPlateSplineTransform, which is a complex function representing a correlation between a set of source and target landmarks.

## Chapter 5

Visualization Techniques

Some basic tools to render and interact with data were presented in the previous chapter. In this chapter we'll show you a variety of visualization techniques. These techniques (implemented as filters) are organized according to the type of data they operate on. Some filters are general and can be applied to any type of data—those filters that accept input of class vtkDataSet (or any subclass). Many filters are more specialized to the type of input they accept (e.g., vtkPolyData). There is one class of filters—those that accept input of type vtkImageData (or its obsolete subclass vtkStructuredPoints)—that are not addressed in this chapter. Instead, filters of this type are described in the next chapter ("Visualization Techniques" on page 83).

Please keep two things to keep in mind while you read this chapter. First, filters generate a variety of output types, and the output type is not necessarily the same as the input type. Second, filters are used in combination to create complex data processing pipelines. Often there are patterns of usage, or common combinations of filters, that are used. In the following examples you may wish to note these combinations.

5.1 Visualizing vtkDataSet (and Subclasses)

In this section, we'll show you how to perform some common visualization operations on data objects of type vtkDataSet. Recall that vtkDataSet is the superclass for all concrete types of visualization data (see **Figure 3–2**). Therefore, the methods described here are applicable to all of the various data types. (In other words, all filters taking vtkDataSet as input will also accept vtkPolyData, vtkImageData, vtkStructuredGrid, vtkRectilinearGrid, and vtkUnstructuredGrid.)

Working With Data Attributes

Data attributes are information associated with the structure of the dataset (as described in "The Visualization Model" on page 23). In VTK, attribute data is associated with points (point attribute data) and cells (cell attribute data). Attribute data, along with the dataset structure, are processed by the many VTK filters to generate new structures and attributes.

A general introduction to attribute data is beyond the scope of this section, but a simple example will demonstrate the basic ideas. (You may wish to refer to "Interface To Field and Attribute Data" on page 270 for more information and **Figure 11–1**.)

Data attributes are simply vtkDataArrays which may be labeled as being one of scalars, vectors, tensors, normals, or texture coordinates. The data attributes may be associated with the points or cells of a vtkDataSet. Every vtkDataArray associated with a vtkDataSet is a concrete subclass of vtkDataArray, such as vtkFloatArray or vtkIntArray. These data arrays can be thought of as contiguous, linear blocks of memory of the named native type. Within this linear block, the data array is thought to consist of subarrays or "tuples." Creating attribute data means instantiating a data array of desired type, specifying the tuple size, inserting data, and associating it with a dataset, as shown in the following Tcl script. The association may have the side effect of labeling the data as scalars, vectors, tensors, texture coordinates, or normals. For example:

```
vtkFloatArray scalars
    scalars InsertTuple1 0 1.0
    scalars InsertTuple1 1 1.2
    ...etc...

vtkDoubleArray vectors
    vectors SetNumberOfComponents 3
    vectors InsertTuple3 0 0.0 0.0 1.0
    vectors InsertTuple3 1 1.2 0.3 1.1
    ...etc...

vtkIntArray justAnArray
    justAnArray SetNumberOfComponents 2
    justAnArray SetNumberOfTuples $numberOfPoints
    justAnArray SetName "Solution Attributes"
    justAnArray SetTuple2 0 1 2
    justAnArray SetTuple2 1 3 4
    ...etc...

vtkPolyData polyData;#A concrete type of vtkDataSet
    [polyData GetPointData] SetScalars scalars
    [polyData GetCellData] SetVectors vectors
    [polyData GetPointData] AddArray justAnArray
```

Here we create three arrays of types `float`, `double`, and `int`. The first array (`scalars`) is instantiated and by default has a tuple size of one. The method InsertTuple1() is used to place data into the array (all methods named Insert___() allocate memory as necessary to hold data). The next data array (`vectors`) is created with a tuple size of three, because vectors are defined as having three components, and InsertTuple3 is used to add data to the array. Finally, we create a general array of tuple size two, and allocate memory using Set-NumberOfTuples(). We then use SetTuple2() to add data; this method assumes that memory has been allocated and is therefore faster than the similar Insert__() methods. Notice that the labelling of what is a scalar, vector, etc. occurs when we associate the data arrays with the point data or cell data of the dataset (using the methods SetScalars() and SetVectors()). Please remember that the number of point attributes (e.g., number of scalars in this example) must equal the number of points in the dataset, and the number of cell attributes (e.g., number of vectors) must match the number of cells in the dataset.

Similarly, to access attribute data, use these methods

```
set scalars [[polyData GetPointData] GetScalars]
set vectors [[polyData GetCellData] GetVectors]
```

You'll find that many of the filters work with attribute data specifically. For example, vtkElevationFilter generates scalar values based on their elevation in a specified direction. Other filters work with the structure of the dataset, and generally ignore or pass the attribute data through the filter (e.g., vtkDecimatePro). And finally, some filters work with (portions of) the attribute data and the structure to generate their output. vtkMarchingCubes is one example. It uses the input scalars in combination with the dataset structure to generate contour primitives (i.e., triangles, lines or points). Other types of attribute data, such as vectors, are interpolated during the contouring process and sent to the output of the filter.

Another important issue regarding attribute data is that some filters will process only one type of attribute (point data versus cell data), ignoring or passing to their output the other attribute data type. You may find that your input data is of one attribute type and you want to process it with a filter that will not handle that type, or you simply want to convert from one attribute type to another. There are two filters that can help you with this: vtkPointDataToCellData and vtkCellDataToPointData, which convert to and from point and cell data attributes. Here's an example of their use (from the Tcl scrip VTK/Examples/DataManipulation/Tcl/pointToCellData.tcl).

```
vtkUnstructuredGridReader reader
    reader SetFileName "$VTK_DATA_ROOT/Data/blow.vtk"
    reader SetScalarsName "thickness9"
    reader SetVectorsName "displacement9"
```

```
vtkPointDataToCellData p2c
    p2c SetInput [reader GetOutput]
    p2c PassPointDataOn
vtkWarpVector warp
    warp SetInput [p2c GetUnstructuredGridOutput]
vtkThreshold thresh
    thresh SetInput [warp GetOutput]
    thresh ThresholdBetween 0.25 0.75
    thresh SetAttributeModeToUseCellData
```

This example is interesting because it demonstrates the conversion between attribute data types (vtkPointDataToCellData), and the use of a filter that can process either cell data or point data (vtkThreshold). The method PassPointDataOn() indicates to vtkPointDataTo-CellData to create cell data and also pass to its output the input point data. The method SetAttributeModeToUseCellData() configures the vtkThreshold filter to use the cell data to perform the thresholding operation.

The conversion between point and cell data and vice versa is performed using an averaging algorithm. Point data is converted to cell data by averaging the values of the point data associated with the points used by a given cell. Cell data is converted to point data by averaging the cell data associated with the cells that use a given point.

Color Mapping

Probably the single most used visualization technique is coloring objects via scalar value, or color mapping. The ideas behind this technique is simple: scalar values are mapped through a lookup table to obtain a color, and the color is applied during rendering to modify the appearance of points or cells. Before proceeding with this section, make sure that you understand how to control the color of an actor (see "Actor Color" on page 59).

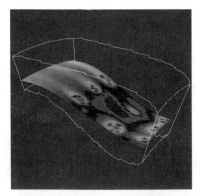

Figure 5–1 Color mapping.

In VTK, color mapping is typically controlled by scalars, which we assume you've created or read from a data file, and the lookup table, which is used by instances of vtkMapper to perform color mapping. It is also possible to use any data array to perform the coloring, just use the method

ColorByArrayComponent(). If not specified, a default lookup table is created by the mapper, but you can create your own (taken from `VTK/Examples/Rendering/Tcl/rainbow.tcl`—see **Figure 5–1**).

```
vtkLookupTable lut
    lut SetNumberOfColors 64
    lut SetHueRange 0.0 0.667
    lut Build
    for {set i 0} {$i<16} {incr i 1} {
        eval lut SetTableValue [expr $i*16] $red 1
        eval lut SetTableValue [expr $i*16+1] $green 1
        eval lut SetTableValue [expr $i*16+2] $blue 1
        eval lut SetTableValue [expr $i*16+3] $black 1
    }
vtkPolyDataMapper planeMapper
    planeMapper SetLookupTable lut
    planeMapper SetInput [plane GetOutput]
    planeMapper SetScalarRange 0.197813 0.710419
vtkActor planeActor
    planeActor SetMapper planeMapper
```

Lookup tables can be manipulated in two different ways, as this example illustrates. First, you can specify a HSVA (Hue-Saturation-Value-Alpha transparency) ramp that is used to generate the colors in the table using linear interpolation in HSVA space (the Build() method actually generates the table). Second, you can manually insert colors at specific locations in the table. Note that the number of colors in the table can be set. Also, you can generate the table with the HSVA ramp, and then replace colors in the table with the SetTableValue() method.

The mapper's SetScalarRange() method controls how scalars are mapped into the table. Scalar values greater than the maximum value are clamped to the maximum value. Scalar values less than the minimum value are clamped to the minimum value. Using the scalar range let's you "expand" a region of the scalar data by mapping more colors to it.

Sometimes the scalar data is actually color, and does not need to be mapped through a lookup table. The mapper provides several methods to control the mapping behavior.

- SetColorModeToDefault() invokes the default mapper behavior. The default behavior treats scalars of data type `unsigned char` as colors and performs no mapping; all other types of scalars are mapped through the lookup table.

- SetColorModeToMapScalars() maps all scalars through the lookup table, regardless of type. If the scalar has more than one component per tuple, then the scalars zeroth component is used perform the mapping.

Another important feature of vtkMapper is controlling which attribute data (i.e., point or cell scalars, or a general data array) is used to color objects. The following methods let you control this behavior. Note that these methods give strikingly different results: point attribute data is interpolated across rendering primitives during the rendering process, whereas cell attribute data colors the cell a constant value.

- SetScalarModeToDefault() invokes the default mapper behavior. The default behavior uses point scalars to color objects unless they are not available, in which case cell scalars are used, if they are available.

- SetScalarModeToUsePointData() always uses point data to color objects. If no point scalar data is available, then the object color is not affected by scalar data.

- SetScalarModeToUseCellData() always uses cell data to color objects. If no cell scalar data is available, then the object color is not affected by scalar data.

- SetScalarModeToUsePointFieldData() indicates that neither the point or cell scalars are to be used, but rather a data array found in the point attribute data. This method should be used in conjunction with ColorByArrayComponent() to specify the data array and component to use as the scalar.

- SetScalarModeToUseCellFieldData() indicates that neither the point or cell scalars are to be used, but rather a data array found in the cell field data. This method should be used in conjunction with ColorByArrayComponent() to specify the data array and component to use as the scalar.

Normally the default behavior works well, unless both cell and point scalar data is available. In this case, you will probably want to explicitly indicate whether to use point scalars or cell scalars to color your object.

Contouring

Another common visualization technique is generating contours. Contours are lines or surfaces of constant scalar value. In VTK, the filter vtkContourFilter is used to perform contouring as shown in the following Tcl example from VTK/Examples/VisualizationAlgorithms/VisQuad.tcl—refer to **Figure 5–2**.

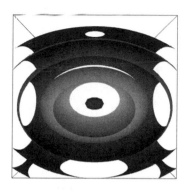

```
# Create 5 surfaces in range specified
vtkContourFilter contours
  contours SetInput [sample GetOutput]
  contours GenerateValues 5 0.0 1.2
vtkPolyDataMapper contMapper
  contMapper SetInput [contours GetOutput]
  contMapper SetScalarRange 0.0 1.2
vtkActor contActor
  contActor SetMapper contMapper
```

Figure 5–2 Generating contours.

You can specify contour values in two ways. The simplest way is to use the SetValue() method to specify the contour number and its value (multiple values can be specified)

```
  contours SetValue 0 0.5
```

The earlier example demonstrated the second way: the GenerateValues(). With this method, you specify the scalar range and the number of contours to be generated in the range (end values inclusive).

Note that there are several objects in VTK that perform contouring specialized to a particular dataset type (and are faster). Examples include vtkMarchingCubes, vtkMarchingSquares, and so on. You do not need to instantiate these directly if you use vtkContourFilter; the filter will select the best contouring function for your dataset type automatically.

Glyphing

Glyphing is a visualization technique that represents data by using symbols, or glyphs (**Figure 5–3**). The symbols can be simple or complex, ranging from oriented cones to show vector data, to complex, multivariate glyphs such as Chernoff faces (symbolic representations of the human face whose expression is controlled by data values). In VTK, the vtkGlyph3D class allows you to create glyphs that can be scaled, colored, and oriented along a direction. The glyphs are copied at each point of the input dataset. The glyph itself is defined by the second input to the filter (which is of type vtkPolyData), the Source instance variable. The following script demonstrates the use of vtkGlyph3D (the Tcl script is taken from VTK/Examples/VisualizationAlgorithms/Tcl/spikeF.tcl).

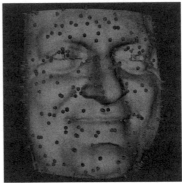

Figure 5–3 Glyphs showing surface normals.

```
vtkPolyDataReader fran
    fran SetFileName "$VTK_DATA_ROOT/Data/fran_cut.vtk"
vtkPolyDataNormals normals
    normals SetInput [fran GetOutput]
    normals FlipNormalsOn
vtkPolyDataMapper franMapper
    franMapper SetInput [normals GetOutput]
vtkActor franActor
    franActor SetMapper franMapper
    eval [franActor GetProperty] SetColor 1.0 0.49 0.25

vtkMaskPoints ptMask
    ptMask SetInput [normals GetOutput]
    ptMask SetOnRatio 10
    ptMask RandomModeOn

# In this case we are using a cone as a glyph. We transform the cone so
# its base is at 0,0,0. This is the point where glyph rotation occurs.
vtkConeSource cone
    cone SetResolution 6
vtkTransform transform
    transform Translate 0.5 0.0 0.0
vtkTransformPolyDataFilter transformF
    transformF SetInput [cone GetOutput]
```

```
    transformF SetTransform transform

vtkGlyph3D glyph
    glyph SetInput [ptMask GetOutput]
    glyph SetSource [transformF GetOutput]
    glyph SetVectorModeToUseNormal
    glyph SetScaleModeToScaleByVector
    glyph SetScaleFactor 0.004
vtkPolyDataMapper spikeMapper
    spikeMapper SetInput [glyph GetOutput]
vtkActor spikeActor
    spikeActor SetMapper spikeMapper
    eval [spikeActor GetProperty] SetColor 0.0 0.79 0.34
```

The purpose of the script is to indicate the direction of surface normals using small, oriented cones. An input dataset (from a Cyberware laser digitizing system) is read and displayed. Next, the filter vtkMaskPoints is used to subsample the points (and associated point attribute data) from the Cyberware data. This serves as the input to the vtkGlyph3D instance. A vtkConeSource is used as the Source for the glyph instance. Notice that the cone is translated (with vtkTransformPolyDataFilter) so that its base is on the origin (0,0,0) (since vtkGlyph3D rotates the source object around the origin).

The vtkGlyph3D object glyph is configured to use the point attribute normals as the orientation vector. (Alternatively, use SetVectorModeToUseVector() to use the vector data instead of the normals.) It also scales the cones by the magnitude of the vector value there, with the given scale factor. (You can scale the glyphs by scalar data or turn data scaling off with the SetScaleModeToScaleByScalar() and SetScaleModeToDataScalingOff().)

It is also possible to color the glyphs with scalar or vector data, or by the scale factor. You can also create a table of glyphs, and use scalar or vector data to index into the table. Refer to the man pages for more information.

Streamlines

A streamline can be thought of as the path that a massless particle takes in a vector field (e.g., velocity field). Streamlines are used to convey the structure of a vector field. Usually multiple streamlines are created to explore interesting features in the field (**Figure 5–4**). Streamlines are computed via numerical integration (integrating the product of velocity times Δt), and are therefore only approximations to the actual streamlines.

Creating a streamlines requires specifying a starting point (or points, if multiple streamlines), an integration direction (along the flow, or opposite the flow direction, or in both directions), and other parameters to control its propagation. The following script shows how to create a single streamline. The streamline is wrapped with a tube whose radius is proportional to the inverse of velocity magnitude. This indicates where the flow is slow (fat tube) and where it is fast (thin tube). This Tcl script is extracted from VTK/Examples/Visualiza-tionAlgorithms/Tcl/officeTube.tcl.

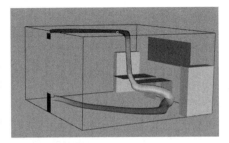

Figure 5–4 Streamline wrapped with a tube.

```
# Read structured grid data
vtkStructuredGridReader reader
    reader SetFileName "$VTK_DATA_ROOT/Data/office.binary.vtk"
    reader Update;#force a read to occur

# Create source for streamtubes
vtkRungeKutta4 integ
vtkStreamLine streamer
    streamer SetInput [reader GetOutput]
    streamer SetStartPosition 0.1 2.1 0.5
    streamer SetMaximumPropagationTime 500
    streamer SetStepLength 0.5
    streamer SetIntegrationDirectionToIntegrateBothDirections
    streamer SetIntegrator integ
vtkTubeFilter streamTube
    streamTube SetInput [streamer GetOutput]
    streamTube SetRadius 0.05
    streamTube SetNumberOfSides 6
    streamTube SetVaryRadiusToVaryRadiusByVector
vtkPolyDataMapper mapStreamTube
    mapStreamTube SetInput [streamTube GetOutput]
    eval mapStreamTube SetScalarRange \
        [[[[reader GetOutput] GetPointData] GetScalars] \
                GetRange];#this is why we did an Update
vtkActor streamTubeActor
    streamTubeActor SetMapper mapStreamTube
```

In this example we've selected a starting point by specifying the world coordinate (0.1,2.1,0.5). It's also possible to specify a starting location by using cellId, cell subId, and parametric coordinates. The MaximumPropagationTime instance variable controls the maximum length of the streamline (measured in units of time), and StepLength controls the size of the output line segments that make up the streamline (which is represented as a polyline). If you want greater accuracy (at the cost of more computation time) set the IntegrationStepLength instance variable to a smaller value. IntegrationStepLength is a number between (0,1) that indicates the step length as a fraction of the current cell size based on the diagonal length of the cells bounding box. Accuracy improvements can also be realized by choosing a different subclass of vtkInitialValueProblemSolver such as vtkRungeKutta4. (By default, the streamer classes use vtkRungeKutta2 to perform the numerical integration.)

You can also control the direction of integration with the methods:

- SetIntegrationDirectionToIntegrateForward()
- SetIntegrationDirectionToIntegrateBackward()
- SetIntegrationDirectionToIntegrateBothDirections()

Lines are often difficult to see and create useful images from. In this example we wrap the lines with a tube filter. The tube filter is configured to vary the radius of the tube inversely proportional to the velocity magnitude (i.e., a flux preserving relationship if the flow field is incompressible). The SetVaryRadiusToVaryRadiusByVector() enables this. You can also vary the radius by scalar value (SetVaryRadiusToVaryRadiusByScalar()) or turn off variable radius (SetVaryRadiusToVaryRadiusOff()).

As suggested earlier, we often wish to generate many streamlines simultaneously. One way to do this is to use the SetSource() method to specify an instance of vtkDataSet whose points are used to seed streamlines. Here's an example of its use (from VTK/Examples/ VisualizationAlgorithms/Tcl/officeTubes.tcl).

```
vtkPointSource seeds
    seeds SetRadius 0.15
    eval seeds SetCenter 0.1 2.1 0.5
    seeds SetNumberOfPoints 6
vtkRungeKutta4 integ
vtkStreamLine streamer
    streamer SetInput [reader GetOutput]
    streamer SetSource [seeds GetOutput]
    streamer SetMaximumPropagationTime 500
    streamer SetStepLength 0.5
    streamer SetIntegrationStepLength 0.05
    streamer SetIntegrationDirectionToIntegrateBothDirections
```

```
     streamer SetIntegrator integ

vtkTubeFilter streamTube
    streamTube SetInput [streamer GetOutput]
    streamTube SetRadius 0.02
    streamTube SetNumberOfSides 12
    streamTube SetVaryRadiusToVaryRadiusByVector
vtkPolyDataMapper mapStreamTube
    mapStreamTube SetInput [streamTube GetOutput]
    eval mapStreamTube SetScalarRange \
        [[[[reader GetOutput] GetPointData] GetScalars] GetRange]
vtkActor streamTubeActor
    streamTubeActor SetMapper mapStreamTube
    [streamTubeActor GetProperty] BackfaceCullingOn
```

Notice that the example uses the source object vtkPointSource to create a spherical cloud of points, which are then set as the source to `streamers`. For every point (inside the input dataset) a streamline will be computed.

Stream Surfaces

Advanced users may want to use VTK's stream surface capability. Stream surfaces are generated in two
parts. First, a rake or series of ordered points are used
to generate a series of streamlines. Then, vtkRuled-
SurfaceFilter is used to create a surface from the
streamlines. It is very important that the points (and
hence streamlines) are ordered carefully because the
vtkRuledSurfaceFilter assumes that the lines lie next
to one another, and are within a specified distance
(DistanceFactor) of the neighbor to the left and right.

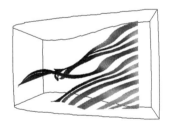

Figure 5–5 Stream surface.

Otherwise, the surface tears or you can obtain poor results. The following script (taken
from VTK/Examples/VisualizationAlgorithms/Tcl/streamSurface.tcl and
shown in **Figure 5–5**.

```
vtkLineSource rake
  rake SetPoint1 15 -5 32
  rake SetPoint2 15 5 32
  rake SetResolution 21
vtkPolyDataMapper rakeMapper
  rakeMapper SetInput [rake GetOutput]
```

```
vtkActor rakeActor
  rakeActor SetMapper rakeMapper

vtkRungeKutta4 integ
vtkStreamLine sl
  sl SetInput [pl3d GetOutput]
  sl SetSource [rake GetOutput]
  sl SetIntegrator integ
  sl SetMaximumPropagationTime 0.1
  sl SetIntegrationStepLength 0.1
  sl SetIntegrationDirectionToBackward
  sl SetStepLength 0.001

vtkRuledSurfaceFilter scalarSurface
  scalarSurface SetInput [sl GetOutput]
  scalarSurface SetOffset 0
  scalarSurface SetOnRatio 2
  scalarSurface PassLinesOn
  scalarSurface SetRuledModeToPointWalk
  scalarSurface SetDistanceFactor 30
vtkPolyDataMapper mapper
  mapper SetInput [scalarSurface GetOutput]
  eval mapper SetScalarRange [[pl3d GetOutput] GetScalarRange]
vtkActor actor
  actor SetMapper mapper
```

A nice feature of the vtkRuledSurfaceFilter is the ability to turn off strips, if multiple lines are provided as input to the filter (the method SetOnRatio()). This helps understand the structure of the surface.

Cutting

Cutting, or slicing, a dataset in VTK entails creating a "cross-section" through the dataset using any type of implicit function. For example, we can slice through a dataset with a plane to create a planar cut. The cutting surface interpolates the data as it cuts, which can then be visualized using any standard visualization technique. The result of cutting is always of type vtkPolyData. (Cutting a *n*-dimensional cell results in a *(n-1)*-dimensional output primitive. For example, cutting a tetrahedron creates either a triangle or quadrilateral.)

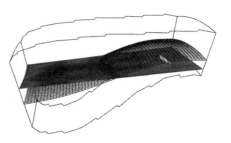

Figure 5–6 Cutting a combustor.

In the following Tcl example, a combustor (structured grid) is cut with a plane as shown in **Figure 5–6**. The example is taken from VTK/Examples/VisualizationAlgorithms/Tcl/probe.tcl.

```
vtkPlane plane
    eval plane SetOrigin [[pl3d GetOutput] GetCenter]
    plane SetNormal -0.287 0 0.9579
vtkCutter planeCut
    planeCut SetInput [pl3d GetOutput]
    planeCut SetCutFunction plane
vtkPolyDataMapper cutMapper
    cutMapper SetInput [planeCut GetOutput]
    eval cutMapper SetScalarRange \
      [[[[pl3d GetOutput] GetPointData] GetScalars] GetRange]
vtkActor cutActor
    cutActor SetMapper cutMapper
```

vtkCutter requires that you specify an implicit function with which to cut. Also, you may wish to specify one or more cut values using the SetValue() or GenerateValues() methods. These values specify the value of the implicit function used to perform the cutting. (Typically the cutting value is zero, meaning that the cut surface is precisely on the implicit function. Values less than or greater than zero are implicit surfaces below and above the implicit surface. The cut value can also be thought of as a "distance" to the implicit surface, which is only strictly true for vtkPlane.)

Merging Data

Up to this point we have seen simple, linear visualization pipelines. However, it is possible for pipelines to have loops, and for pieces of data to move from one leg of the pipeline to another. In this section and the following, we introduce two filters that allow you to build datasets from other datasets. We'll start with vtkMergeFilter.

vtkMergeFilter merges pieces of data from several datasets into a new dataset. For example, you can take the structure (topology and geometry) from one dataset, the scalars from a second, and the vectors from a third dataset, and combine them into a single dataset. Here's an example of its use (From the Tcl script VTK/Examples/VisualizationAlgorithms/Tcl/imageWarp.tcl). (Please ignore those filters that you don't recognize, focus on the use of vtkMergeFilter. We'll describe more fully the details of the script in "Warp Based On Scalar Values" on page 125.)

```
vtkBMPReader reader
  reader SetFileName $VTK_DATA_ROOT/Data/masonry.bmp
vtkImageLuminance luminance
  luminance SetInput [reader GetOutput]
vtkImageDataGeometryFilter geometry
  geometry SetInput [luminance GetOutput]
vtkWarpScalar warp
  warp SetInput [geometry GetOutput]
  warp SetScaleFactor -0.1

# use merge to put back scalars from image file
vtkMergeFilter merge
  merge SetGeometry [warp GetOutput]
  merge SetScalars  [reader GetOutput]
vtkDataSetMapper mapper
  mapper SetInput [merge GetOutput]
  mapper SetScalarRange 0 255
  mapper ImmediateModeRenderingOff
vtkActor actor
  actor SetMapper mapper
```

What's happening here is that the dataset (or geometry) from vtkWarpScalar (which happens to be of type vtkPolyData) is combined with the scalar data from the vtkPNMReader. The pipeline has split and rejoined because the geometry had to be processed separately (in the imaging pipeline) from the scalar data.

When merging data, the number of tuples found in the data arrays that make up the point attribute data must equal the number of points. This is also true for the cell data.

Appending Data

Like vtkMergeFilter, vtkAppendFilter (and its specialized cousin vtkAppendPolyData) builds a new dataset by appending datasets. The append filters take a list of inputs, each of which must be the same type. During the append operation, only those data attributes that are common to all input datasets are appended together. A great example of its application is shown in the example in the following section ("Probing" on page 98).

Probing

Probing is a process of sampling one dataset with another dataset. In VTK, you can use any dataset as a probe geometry onto which point data attributes are mapped from another dataset. For example, the following Tcl script (taken from VTK/Examples/Visual-izationAlgorithms/Tcl/probeComb.tcl) creates three planes (which serve as the probe geometry) used to sample a structured grid dataset. The planes are then processed with vtkContourFilter to generate contour lines.

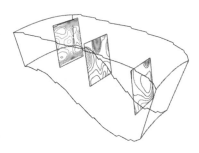

Figure 5–7 Probing data.

```
# Create pipeline
vtkPLOT3DReader pl3d
    pl3d SetXYZFileName "$VTK_DATA_ROOT/Data/combxyz.bin"
    pl3d SetQFileName "$VTK_DATA_ROOT/Data/combq.bin"
    pl3d SetScalarFunctionNumber 100
    pl3d SetVectorFunctionNumber 202
    pl3d Update;#force data read

# Create the probes. Transform them into right place.
vtkPlaneSource plane
    plane SetResolution 50 50
vtkTransform transP1
    transP1 Translate 3.7 0.0 28.37
    transP1 Scale 5 5 5
    transP1 RotateY 90
```

```
vtkTransformPolyDataFilter tpd1
    tpd1 SetInput [plane GetOutput]
    tpd1 SetTransform transP1
vtkOutlineFilter outTpd1
    outTpd1 SetInput [tpd1 GetOutput]
vtkPolyDataMapper mapTpd1
    mapTpd1 SetInput [outTpd1 GetOutput]
vtkActor tpd1Actor
    tpd1Actor SetMapper mapTpd1
    [tpd1Actor GetProperty] SetColor 0 0 0

vtkTransform transP2
    transP2 Translate 9.2 0.0 31.20
    transP2 Scale 5 5 5
    transP2 RotateY 90
vtkTransformPolyDataFilter tpd2
    tpd2 SetInput [plane GetOutput]
    tpd2 SetTransform transP2
vtkOutlineFilter outTpd2
    outTpd2 SetInput [tpd2 GetOutput]
vtkPolyDataMapper mapTpd2
    mapTpd2 SetInput [outTpd2 GetOutput]
vtkActor tpd2Actor
    tpd2Actor SetMapper mapTpd2
    [tpd2Actor GetProperty] SetColor 0 0 0

vtkTransform transP3
    transP3 Translate 13.27 0.0 33.30
    transP3 Scale 5 5 5
    transP3 RotateY 90
vtkTransformPolyDataFilter tpd3
    tpd3 SetInput [plane GetOutput]
    tpd3 SetTransform transP3
vtkOutlineFilter outTpd3
    outTpd3 SetInput [tpd3 GetOutput]
vtkPolyDataMapper mapTpd3
    mapTpd3 SetInput [outTpd3 GetOutput]
vtkActor tpd3Actor
    tpd3Actor SetMapper mapTpd3
    [tpd3Actor GetProperty] SetColor 0 0 0

vtkAppendPolyData appendF
    appendF AddInput [tpd1 GetOutput]
    appendF AddInput [tpd2 GetOutput]
    appendF AddInput [tpd3 GetOutput]
vtkProbeFilter probe
```

```
    probe SetInput [appendF GetOutput]
    probe SetSource [pl3d GetOutput]
vtkContourFilter contour
    contour SetInput [probe GetOutput]
    eval contour GenerateValues 50 [[pl3d GetOutput]\
                                 GetScalarRange]
vtkPolyDataMapper contourMapper
    contourMapper SetInput [contour GetOutput]
    eval contourMapper SetScalarRange [[pl3d GetOutput]\
                                 GetScalarRange]
vtkActor planeActor
    planeActor SetMapper contourMapper
```

Notice that the probe is set as the input to vtkProbeFilter, and the dataset to probe is set to the Source of vtkProbeFilter.

Another useful application of probing is resampling data. For example, if you have an unstructured grid and wish to visualize it with tools specific to vtkImageData (such as volume rendering—see "Volume Rendering" on page 136), you can use vtkProbeFilter to sample the unstructured grid with a volume, and then visualize the volume. It is also possible to probe data with lines (or curves) and use the output to perform x-y plotting.

One final note: cutting and probing can give similar results, although there is a difference in resolution. Similar to the example described in "Cutting" on page 96, vtkProbeFilter could be used with a vtkPlaneSource to generate a plane with data attributes from the structured grid. However, cutting creates surfaces with a resolution dependent on the resolution of the input data. Probing creates surfaces (and other geometries) with a resolution independent of the input data. Care must be taken when probing data to avoid under- or oversampling. Undersampling can result in errors in visualization, and oversampling can consume excessive computation time.

Color An Isosurface With Another Scalar

A common visualization task is to generate an isosurface and then color it with another scalar. While you might do this with a probe, their is a much more efficient way when the dataset that you isosurface contains the data you wish to color the isosurface with. This is because the vtkContourFilter (which generates the isosurface) interpolates all data to the isosurface during the generation process. The interpolated data can then be used during the mapping process to color the isosurface. Here's an example from the Tcl script VTK/ Examples/VisualizationAlgorithms/Tcl/ ColorIsosurface.tcl.

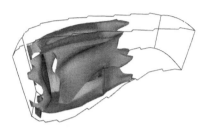

Figure 5–8 Coloring an isosurface with another scalar.

```
vtkPLOT3DReader pl3d
    pl3d SetXYZFileName "$VTK_DATA_ROOT/Data/combxyz.bin"
    pl3d SetQFileName "$VTK_DATA_ROOT/Data/combq.bin"
    pl3d SetScalarFunctionNumber 100
    pl3d SetVectorFunctionNumber 202
    pl3d AddFunction 153
    pl3d Update
vtkContourFilter iso
    iso SetInput [pl3d GetOutput]
    iso SetValue 0 .24
vtkPolyDataNormals normals
    normals SetInput [iso GetOutput]
    normals SetFeatureAngle 45
vtkPolyDataMapper isoMapper
    isoMapper SetInput [normals GetOutput]
    isoMapper ScalarVisibilityOn
    isoMapper SetScalarRange 0 1500
    isoMapper SetScalarModeToUsePointFieldData
    isoMapper ColorByArrayComponent "Velocity Magnitude" 0
vtkLODActor isoActor
    isoActor SetMapper isoMapper
    isoActor SetNumberOfCloudPoints 1000
```

First, the dataset is read with a vtkPLOT3DReader. Here we add a function to be read (function number 153) which we know to be named "Velocity Magnitude." An isosurface is generated which also interpolates all its input data arrays including the velocity magnitude data. We then use the velocity magnitude to color the contour by invoking the method

SetScalarModeToUsePointFieldData() and specifying the data array to use to color with the ColorByArrayComponent() method.

Extract Subset of Cells

Visualization data is often large and processing such data can be quite costly in execution time and memory requirements. As a result, the ability to extract pieces of data is important. Many times only a subset of the data contains meaningful information, or the resolution of the data can be reduced without significant loss of accuracy.

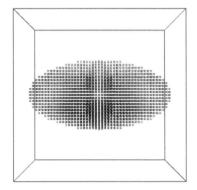

The *Visualization Toolkit* offers several tools to extract portions of, or subsample data. We've already seen how vtkProbeFilter can be used to subsample data (see "Probing" on page 98). Other tools include classes to subsample data, and tools to extract cells within a region

Figure 5–9 Extracting cells.

in space. (Subsampling tools are specific to a type of dataset. See "Subsampling Image Data" on page 124 for information about subsampling structured points datasets, and "Subsampling Structured Grids" on page 115 for information about subsampling structured grids.) In this section, we describe how to extract pieces of a dataset contained within a region in space.

The class vtkExtractGeometry extracts all cells in a dataset that lie either inside or outside of a vtkImplicitFunction (remember, implicit functions can consist of boolean combinations of other implicit functions). The following script creates a boolean combination of two ellipsoids that is used as the extraction region. A vtkShrinkFilter is also used to shrink the cells so you can see what's been extracted. (The Tcl script is from VTK/Examples/ VisualizationAlgorithms/Tcl/ExtractGeometry.tcl.)

```
vtkQuadric quadric
    quadric SetCoefficients .5 1 .2 0 .1 0 0 .2 0 0
vtkSampleFunction sample
    sample SetSampleDimensions 50 50 50
    sample SetImplicitFunction quadric
    sample ComputeNormalsOff
vtkTransform trans
    trans Scale 1 .5 .333
vtkSphere sphere
```

```
    sphere SetRadius 0.25
    sphere SetTransform trans
vtkTransform trans2
    trans2 Scale .25 .5 1.0
vtkSphere sphere2
    sphere2 SetRadius 0.25
    sphere2 SetTransform trans2
vtkImplicitBoolean union
    union AddFunction sphere
    union AddFunction sphere2
    union SetOperationType 0;#union

vtkExtractGeometry extract
    extract SetInput [sample GetOutput]
    extract SetImplicitFunction union
vtkShrinkFilter shrink
    shrink SetInput [extract GetOutput]
    shrink SetShrinkFactor 0.5
vtkDataSetMapper dataMapper
    dataMapper SetInput [shrink GetOutput]
vtkActor dataActor
    dataActor SetMapper dataMapper
```

The output of vtkExtractGeometry is always a vtkUnstructuredGrid. This is because the extraction process generally disrupts the topological structure of the dataset, and the most general dataset form (i.e., vtkUnstructuredGrid) must be used to represent the output.

As a side note: implicit functions can be transformed by assigning them a vtkTransform. If specified, the vtkTransform is used to modify the evaluation of the implicit function. You may wish to experiment with this capability.

Extract Cells As Polygonal Data

Most dataset types cannot be directly rendered by graphics hardware or libraries. Only polygonal data (vtkPolyData) is commonly supported by rendering systems. Structured points datasets, especially images and sometimes volumes, are also supported by graphics systems. All other datasets require special processing if they are to be rendered. In VTK, one approach to rendering non-polygonal datasets is to convert them to polygonal data. This is the function of vtkGeometryFilter.

vtkGeometryFilter accepts as input any type of vtkDataSet, and generates vtkPolyData on output. It performs the conversion using the following rules. All input cells of topological dimension 2 or less (e.g., polygons, lines, vertices) are passed to the output. The faces of cells of dimension 3 are sent to the output if they are on the boundary of the dataset. (A face is on the boundary if it is used by only one cell.) In addition, vtkGeometryFilter has methods that allows you to extract cells based on a range of point ids, cell ids, or whether the cells lie in a particular rectangular region in space.

The principal use of vtkGeometryFilter is as a conversion filter. The following example from VTK/Examples/DataManipulation/Tcl/pointToCellData.tcl uses vtk-GeometryFilter to convert a 2D unstructured grid into polygonal data for later processing by filters that accept vtkPolyData as input. Here, the vtkConnectivityFilter extracts data as vtkUnstructuredGrid which is then converted into polygons using vtkGeometryFilter.

```
vtkConnectivityFilter connect2
    connect2 SetInput [thresh GetOutput]
vtkGeometryFilter parison
    parison SetInput [connect2 GetOutput]
vtkPolyDataNormals normals2
    normals2 SetInput [parison GetOutput]
    normals2 SetFeatureAngle 60
vtkLookupTable lut
    lut SetHueRange 0.0 0.66667
vtkPolyDataMapper parisonMapper
    parisonMapper SetInput [normals2 GetOutput]
    parisonMapper SetLookupTable lut
    parisonMapper SetScalarRange 0.12 1.0
vtkActor parisonActor
    parisonActor SetMapper parisonMapper
```

In fact, the vtkDataSetMapper mapper uses vtkGeometryFilter internally to convert datasets of any type into polygonal data. (The filter is smart enough to pass input vtkPoly-Data straight to its output without processing.)

vtkGeometryFilter extracts pieces of datasets based on point and cell ids using the methods PointClippingOn(), SetPointMinimum(), SetPointMaximum() and CellClippingOn(), SetCellMinimum(), SetCellMaximum(). The minimum and maximum values specify a range of ids which are extracted. Also, you can use a rectangular region in space to limit what's extracted. Use the ExtentClippingOn() and SetExtent() to enable extent clipping and specify the extent. (The extent consists of six values defining a bounding box in space—$(x_{min}, x_{max}, y_{min}, y_{max}, z_{min}, z_{max})$.) You can use point, cell, and extent clipping in any combination. This is a useful feature when debugging data, or when you only want to look at a portion of it.

5.2 Visualizing Polygonal Data

Polygonal data (vtkPolyData) is an important form of visualization data. Its importance is due to it use as the geometry interface into the graphics hardware/rendering engine. Other data types must be converted into polygonal data in order to be rendered (with the exception of vtkImageData (images and volumes) which uses special imaging or volume rendering techniques). You may wish to refer to "Extract Cells As Polygonal Data" on page 103 to see how this conversion is performed.

Polygonal data (vtkPolyData) consists of combinations of vertices and polyvertices; lines and polylines, triangles, quadrilaterals, and polygons; and triangle strips. Most filters (that input vtkPolyData) will process any combination of this data; however, some filters (like vtkDecimatePro and vtkTubeFilter) will only process portions of the data (triangle meshes and lines).

Manually Create vtkPolyData

Polygonal data can be constructed several different ways. Typically, you'll create a vtk-Points to represent the points, and then one to four vtkCellArrays to represent vertex, line, polygon, and triangle strip connectivity. Here's an example taken from VTK/Examples/DataManipulation/Tcl/CreateStrip.tcl. It creates a vtkPolyData with a single triangle strip.

```
vtkPoints points
    points InsertPoint 0 0.0 0.0 0.0
    points InsertPoint 1 0.0 1.0 0.0
    points InsertPoint 2 1.0 0.0 0.0
    points InsertPoint 3 1.0 1.0 0.0
    points InsertPoint 4 2.0 0.0 0.0
    points InsertPoint 5 2.0 1.0 0.0
    points InsertPoint 6 3.0 0.0 0.0
    points InsertPoint 7 3.0 1.0 0.0
vtkCellArray strips
    strips InsertNextCell 8;#number of points
    strips InsertCellPoint 0
    strips InsertCellPoint 1
    strips InsertCellPoint 2
    strips InsertCellPoint 3
    strips InsertCellPoint 4
    strips InsertCellPoint 5
```

```
    strips InsertCellPoint 6
    strips InsertCellPoint 7
vtkPolyData profile
    profile SetPoints points
    profile SetStrips strips
vtkPolyDataMapper map
    map SetInput profile
vtkActor strip
    strip SetMapper map
    [strip GetProperty] SetColor 0.3800 0.7000 0.1600
```

In C++, here's another example showing how to create a cube (Cube.cxx). This time we create six quadrilateral polygons, as well as scalar values at the vertices of the cube.

```
int i;
static float x[8][3]={{0,0,0}, {1,0,0}, {1,1,0}, {0,1,0},
                      {0,0,1}, {1,0,1}, {1,1,1}, {0,1,1}};
static vtkIdType pts[6][4]={{0,1,2,3}, {4,5,6,7}, {0,1,5,4},
                            {1,2,6,5}, {2,3,7,6}, {3,0,4,7}};

// We'll create the building blocks of polydata including data attributes.
vtkPolyData *cube = vtkPolyData::New();
vtkPoints *points = vtkPoints::New();
vtkCellArray *polys = vtkCellArray::New();
vtkFloatArray *scalars = vtkFloatArray::New();

// Load the point, cell, and data attributes.
for (i=0; i<8; i++) points->InsertPoint(i,x[i]);
for (i=0; i<6; i++) polys->InsertNextCell(4,pts[i]);
for (i=0; i<8; i++) scalars->InsertTuple1(i,i);

// We now assign the pieces to the vtkPolyData.
cube->SetPoints(points);
points->Delete();
cube->SetPolys(polys);
polys->Delete();
cube->GetPointData()->SetScalars(scalars);
scalars->Delete();
```

vtkPolyData can be constructed with any combination of vertices, lines, polygons, and triangle strips. Also, vtkPolyData supports an extensive set of operators that allows you to edit and modify the underlying structure. Refer to "Interface To vtkPolyData" on page 253 for more information.

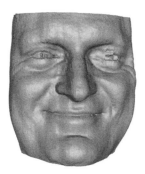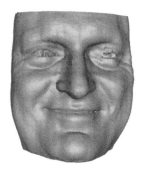

Figure 5–10 Comparing a mesh with and without surface normals.

Generate Surface Normals

When you render a polygonal mesh, you may find that the image clearly shows the faceted nature of the mesh (**Figure 5–10**). The image can be improved by using Gouraud shading (see "Actor Properties" on page 58). However, Gouraud shading depends on the existence of normals at each point in the mesh. The vtkPolyDataNormals filter can be used to generate normals on the mesh. The scripts in "Sampling Implicit Functions" on page 167, "Glyphing" on page 90, and "Color An Isosurface With Another Scalar" on page 101 all use vtkPolyDataNormals, refer to them to see how the filter is used.

Two important instance variables are Splitting and FeatureAngle. If splitting is on, feature edges (defined as edges where the polygonal normals on either side of the edge make an angle greater than or equal to the feature angle) are "split," that is, points are duplicated along the edge, and the mesh is separated on either side of the feature edge (see *The Visualization Toolkit* text). This creates new points, but allows sharp corners to be rendered crisply. Another important instance variable is FlipNormals. Invoking FlipNormalsOn() causes the filter to reverse the direction of the normals (and the ordering of the polygon connectivity list).

Decimation

Polygonal data, especially triangle meshes, are a common form of graphics data. Filters such as vtkContourFilter generate triangle meshes. Often, these meshes are quite large and cannot be rendered or processed quickly enough for interactive application. Decimation techniques have been developed to address this problem. Decimation, also referred to as polygonal reduction, mesh simplification, or multiresolution modeling, is a process to reduce the number of triangles in a triangle mesh, while maintaining a faithful approximation to the original mesh.

VTK supports four decimation objects: vtkDecimate, vtkDecimatePro, vtkQuadricClustering, and vtkQuadricDecimation. All are similar in usage and application, although they each offer advantages and disadvantages as follows:

*   vtkDecimatePro is relatively fast and has the ability to modify topology during the reduction process. It uses an edge collapse process to eliminate vertices and triangles. It's error metric is based on distance to plane/distance to edge. A nice feature of vtkDecimatePro is that you can achieve any level of reduction requested, since the algorithm will begin tearing the mesh into pieces to achieve this (if topology modification is allowed).

*   vtkDecimate is patented (be careful if you use it in commercial application), and it has the slight advantage that it uses a better triangulation technique during processing (i.e., results might be slightly better) than some of the other methods. It's major feature is that it is one of the first decimation algorithms, and is relatively easy to understand and modify.

*   vtkQuadricDecimation uses the quadric error measure proposed by Garland and Heckbert in Siggraph '97 *Surface Simplification Using Quadric Error Metrics*. It uses an edge collapse to eliminate vertices and triangles. The quadric error metric is generally accepted as one of the better error metrics.

*   vtkQuadricClustering is the fastest algorithm. It is based on the algorithm presented by Peter Lindstrom in his Siggraph 2000 paper *Out-of-Core Simplification of Large Polygonal Models*. It is capable of quickly reducing huge meshes, and the class supports the ability to process pieces of a mesh (using the StartAppend(), Append(), and EndAppend() methods). This enables the user to avoid reading an entire mesh into memory. This algorithm works well with large meshes; the triangulation process does not work well as meshes are become smaller. (Combining this algorithm with

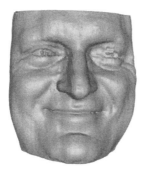

Figure 5–11 Triangle mesh before (left) and after (right) 90% decimation.

one of the other algorithms is a good approach.)

Here's an example using vtkDecimatePro. It's been adapted from the Tcl script VTK/
Examples/VisualizationAlgorithms/Tcl/deciFran.tcl (**Figure 5–11**).

```
vtkDecimatePro deci
    deci SetInput [fran GetOutput]
    deci SetTargetReduction 0.9
    deci PreserveTopologyOn
vtkPolyDataNormals normals
    normals SetInput [fran GetOutput]
    normals FlipNormalsOn
vtkPolyDataMapper franMapper
    franMapper SetInput [normals GetOutput]
vtkActor franActor
    franActor SetMapper franMapper
    eval [franActor GetProperty] SetColor 1.0 0.49 0.25
```

Two important instance variables of vtkDecimatePro are TargetReduction and PreserveTopology. The TargetReduction is the requested amount of reduction (e.g., a value of 0.9
means that we wish to reduce the number of triangles in the mesh by 90%). Depending on
whether you allow topology to change or not (PreserveTopologyOn/Off()), you may or
may not achieve the requested reduction. If PreserveTopology is off, then vtkDecimatePro
will give you the requested reduction.

A final note: the decimation filters take triangle data as input. If you have a polygonal
mesh you can convert the polygons to triangles with vtkTriangleFilter.

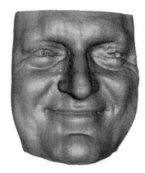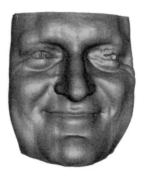

Figure 5–12 Smoothing a polygonal mesh. Right image shows the effect of smoothing.

Smooth Mesh

Polygonal meshes often contain noise or excessive roughness that affect the quality of the rendered image. For example, isosurfacing low resolution data can show aliasing, or stepping effects. One way to treat this problem is to use smoothing. Smoothing is a process that adjusts the positions of points to reduce the noise content in the surface.

VTK offers two smoothing objects: vtkSmoothPolyDataFilter and vtkWindowedSinc-PolyDataFilter. Of the two, the vtkWindowedSincPolyDataFilter gives the best results and is slightly faster. The following example shows how to use the smoothing filter. The example is the same as the one in the previous section, except that a smoothing filter has been added. **Figure 5–12** shows the effects of smoothing on the decimated mesh.

```
# decimate and smooth data
vtkDecimatePro deci
    deci SetInput [fran GetOutput]
    deci SetTargetReduction 0.9
    deci PreserveTopologyOn
vtkSmoothPolyDataFilter smoother
    smoother SetInput [deci GetOutput]
    smoother SetNumberOfIterations 50
vtkPolyDataNormals normals
    normals SetInput [smoother GetOutput]
    normals FlipNormalsOn
vtkPolyDataMapper franMapper
    franMapper SetInput [normals GetOutput]
vtkActor franActor
```

```
franActor SetMapper franMapper
eval [franActor GetProperty] SetColor 1.0 0.49 0.25
```

Both smoothing filters are used similarly. There are optional methods for controlling the effects of smoothing along feature edges and on boundaries. Check the man pages and/or .h files for more information.

Clip Data

Clipping, like cutting (see "Cutting" on page 96), uses an implicit function to define a surface with which to clip. Clipping separates a polygonal mesh into pieces, as shown in **Figure 5–13**. Clipping will break polygonal primitives into separate parts on either side of the clipping surface. Like cutting, clipping allows you to set a clip value defining the value of the implicit clipping function.

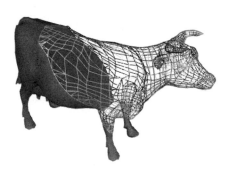

Figure 5–13 Clipping a model.

The following example uses a plane to clip a polygonal model of a cow. The clip value is used to move the plane along its normal so that the model can be clipped at different locations. The example Tcl script shown below is taken from `VTK/Examples/Visualization-Algorithms/Tcl/ClipCow.tcl`.

```
# Read the polygonal data and generate vertex normals
vtkBYUReader cow
  cow SetGeometryFileName "$VTK_DATA_ROOT/Data/Viewpoint/cow.g"
vtkPolyDataNormals cowNormals
  cowNormals SetInput [cow GetOutput]

# Define a clip plane to clip the cow in half
vtkPlane plane
    plane SetOrigin 0.25 0 0
    plane SetNormal -1 -1 0
vtkClipPolyData clipper
    clipper SetInput [cowNormals GetOutput]
    clipper SetClipFunction plane
    clipper GenerateClippedOutputOn
    clipper SetValue 0.5
vtkPolyDataMapper clipMapper
    clipMapper SetInput [clipper GetOutput]
```

```
vtkActor clipActor
    clipActor SetMapper clipMapper
    eval [clipActor GetProperty] SetColor $peacock

# Create the rest of the cow in wireframe
vtkPolyDataMapper restMapper
  restMapper SetInput [clipper GetClippedOutput]
vtkActor restActor
  restActor SetMapper restMapper
  [restActor GetProperty] SetRepresentationToWireframe
```

The GenerateClippedOutputOn() method causes the filter to create a second output: the data that was clipped away. This output is shown in wireframe in the figure. If the Set-Value() method is used to change the clip value, the implicit function will cut at a point parallel to the original plane, but above or below it. (You could also change the definition of vtkPlane to achieve the same result.)

Generate Texture Coordinates

Several filters are available to generate texture coordinates: vtkTextureMapToPlane, vtk-TextureMapToCylinder, and vtkTextureMapToSphere. These objects generated texture coordinates based on a planar, cylindrical, and spherical coordinate system, respectively. Also, the class vtkTransformTextureCoordinates allows you to position the texture map on the surface by translating and scaling the texture coordinates. The following example shows using vtkTextureMapToCylinder to create texture coordinates for an unstructured grid generated from the vtkDelaunay3D object (see "Delaunay Triangulation" on page 171 for more information). The full example can be found at VTK/Examples/VisualizationAlgorithms/Tcl/GenerateTextureCoordinates.tcl.

```
vtkPointSource sphere
  sphere SetNumberOfPoints 25

vtkDelaunay3D del
  del SetInput [sphere GetOutput]
  del SetTolerance 0.01

vtkTextureMapToCylinder tmapper
  tmapper SetInput [del GetOutput]
  tmapper PreventSeamOn

vtkTransformTextureCoords xform
  xform SetInput [tmapper GetOutput]
```

```
    xform SetScale 4 4 1

vtkDataSetMapper mapper
    mapper SetInput [xform GetOutput]

vtkBMPReader bmpReader
    bmpReader SetFileName "$VTK_DATA_ROOT/Data/masonry.bmp"
vtkTexture atext
    atext SetInput [bmpReader GetOutput]
    atext InterpolateOn
vtkActor triangulation
    triangulation SetMapper mapper
    triangulation SetTexture atext
```

In this example a random set of points in the unit sphere is triangulated. The triangulation then has texture coordinates generated over it. These texture coordinates are then scaled in the *i-j* texture coordinate directions in order to cause texture repeats. Finally, a texture map is read in and assigned to the actor.

As a side note: instances of vtkDataSetMapper are mappers that accept any type of data as input. They use an internal instance of vtkGeometryFilter followed by vtkPolyDataMapper to convert the data into polygonal primitives that can then be passed to the rendering engine. See "Extract Cells As Polygonal Data" on page 103 for further information.

5.3 Visualizing Structured Grids

Structured grids are regular in topology, and irregular in geometry (see **Figure 3–2**(c)). Structured grids are often used in numerical analysis (e.g., computational fluid dynamics). The vtkStructuredGrid dataset is composed of hexahedral (vtkHexahedron) or quadrilateral (vtkQuad) cells.

Manually Create vtkStructuredGrid

Structured grids are created by specifying grid dimensions (to define topology) along with a vtkPoints object defining the *x-y-z* point coordinates (to define geometry). This code was derived from VTK/Examples/DataManipulation/Cxx/SGrid.cxx.

```
vtkPoints points
    points InsertPoint 0 0.0 0.0 0.0
```

```
...etc...
```

```
vtkStructuredGrid sgrid
    sgrid SetDimensions 13 11 11
    sgrid SetPoints points
```

Make sure that the number of points in the vtkPoints object is consistent with the number of points defined by the product of the three dimension values in the *i, j*, and *k* topological directions.

Extract Computational Plane

In most cases, structured grids are processed by filters that accept vtkDataSet as input (see "Visualization Techniques" on page 83). One filter that directly accepts vtkStructuredGrid as input is the vtkStructuredGridGeometryFilter. This filter is used to extract pieces of the grid as points, lines, or polygonal "planes", depending on the specification of the Extent instance variable. (Extent is a 6-vector that describes a $(i_{min}, i_{max}, j_{min}, j_{max}, k_{min}, k_{max})$ topological region.)

In the following example, we read a structured grid, extract three planes, and warp the planes with the associated vector data (from VTK/Examples/VisualizationALgorithms/Tcl/warpComb.tcl).

```
vtkPLOT3DReader pl3d
    pl3d SetXYZFileName "$VTK_DATA_ROOT/Data/combxyz.bin"
    pl3d SetQFileName "$VTK_DATA_ROOT/Data/combq.bin"
    pl3d SetScalarFunctionNumber 100
    pl3d SetVectorFunctionNumber 202
    pl3d Update
vtkStructuredGridGeometryFilter plane
    plane SetInput [pl3d GetOutput]
    plane SetExtent 10 10 1 100 1 100
vtkStructuredGridGeometryFilter plane2
    plane2 SetInput [pl3d GetOutput]
    plane2 SetExtent 30 30 1 100 1 100
vtkStructuredGridGeometryFilter plane3
    plane3 SetInput [pl3d GetOutput]
    plane3 SetExtent 45 45 1 100 1 100
vtkAppendPolyData appendF
    appendF AddInput [plane GetOutput]
    appendF AddInput [plane2 GetOutput]
    appendF AddInput [plane3 GetOutput]
```

```
vtkWarpScalar warp
    warp SetInput [appendF GetOutput]
    warp UseNormalOn
    warp SetNormal 1.0 0.0 0.0
    warp SetScaleFactor 2.5
vtkPolyDataNormals normals
    normals SetInput [warp GetPolyDataOutput]
    normals SetFeatureAngle 60
vtkPolyDataMapper planeMapper
    planeMapper SetInput [normals GetOutput]
    eval planeMapper SetScalarRange [[pl3d GetOutput] GetScalarRange]
vtkActor planeActor
    planeActor SetMapper planeMapper
```

Subsampling Structured Grids

Structured grids can be subsampled similar to structured points (see "Subsampling Image Data" on page 124). The vtkExtractGrid performs the subsampling and data extraction.

```
vtkPLOT3DReader pl3d
    pl3d SetXYZFileName "$VTK_DATA_ROOT/Data/combxyz.bin"
    pl3d SetQFileName "$VTK_DATA_ROOT/Data/combq.bin"
    pl3d SetScalarFunctionNumber 100
    pl3d SetVectorFunctionNumber 202
    pl3d Update
vtkExtractGrid extract
    extract SetInput [pl3d GetOutput]
    extract SetVOI 30 30 -1000 1000 -1000 1000
    extract SetSampleRate 1 2 3
    extract IncludeBoundaryOn
```

In this example, a subset of the original structured grid (which has dimensions 57x33x25) is extracted with a sampling rate of (1,2,3) resulting in a structured grid with dimensions (1,17,9). The IncludeBoundaryOn method makes sure that the boundary is extracted even if the sampling rate does not pick up the boundary.

5.4 Visualizing Rectilinear Grids

Rectilinear grids are regular in topology, and semi-regular in geometry (see **Figure 3–2**(b)). Rectilinear grids are often used in numerical analysis. The vtkRectilinearGrid dataset is composed of voxel (vtkVoxel) or pixel (vtkPixel) cells.

Manually Create vtkRectilinearGrid

Rectilinear grids are created by specifying grid dimensions (to define topology) along with three scalar arrays to define point coordinates along the *x-y-z* axes (to define geometry). This code was modified from `VTK/Examples/DataManipulation/Cxx/RGrid.cxx`.

```
vtkFloatArray *xCoords = vtkFloatArray::New();
  for (i=0; i<47; i++) xCoords->InsertNextValue(x[i]);

  vtkFloatArray *yCoords = vtkFloatArray::New();
  for (i=0; i<33; i++) yCoords->InsertNextValue(y[i]);

  vtkFloatArray *zCoords = vtkFloatArray::New();
  for (i=0; i<44; i++) zCoords->InsertNextValue(z[i]);

  vtkRectilinearGrid *rgrid = vtkRectilinearGrid::New();
    rgrid->SetDimensions(47,33,44);
    rgrid->SetXCoordinates(xCoords);
    rgrid->SetYCoordinates(yCoords);
    rgrid->SetZCoordinates(zCoords);
```

Make sure that the number of scalars in the *x*, *y*, and *z* directions equals the three dimension values in the *i, j,* and *k* topological directions.

Extract Computational Plane

In most cases, rectilinear grids are processed by filters that accept vtkDataSet as input (see "Visualization Techniques" on page 83). One filter that directly accepts vtkRectilinear-Grid as input is the vtkRectilinearGridGeometryFilter. This filter is used to extract pieces of the grid as points, lines, or polygonal "planes", depending on the specification of the Extent instance variable. (Extent is a 6-vector that describes a $(i_{min}, i_{max}, j_{min}, j_{max}, k_{min}, k_{max})$ topological region.)

The following example, which we continue from the previous found in `VTK/Examples/ DataManipulation/Cxx/RGrid.cxx` we extract a plane as follows

```
vtkRectilinearGridGeometryFilter *plane =
                              vtkRectilinearGridGeometryFilter::New();
    plane->SetInput(rgrid);
    plane->SetExtent(0,46, 16,16, 0,43);
```

5.5 Visualizing Unstructured Grids

Unstructured grids are irregular in both topology and geometry (see **Figure 3–2**(f)). Unstructured grids are often used in numerical analysis (e.g., finite element analysis). Any and all cell types can be represented in an unstructured grid.

Manually Create vtkUnstructuredGrid

Unstructured grids are created by defining geometry via a vtkPoints instance, and defining topology by inserting cells. (This script was derived from the example VTK/Examples/ DataManipulation/Tcl/BuildUGrid.tcl.)

```
vtkPoints tetraPoints
  tetraPoints SetNumberOfPoints 4
  tetraPoints InsertPoint 0 0 0 0
  tetraPoints InsertPoint 1 1 0 0
  tetraPoints InsertPoint 2 .5 1 0
  tetraPoints InsertPoint 3 .5 .5 1
vtkTetra aTetra
  [aTetra GetPointIds] SetId 0 0
  [aTetra GetPointIds] SetId 1 1
  [aTetra GetPointIds] SetId 2 2
  [aTetra GetPointIds] SetId 3 3
vtkUnstructuredGrid aTetraGrid
  aTetraGrid Allocate 1 1
  aTetraGrid InsertNextCell [aTetra GetCellType] [aTetra GetPointIds]
  aTetraGrid SetPoints tetraPoints
  ...insert other cells if any...
```

It is mandatory that you invoke the Allocate() method prior to inserting cells into an instance of vtkUnstructuredGrid. The values supplied to this method are the initial size of the data, and the size to extend the allocation by when additional memory is required. Larger values generally give better performance (since fewer memory reallocations are required).

Extract Portions of the Mesh

In most cases, unstructured grids are processed by filters that accept vtkDataSet as input (see "Visualization Techniques" on page 83). One filter that directly accepts vtkUnstruc-

turedGrid as input is the vtkExtractUnstructuredGrid. This filter is used to extract portions
of the grid using a range of point ids, cell ids, or geometric bounds (the Extent instance
variable which defines a bounding box). This script was derived from VTK/Examples/
VisualizationAlgorithms/Tcl/ExtractUGrid.tcl.

```
vtkDataSetReader reader
    reader SetFileName "$VTK_DATA_ROOT/Data/blow.vtk"
    reader SetScalarsName "thickness9"
    reader SetVectorsName "displacement9"
vtkCastToConcrete castToUnstructuredGrid
    castToUnstructuredGrid SetInput [reader GetOutput]
vtkWarpVector warp
    warp SetInput [castToUnstructuredGrid GetUnstructuredGridOutput]

vtkConnectivityFilter connect
    connect SetInput [warp GetOutput]
    connect SetExtractionModeToSpecifiedRegions
    connect AddSpecifiedRegion 0
    connect AddSpecifiedRegion 1
vtkDataSetMapper moldMapper
    moldMapper SetInput [reader GetOutput]
    moldMapper ScalarVisibilityOff
vtkActor moldActor
    moldActor SetMapper moldMapper
    [moldActor GetProperty] SetColor .2 .2 .2
    [moldActor GetProperty] SetRepresentationToWireframe

vtkConnectivityFilter connect2
    connect2 SetInput [warp GetOutput]
    connect2 SetExtractionModeToSpecifiedRegions
    connect2 AddSpecifiedRegion 2
vtkExtractUnstructuredGrid extractGrid
    extractGrid SetInput [connect2 GetOutput]
    extractGrid CellClippingOn
    extractGrid SetCellMinimum 0
    extractGrid SetCellMaximum 23
vtkGeometryFilter parison
    parison SetInput [extractGrid GetOutput]
vtkPolyDataNormals normals2
    normals2 SetInput [parison GetOutput]
    normals2 SetFeatureAngle 60
vtkLookupTable lut
    lut SetHueRange 0.0 0.66667
vtkPolyDataMapper parisonMapper
    parisonMapper SetInput [normals2 GetOutput]
```

```
    parisonMapper SetLookupTable lut
    parisonMapper SetScalarRange 0.12 1.0
vtkActor parisonActor
    parisonActor SetMapper parisonMapper
```

In this example, we are using cell clipping (i.e., using cell ids) in combination with a connectivity filter to extract portions of the mesh. Similarly, we could use point ids and a geometric extent to extract portions of the mesh. The vtkConnectivityFilter (and a related class vtkPolyDataConnectivityFilter) are used to extract connected portions of a dataset. (Cells are connected when they share points.) The SetExtractionModeToSpecifiedRegions() method indicates to the filter which connected region to extract. By default, the connectivity filters extract the largest connected regions encountered. However, it is also possible to specify a particular region as this example does, which of course requires some experimentation to determine which region is which.

Contour Unstructured Grids

A special contouring class is available to generate isocontours for unstructured grids. The class vtkContourGrid is a higher-performing version than the generic vtkContourFilter isocontouring filter. Normally you do not need to instantiate this class directly since vtkContourFilter will automatically create an internal instance of vtkContourGrid if it senses that its input is of type vtkUnstructuredGrid.

This concludes our overview of visualization techniques. You may also wish to refer to the next chapter which describes image processing and volume rendering. Also, see "Summary Of Filters" on page 332 for a summary of the filters in VTK.

## Chapter 6

Visualizing Image & Volume Data

Image datasets, represented by the class vtkImageData, are regular in topology and geometry as shown in **Figure 6–1**. This data type is structured, meaning that the locations of the data points are implicitly defined using just the few parameters origin, spacing and dimensions. Medical and scientific scanning devices such as CT, MRI, and ultrasound scanners, and confocal microscopes often produce data of this type. Conceptually, the vtkImageData dataset is composed of voxel (vtkVoxel) or pixel (vtkPixel) cells. However, the structured nature of this dataset allows us to store the data values in a simple array rather than explicitly creating the vtkVoxel or vtkPixel cells.

In VTK, image data is a special data type that can be processed and rendered in several ways. Although not an exhaustive classification, most of the operations performed on image data in VTK fall into one of the three categories—image processing, geometry extraction, or direct rendering. Dozens of image processing filters exist that can operate on image datasets. These filters take vtkImageData as input and produce vtkImageData as output. Geometry extraction filters exist that convert vtkImageData into vtkPolyData. For example, the vtkContourFilter can extract iso-valued contours in triangular patches from the image dataset. Finally, there are various mappers and specialized actors to render vtkImageData, including techniques ranging from simple 2D image display to volume rendering.

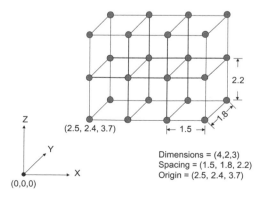

Figure 6–1 The vtkImageData structure is defined by dimensions, spacing, and origin. The dimensions are the number of voxels or pixels along each of the major axes. The origin is the world coordinate position of the lower left corner of the first slice of the data. The spacing is the distance between pixels along each of the three major axes.

In this chapter we examine some important image processing techniques. We will discuss basic image display, image processing, and geometry extraction as elevation maps. In addition, we will cover volume rendering in detail in this chapter. Other geometry extraction techniques such as contouring are covered in Chapter 5.

6.1 Historical Note on vtkStructuredPoints

Initially, VTK contained only the class vtkStructuredPoints for representing image datasets. When extensive image processing functionality was added to VTK, the class vtkImageData was developed. This class was more flexible than vtkStructuredPoints, allowing for parallel processing and streaming of data. Over the next several releases of VTK, the image and graphics pipelines were merged. This caused vtkImageData and vtk-StructuredPoints to become functionally quite similar, until vtkStructuredPoints became a nearly empty subclass of vtkImageData. Although it will likely require several more releases of VTK to remove all references to "structured points," the class vtkStructured-Points has been deprecated and should not be used.

6.2 Manually Creating vtkImageData

Creating image data is straightforward: you need only define the dimensions, origin, and spacing of the dataset. The origin is the world coordinate position of the lower left hand corner of the dataset. The dimensions are the number of voxels or pixels along each of the three major axes. The spacing is the height, length, and width of a voxel or the distance between neighboring pixels, depending on whether you view your data as homogeneous boxes or sample points in a continuous function.

In this first example we will assume that we have an array of unsigned character values pointed to by the variable data, and is size[0] by size[1] by size[2] samples. We generated this data outside of VTK, and now want to get this data into a vtkImageData so that we might use the VTK filtering and rendering operations. We will give VTK a pointer into the memory, but we will manage the deletion of the memory ourselves.

The first thing we need to do is create an array of unsigned chars to store the data. We use the SetVoidArray() method to specify the pointer to the data and its size, with the final argument indicating that VTK should not free this memory.

```
vtkUnsignedCharArray *array = vtkUnsignedCharArray::New();
array->SetVoidArray( data, size[0]*size[1]*size[2], 1);
```

The second step is to create the image data. We must take care that all values match—the scalar type of the image data must be unsigned char, and the dimensions of the image data must match the size of the data.

```
imageData = vtkImageData::New();
imageData->GetPointData()->SetScalars(array);
imageData->SetDimensions(size);
imageData->SetScalarType(VTK_UNSIGNED_CHAR);
imageData->SetSpacing(1.0, 1.0, 1.0 );
imageData->SetOrigin(0.0, 0.0, 0.0 );
```

What's important about image datasets is that because the geometry and topology are implicitly defined by the dimensions, origin, and spacing, the storage required to represent the dataset *structure* is tiny. Also, computation on the structure is fast because of its regular arrangement. What does require storage is the attribute data that goes along with the dataset.

In this next example, we will use C++ to create the image data. Instead of manually creating the data array and associating them with the image data, we will have the vtkImageData object create the scalar data for us. This eliminates the possibility of mismatching the size of the scalars with the dimensions of the image data.

```
// Create the image data
vtkImageData *id = vtkImageData::New();
   id->SetDimensions(10,25,100);
   id->SetScalarTypeToUnsignedShort();
   id->SetNumberOfScalarComponents(1);
   id->AllocateScalars();

// Fill in scalar values
unsigned short *ptr = (unsigned short *) id->GetScalarPointer();
for (int i=0; i<10*25*100; i++)
   {
   *ptr++ = i;
   }
```

In this example, the convenience method AllocateScalars() is used to allocate storage for the image data. Notice that this call is made *after* the scalar type and number of scalar components have been set (up to four scalar components can be set). Then the method GetScalarPointer(), which returns a void*, is invoked and the result is cast to unsigned short. We can do this knowing that the type is `unsigned short` because we specified this earlier. (In VTK's imaging filters, many Execute() methods query the scalar type and then switch on the type into a templated function in a similar manner.)

6.3 Subsampling Image Data

As we saw in "Extract Subset of Cells" on page 102, extracting parts of a dataset is often desirable. The filter vtkExtractVOI extracts pieces of the input image dataset, and can also perform subsampling on it. The output of the filter is also of type vtkImageData.

There are actually two similar filters that perform this clipping functionality in VTK: vtkExtractVOI and vtkImageClip. The reason that there are two versions is historical—the imaging pipeline used to be separate from the graphics pipeline, with vtkImageClip working only on vtkImageData in the imaging pipeline and vtkExtractVOI working only on vtkStructuredPoints in the graphics pipeline. These distinctions are gone now, but there are still some differences between these filters. vtkExtractVOI will extract a subregion of the volume and produce a vtkImageData that contains exactly this information. In addition, vtkExtractVOI can be used to resample the volume within the VOI. On the other hand, vtkImageClip by default will pass the input data through to the output unchanged except for the extent information. A flag may be set on this filter to force it to produce the exact amount of data only, in which case the region will be copied into the output vtkImageData. The vtkImageClip filter cannot resample the volume.

The following Tcl example (taken from `VTK/Examples/ImageProcessing/Tcl/Contours2D.tcl`) demonstrates how to use vtkExtractVOI. It extracts a piece of the input volume, and then subsamples it. The output is fed into a vtkContourFilter. (You may want to try removing vtkExtractVOI and compare the results.)

```
# Quadric definition
vtkQuadric quadric
    quadric SetCoefficients .5 1 .2 0 .1 0 0 .2 0 0
vtkSampleFunction sample
    sample SetSampleDimensions 30 30 30
    sample SetImplicitFunction quadric
    sample ComputeNormalsOff
vtkExtractVOI extract
    extract SetInput [sample GetOutput]
    extract SetVOI 0 29 0 29 15 15
    extract SetSampleRate 1 2 3
vtkContourFilter contours
```

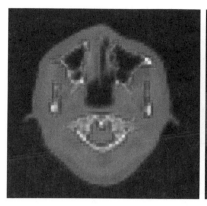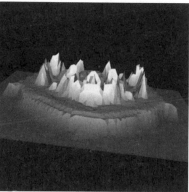

Figure 6–2 Image warped by scalar values.

```
    contours SetInput [extract GetOutput]
    contours GenerateValues 13 0.0 1.2
vtkPolyDataMapper contMapper
    contMapper SetInput [contours GetOutput]
    contMapper SetScalarRange 0.0 1.2
vtkActor contActor
    contActor SetMapper contMapper
```

Note that this script extracts a plane from the original data by specifying the volume of interest (VOI) as (0,29,0,29,15,15) ($i_{min}, i_{max}, j_{min}, j_{max}, k_{min}, k_{max}$), and the sample rate is set differently along each of the *i-j-k* topological axes. You could also extract a subvolume or even a line or point by modifying the VOI specification. (The volume of interest is specified using 0-offset values.)

6.4 Warp Based On Scalar Values

One common use of image data is to store elevation values as an image. These images are frequently called range maps or elevation maps. The scalar value for each pixel in the image represents an elevation, or range value. A common task in visualization is to take such an image and warp it to produce an accurate 3D geometry representing the elevation or range data. Consider **Figure 6–2** which shows an image that has been warped based on its scalar value. The left image shows the original image while the right view shows the image after warping to produce a 3D surface.

The pipeline to perform this visualization is fairly simple but there is an important concept to understand. The original data is an image which has implicit geometry and topology. Warping the image will result in a 3D surface where geometry is no longer implicit. To support this we first convert the image to a vtkPolyData representation using vtkImage-DataGeometryFilter. The we perform the warp and connect to a mapper. In the script below you'll note that we also make use of vtkWindowLevelLookupTable to provide a greyscale lookup-table instead of the default red to blue lookup table.

```
vtkImageReader reader
reader SetDataByteOrderToLittleEndian
reader SetDataExtent 0 63 0 63 40 40
reader SetFilePrefix "$VTK_DATA_ROOT/Data/headsq/quarter"
reader SetDataMask 0x7fff

vtkImageDataGeometryFilter geometry
  geometry SetInput [reader GetOutput]

vtkWarpScalar warp
  warp SetInput [geometry GetOutput]
  warp SetScaleFactor 0.005

vtkWindowLevelLookupTable wl

vtkPolyDataMapper mapper
  mapper SetInput [warp GetPolyDataOutput]
  mapper SetScalarRange 0 2000
  mapper ImmediateModeRenderingOff
  mapper SetLookupTable wl

vtkActor actor
  actor SetMapper mapper
```

This example is often combined with other techniques. If you want to warp the image with its scalar value and then color it with a different scalar field you would use the vtkMerge-Filter. Another common operation is to reduce the number of polygons in the warped surface. Because these surfaces were generated from images they tend to have a large number of polygons. You can use vtkDecimatePro to reduce the number. You should also consider using vtkTriangleFilter followed by vtkStripper to convert the polygons (squares) into triangle strips which tend to render faster and consume less memory.

6.5 Image Display

There are several ways to directly display image data. Two methods that are generally applicable for displaying 2D images are described in this section. Volume rendering is the method for directly displaying 3D images (volumes) and is described in detail later in this chapter.

Image Viewer

vtkImageViewer is a convenient class for displaying images. It manages several objects internally—vtkImageWindow, vtkImager, vtkActor2D, and vtkImageMapper—providing an easy-to-user class that can be dropped into your application. A typical usage pattern for vtkImageViewer is to set its input, specify a z-slice to display (assuming that the input is a volume), and then specify window and level transfer function values. (Refer to "Image Reslice" on page 135 for an example of this class used in application.)

```
vtkImageViewer viewer
  viewer SetInput [reslice GetOutput]
  viewer SetZSlice 120
  viewer SetColorWindow 2000
  viewer SetColorLevel 1000
```

The window-level transfer function is defined as shown in **Figure 6–3**. The level is the data value that centers the a window. The slope of the resulting transfer function determines the amount of contrast in the final image. The width (i.e., window) defines the data values that are mapped to the display. All data values outside of the window are clamped to the data values at the boundaries of the window.

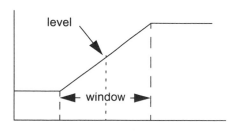

Figure 6–3 Window-level transfer function.

Image Actor

Using a vtkImageViewer is convenient when you would simply like to display the image in a window by itself, or accompanied by some simple 2D annotation. The vtkImageActor composite actor class is useful when you want to display your image in a 3D rendering window. The image is displayed by creating a polygon representing the bounds of the image and using hardware texture mapping to paste the image onto the polygon. On most platforms this enables you to rotate, pan, and zoom your image with bilinear interpolation in real-time. By changing the interactor to a vtkInteractorStyleImage you can limit rotations so that the 3D render window operates as a 2D image viewer (see "Interactor Styles" on page 50 and "vtkRenderWindow Interaction Style" on page 303 for more information about interactor styles). The advantage to using the 3D render window for image display is that you can easily embed multiple images and complex 3D annotation into one window.

The vtkImageActor object is a composite class that encapsulates both an actor and a mapper into one class. It is simple to use, as can be seen in this example.

```
vtkPNMReader pnmReader
pnmReader SetFileName "$VTK_DATA_ROOT/Data/masonry.ppm"

vtkImageActor imageActor
imageActor SetInput [pnmReader GetOutput]
```

This imageActor can then be added to the renderer using the AddProp() method. The vtkImageActor class expects that its input will have a length of 1 along one of the three dimensions, with the image extending along the other two dimensions. This allows the vtkImageActor to be connected to a volume through the use of a clipping filter without the need to reorganize the data if the clip is performed along the X or Y axis. (Note: the input image to vtkImageActor must be if type unsigned char. If your image type is different, you can use vtkImageCast or vtkImageShiftScale to convert to unsigned char.)

6.6 Image Sources

There are some image processing objects that produce output but do not take any data objects as input. These are known as image sources, and some of the VTK image sources are described here. Refer to "Source Objects" on page 332, or the Doxygen documentation on the CD, for a more complete list of available image sources.

ImageCanvasSource2D

The vtkImageCanvasSource2D class creates a blank two-dimensional image of a specified size and type, and provides methods for drawing various primitives into this blank image. Primitives include boxes, lines, and circles, and a flood fill operation is also provided. The following example illustrates the use of this source by creating a 512x512 pixel images and drawing several primitives into this image. The resulting image is shown in **Figure 6–4**.

```
#set up the size and type of the image canvas
vtkImageCanvasSource2D imCan
imCan SetScalarType $VTK_UNSIGNED_CHAR
imCan SetExtent 0 511 0 511 0 0

# Draw various primitives
imCan SetDrawColor 86
imCan FillBox 0 511 0 511
imCan SetDrawColor 0
imCan FillTube 500 20 30 400 5
imCan SetDrawColor 255
imCan DrawSegment 10 20 500 510
imCan SetDrawColor 0
imCan DrawCircle 400 350 80.0
imCan SetDrawColor 255
imCan FillPixel 450 350
imCan SetDrawColor 170
imCan FillTriangle 100 100  300 150  150 300

#Show the resulting image
vtkImageViewer viewer
viewer SetInput [imCan GetOutput]
viewer SetColorWindow 256
viewer SetColorLevel 127.5
```

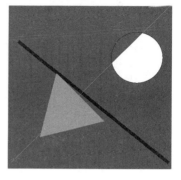

Figure 6–4 The results from a vtkImageCanvasSource2D source after drawing various primitives.

ImageEllipsoidSource

If you would like to write your own image source using a templated execute function, vtkImageEllipsoidSource is a good starting point. This object produces a binary image of an ellipsoid as output based on a center position, a radius along each axis, and the inside and outside values. The output scalar type can also be specified, and this is why the execute function is templated. This source is used internally by some of the imaging filters such as vtkImageDilateErode3D.

If you want to create a vtkImageBoxSource, for example, to produce a binary image of a box you could start by copying the vtkImageEllipsoidSource source and header files and doing a global search and replace. You would probably change the instance variable

Radius to be Length since this is a more appropriate description for a box source. Finally, you would replace the code within the templated function vtkImageBoxSourceExecute to create the box image rather than the ellipsoid image. (For more information on creating image processing filters see "How To Write An Imaging Filter" on page 295.)

ImageGaussianSource

The vtkImageGaussianSource object produces an image with pixel values determined according to a Gaussian distribution using a center location, a maximum value, and a standard deviation. The output of this image source is always floating point values.

If you would like to write your own source that produces just one type of output image, for example float, than this might be a good class to use as a starting point. Comparing the source code for vtkImageGaussianSource with that for vtkImageEllipsoidSource, you will notice that the filter implementation is in the Execute() method for vtkImageGaussian-Source, whereas in vtkImageEllipsoidSource the Execute() method calls a templated function that contains the implementation.

ImageGridSource

If you would like to annotate your image with a 2D grid, vtkImageGridSource can be used to create an image with the grid pattern (**Figure 6–5**). The following example illustrates this use by blending a grid pattern with a slice from a CT dataset. The reader is a vtkImageReader that produces a 64 by 64 image.

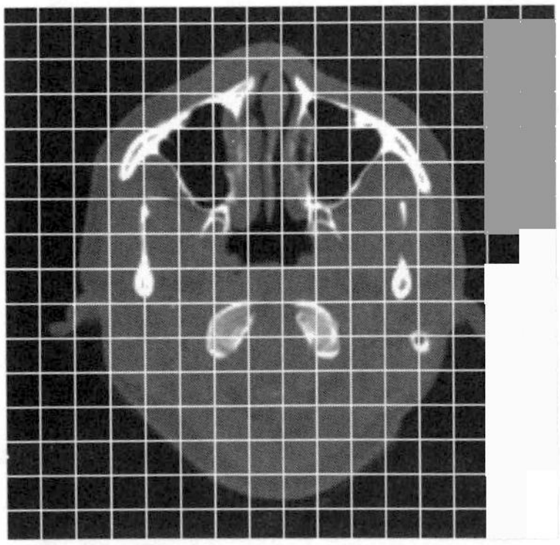

Figure 6–5 A grid pattern created by a vtkImageGridSource is overlayed on a slice of a CT dataset.

```
imageGrid SetGridSpacing 16 16 0
imageGrid SetGridOrigin 0 0 0
imageGrid SetDataExtent 0 63 0 63 0 0
imageGrid SetLineValue 4095
imageGrid SetFillValue 0
imageGrid SetDataScalarTypeToShort

vtkImageBlend blend
blend SetOpacity 0 0.5
blend SetOpacity 1 0.5
blend SetInput 0 [reader GetOutput]
blend SetInput 1 [imageGrid GetOutput]
```

```
vtkImageViewer viewer
viewer SetInput [blend GetOutput]
viewer SetColorWindow 1000
viewer SetColorLevel 500
viewer Render
```

ImageNoiseSource

The vtkImageNoiseSource image source can be used to generate an image filled with random numbers between some specified minimum and maximum values. The type of the output image is floating point.

One thing to note about vtkImageNoiseSource is that it will produce a different image every time it executes. Normally, this is the desired behavior of a noise source, but this has negative implications in a streaming pipeline with overlap in that the overlapping region will not have the same values across the two requests. For example, assume you set up a pipeline with a vtkImageNoiseSource connected to an ImageMedianFilter which is in turn connected to a vtkImageDataStreamer. If you specify a memory limit in the streamer such that the image will be computed in two halves, the first request the streamer makes would be for half the image. The median filter would need slightly more than half of the input image (based on the extent of the kernel) to produce requested output image. When the median filter executes the second time to produce the second half of the output image, it will again request the overlap region, but this region will contain different values, causing any values computed using the overlap region to be inaccurate.

ImageSinusoidSource

The vtkImageSinusoidSource object can be used to create an image of a specified size where the pixel values are determined by a sinusoid function given direction, period, phase, and amplitude values. The output of the sinusoid source is floating point. In the image below, the output of the sinusoid source shown on the left has been converted to unsigned char

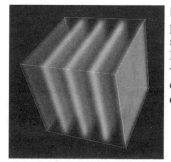

Figure 6–6 The output of the sinusoid source shown on the left has been converted to unsigned char and volume rendered.

values and volume rendered. This same output was passed through an outline filter to create the bounding box seen in the image.

```
vtkImageSinusoidSource ss
   ss SetWholeExtent 0 99 0 99 0 99
   ss SetAmplitude 63
   ss SetDirection 1 0 0
   ss SetPeriod 25
```

6.7 Image Processing

Now we will consider a few examples that process image data. This is not an exhaustive description of all filters, but it will get you started using VTK's image processing filters. You may wish to refer to the Doxygen documentation on CD, and image processing texts for more information.

Gradient

vtkImageGradient is the filter that computes the gradient of an image or volume. You can control whether it computes a two- or three-dimensional gradient using the SetDimensionality() method. It will produce an output with either two or three scalar components per pixel depending on the dimensionality you specified. The scalar components correspond to the x, y, and optionally z components of the gradient vector. If you only want the gradient magnitude you can use the vtkImageGradientMagnitude filter or vtkImageGradient followed by vtkImageMagnitude.

vtkImageGradient computes the gradient by using central differences. This means that to compute the gradient for a pixel we must look at its left and right neighbors. This creates a problem for the pixels on the outside edges of the image since they will be missing one of their two neighbors. There are two solutions to this problem and they are controlled by the HandleBoundaries instance variable. If HandleBoundaries is on, then vtkImageGradient will use a modified gradient calculation for all of the edge pixels. If HandleBoundaries is off, vtkImageGradient will ignore those edge pixels and produce a resulting image that is smaller than the original input image.

In the following example we use a vtkImageReader to read in the raw medical data for a CT scan. We then pass this data through a 3D vtkImageGradient and display the result as a color image.

```
vtkImageReader reader
  reader SetDataByteOrderToLittleEndian
  reader SetDataExtent 0 63 0 63 1 93
  reader SetFilePrefix "$VTK_DATA_ROOT/Data/headsq/quarter"
  reader SetDataMask 0x7fff

vtkImageGradient gradient
  gradient SetInput [reader GetOutput]
  gradient SetDimensionality 3

vtkImageViewer viewer
  viewer SetInput [gradient GetOutput]
  viewer SetZSlice 22
  viewer SetColorWindow 400
  viewer SetColorLevel 0
```

Gaussian Smoothing

Smoothing an image with a Gaussian kernel is similar to the gradient calculation done above. It has a dimensionality that controls what dimension Gaussian kernel to convolve against. It also has SetStandardDeviations() and SetRadiusFactors() methods that control the shape of the Gaussian kernel and when to truncate it. The example provided below is very similar to the gradient calculation. We start with a vtkImageReader connected to the vtkImageGaussianSmooth which finally connects to the vtkImageViewer.

```
vtkImageReader reader
  reader SetDataByteOrderToLittleEndian
  reader SetDataExtent 0 63 0 63 1 93
  reader SetFilePrefix "$VTK_DATA_ROOT/Data/headsq/quarter"
  reader SetDataMask 0x7fff

vtkImageGaussianSmooth smooth
  smooth SetInput [reader GetOutput]
  smooth SetDimensionality 2
  smooth SetStandardDeviations 2 10

vtkImageViewer viewer
  viewer SetInput [smooth GetOutput]
  viewer SetZSlice 22
  viewer SetColorWindow 2000
  viewer SetColorLevel 1000
```

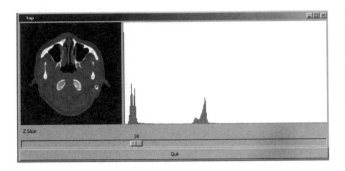

Figure 6–7 The vtkImageAccumulate class is used to generate the one dimensional histogram from the one-component input image.

Histogram

vtkImageAccumulate is an image filter that will produce generalized histograms of up to four dimensions. This is done by dividing the component space into discrete bins, then counting the number of pixels corresponding to each bin. The input image may be of any scalar type, but the output image will always be of integer type. If the input image has only one scalar component, then the output image will be one-dimensional, as shown in **Figure 6–7**. (This example is taken from VTK/Examples/ImageProcessing/Tcl/Histogram.tcl.)

Image Logic

vtkImageLogic is an image processing filter that takes one or two inputs and performs a boolean logic operation on them (**Figure 6–8**). Most standard operations are supported including AND, OR, XOR, NAND, NOR, and NOT. This filter has two inputs although for unary operations such as NOT, only the first input is required. In the example provided below you will notice we use vtkImageEllipseSource to generate the two input images. vtkImageEllipseSource is one of a few image sources that can procedurally generate images. Similar classes are vtkImageGaussianSource and vtkImageNoiseSource.

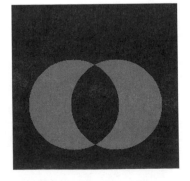

Figure 6–8 Result of image logic.

```
vtkImageEllipsoidSource sphere1
   sphere1 SetCenter 95 100 0
   sphere1 SetRadius 70 70 70

vtkImageEllipsoidSource sphere2
   sphere2 SetCenter 161 100 0
   sphere2 SetRadius 70 70 70

vtkImageLogic xor
   xor SetInput1 [sphere1 GetOutput]
   xor SetInput2 [sphere2 GetOutput]
   xor SetOutputTrueValue 150
   xor SetOperationToXor

vtkImageViewer viewer
   viewer SetInput [xor GetOutput]
   viewer SetColorWindow 255
   viewer SetColorLevel 127.5
```

Image Reslice

vtkImageReslice is a contributed class (David Gobbi is the author) that offers high-performance image resampling along an arbitrarily oriented volume (or image). The extent, origin, and sampling density of the output data can also be set. This class provides several other imaging filters: it can permute, flip, rotate, scale, resample, and pad image data in any combination. It can also extract oblique slices from image volumes, which no other VTK imaging filter can do. The following script, taken from VTK/Examples/Imaging/ Tcl/TestReslice.tcl demonstrates how to use vtkImageReslice.

```
vtkImageReader reader
   reader ReleaseDataFlagOff
   reader SetDataByteOrderToLittleEndian
   reader SetDataExtent 0 63 0 63 1 93
   reader SetDataOrigin -32.5 -32.5 -47
   reader SetFilePrefix "$VTK_DATA_ROOT/Data/headsq/quarter"
   reader SetDataMask 0x7fff
   reader Update
vtkTransform transform
   transform RotateX 10
   transform RotateY 20
   transform RotateZ 30
vtkImageReslice reslice
   reslice SetInput [reader GetOutput]
```

```
reslice SetResliceTransform transform
reslice InterpolateOn
reslice SetBackgroundLevel 1023
vtkImageViewer viewer
  viewer SetInput [reslice GetOutput]
  viewer SetZSlice 120
  viewer SetColorWindow 2000
  viewer SetColorLevel 1000
  viewer Render
```

In this example (**Figure 6–9**) a volume of size 64^2 x 93 is read. A transform is used to position a volume on which to resample (or reslice) the data. Linear interpolation is used, and a background gray level (since the volume is single-component) is set that defines the color of resample points outside the original volume. By default, the spacing of the output volume is set at 1.0, and the output origin and extent are adjusted to enclose the input volume. A viewer is used to display one z-slice of the resulting volume.

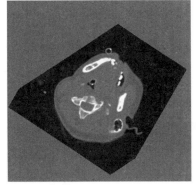

Figure 6–9 Output of vtkImage-Reslice with a gray background level set.

6.8 Volume Rendering

Volume rendering is a term used to describe a rendering process applied to 3D data where information exists throughout a 3D space instead of simply on 2D surfaces defined in 3D space. There is not a clear dividing line between volume rendering and geometric rendering techniques. Often two different approaches can produce similar results, and in some cases one approach may be considered both a volume rendering and a geometric rendering technique. For example, you can use a contouring technique to extract triangles representing an isosurface in a structured points dataset (see "Contouring" on page 89) and then use geometric rendering techniques to display these triangles, or you can use a volumetric ray casting technique on the image dataset and terminate the ray traversal at a particular isovalue. These two different approaches produce similar (although not necessarily identical) results. Another example is the technique of employing texture mapping hardware in order to perform composite volume rendering. This one method maybe considered a volume rendering technique since it works on image data, or a geometric technique since it uses geometric primitives and standard graphics hardware.

In VTK, volume rendering techniques have been implemented for image datasets. The SetInput() method of vtkVolumeMapper accepts a pointer to vtkImageData. Unstructured datasets cannot (at this time) be directly volume rendered. However, you can resample an unstructured grid into a regular image data format in order to take advantage of the techniques described in this section (see "Probing" on page 98).

There are three main volume rendering techniques currently implemented in VTK: ray casting, 2D texture mapping, and support for the VolumePro volume rendering hardware (if you have one of these boards installed on your system). More information on the VolumePro board can be found at the TeraRecon web site: http://www.terarecon.com.

We will begin this section with a simple example written using the three different volume rendering techniques. Then we will cover the objects / parameters common to all of these techniques. Next, each of the three volume rendering techniques will be discussed in more detail, including information on parameters specific to that rendering method. This will be followed by a discussion on achieving interactive rendering rates, and finally a summary of the features supported by each volume rendering approach.

A Simple Example

Consider the simple volume rendering example shown below (and illustrated in **Figure 6–10**) that is nearly the simplest Tcl script that can be written to render a volume (refer to VTK/Examples/VolumeRendering/Tcl/SimpleRayCast.tcl). This example is written for volumetric ray casting, but only the portion of the Tcl script highlighted with bold text is specific to this rendering technique. Following this example you will find the alternate versions of the bold portion of the script that would instead perform the volume rendering task with a 2D texture mapping approach, or using the VolumePro hardware support. You will notice that switching volume rendering techniques, at least in this simple case, requires only a few minor changes to the script.

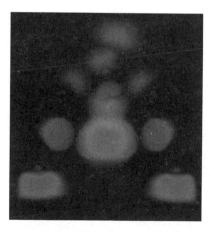

Figure 6–10 Volume rendering.

```
vtkRenderer ren1
vtkRenderWindow renWin
    renWin AddRenderer ren1
vtkRenderWindowInteractor iren
    iren SetRenderWindow renWin

# Create the reader for the data
vtkStructuredPointsReader reader
    reader SetFileName "$VTK_DATA_ROOT/Data/ironProt.vtk"

# Create transfer mapping scalar value to opacity
vtkPiecewiseFunction opacityTransferFunction
    opacityTransferFunction AddPoint  20    0.0
    opacityTransferFunction AddPoint  255   0.2

# Create transfer mapping scalar value to color
vtkColorTransferFunction colorTransferFunction
    colorTransferFunction AddRGBPoint     0.0 0.0 0.0 0.0
    colorTransferFunction AddRGBPoint    64.0 1.0 0.0 0.0
    colorTransferFunction AddRGBPoint   128.0 0.0 0.0 1.0
    colorTransferFunction AddRGBPoint   192.0 0.0 1.0 0.0
    colorTransferFunction AddRGBPoint   255.0 0.0 0.2 0.0

# The property describes how the data will look
vtkVolumeProperty volumeProperty
    volumeProperty SetColor colorTransferFunction
    volumeProperty SetScalarOpacity opacityTransferFunction

# The mapper / ray cast functions know how to render the data
vtkVolumeRayCastCompositeFunction  compositeFunction
vtkVolumeRayCastMapper volumeMapper
    volumeMapper SetVolumeRayCastFunction compositeFunction
    volumeMapper SetInput [reader GetOutput]

# The volume holds the mapper and the property and
# can be used to position/orient the volume
vtkVolume volume
    volume SetMapper volumeMapper
    volume SetProperty volumeProperty

ren1 AddProp volume
renWin Render
```

In this example we start by reading in a data file from disk. We then define the functions that map scalar value into opacity and color which are used in the vtkVolumeProperty.

Next we create the objects specific to volumetric ray casting—a vtkVolumeRayCastCompositeFunction that performs the compositing of samples along the ray, and a vtkVolumeRayCastMapper that performs some of the basic ray casting operations such as transformations and clipping. We set the input of the mapper to the data we read off the disk, and we create a vtkVolume (a subclass of vtkProp3D similar to vtkActor) to hold the mapper and property. Finally, we create the standard graphics display objects, add the volume to the renderer, and render the scene.

If you decided to implement the above script with a 2D texture mapping approach instead of volumetric ray casting, the bolded portion of the script would instead be:

```
# Create the objects specific to 2D texture mapping approach
vtkVolumeTextureMapper2D volumeMapper
```

If you have a VolumePro volume rendering board on your system, and you have compiled in the support for this device as described later in this section, you could use the following script fragment to replace the volumetric ray casting specific section with a VolumePro volume mapper:

```
# Create the objects specific to VolumePro volume rendering hardware
vtkVolumeProMapper volumeMapper
```

Why Multiple Volume Rendering Techniques?

As you can see, in this simple example the only thing that changes between rendering strategies is the type of volume mapper that is instantiated; and in the case of ray casting, a ray cast function also needs to be created. This may lead you to the following questions: why are there different volume rendering strategies in VTK? Why can't VTK simply pick the strategy that would work best on my platform? First, it is not always easy to predict which strategy will work best—ray casting may out-perform texture mapping if the image size is reduced, more processors become available, or the graphics hardware is the bottleneck to the rendering rate. These are things that can change continuously at run time. Second, due to its computational complexity, most volume rendering techniques only produce an approximation of the desired rendering equation. For example, techniques which take samples through the volume and composite them with an alpha blending function are only approximating the true integral through the volume. Under different circumstances, different techniques perform better or worse than others in terms of both quality and speed. In addition, some techniques work only under certain special conditions. For example, the VolumePro rendering board only supports parallel camera projections while ray casting and texture mapping both support parallel and perspective camera transformations. The last portion of this section provides a summary chart of the capabilities / limitations of each of these volume rendering techniques (see **Table 6–1**).

Creating a vtkVolume

A vtkVolume is a subclass of vtkProp3D that is intended for use in volume rendering. Similar to a vtkActor (that is intended for geometric rendering), a vtkVolume holds the transformation information such as position, orientation, and scale, and pointers to the mapper and property for the volume. Additional information on how to control the transformation of a vtkVolume is covered in "Volumes" on page 63.

The vtkVolume class accepts objects that are subclasses of vtkVolumeMapper as input to SetMapper(), and accepts a vtkVolumeProperty object as input to SetProperty(). vtkActor and vtkVolume are two separate objects in order to enforce the different types of the mappers and properties. These different types are necessary due to the fact that some parameters of geometric rendering do not make sense in volume rendering and vice versa. For example, the SetRepresentationToWireframe() method of vtkProperty is meaningless in volume rendering, while the SetInterpolationTypeToNearest() method of vtkVolumeProperty has no value in geometric rendering.

Using vtkPiecewiseFunction

In order to control the appearance of a 3D volume of scalar values, three mappings or transfer functions must be defined. The first transfer function, known as the *scalar opacity transfer function*, maps the scalar value into an opacity or an opacity per unit length value. The second transfer function, referred to simply as the *color transfer function*, maps the scalar value into a color. The third transfer function, called the *gradient opacity transfer function*, maps the magnitude of the gradient of the scalar value into an opacity multiplier. Any of these mappings can be defined as a single value to single value mapping, which can be represented with a vtkPiecewiseTransferFunction. For the scalar value to color mapping, a vtkColorTransferFunction can also be used to define RGB rather than grey-scale colors.

From a user's point of view, vtkPiecewiseFunction has two types of methods—those that add information to the mapping, and those that clear out information from the mapping. When information is added to a mapping, it is considered to be a point sample of the mapping with linear interpolation used to determine values between the specified ones. For example, consider the following section of a script on the left that produces the transfer function draw on the right:

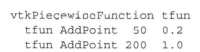

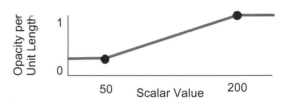

The value of the mapping for the scalar values of 50 and 200 are given as 0.2 and 1.0 respectively, and all other mapping values can be obtained by interpolating between these two values. If Clamping is on (it is by default) then the mapping of any value below 50 will be 0.2, and the mapping of any value above 200 will be 1.0. If Clamping was turned off, then out-of-range values map to 0.0.

Points can be added to the mapping at any time. If a mapping is redefined it replaces the existing mapping. In addition to adding a single point, a segment can be added which will define two mapping points and clear any existing points between the two. As an example, consider the following two modification steps and the corresponding pictorial representations of the transfer functions:

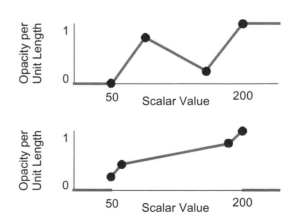

In the first step, we change the mapping of scalar value 50 by removing the point and then adding it again, and we add a segment. In the second step, we change the mapping of scalar value 50 by simply adding a new mapping without first removing the old one. We also add a new segment which eliminates the mappings for 100 and 150 since they lie within the new segment, and we turn clamping off.

Using vtkColorTransferFunction

A vtkColorTransferFunction can be used to specify a mapping of scalar value to color using either an RGB or HSV color space. The methods available are similar to those provided by vtkPiecewiseFunction, but tend to come in two flavors. For example, AddRGB-Point() and AddHSVPoint() both add a point into the transfer function with one accepting an RGB value as input and the other accepting an HSV value as input.

The following Tcl example shows how to specify a transfer function from red to green to blue with RGB interpolation performed for values in between those specified:

```
vtkColorTransferFunction ctfun
  ctfun SetColorSpaceToRGB
  ctfun AddRGBPoint 0 1 0 0
  ctfun AddRGBPoint 127 0 1 0
  ctfun AddRGBPoint 255 0 0 1
```

Controlling Color / Opacity with a vtkVolumeProperty

In the previous two sections we have discussed the basics of creating transfer functions, but we have not yet discussed how these control the appearance of the volume. Typically, defining the transfer functions is the hardest part of achieving an effective volume visualization since you are essentially performing a classification operation that requires you to understand the meaning of the underlying data values.

For rendering techniques that map a pixel to a single location in the volume (such as an isosurface rendering or a maximum intensity projection) the ScalarOpacity transfer function maps the scalar value to an opacity. When a compositing technique is used, the ScalarOpacity function maps scalar value to an opacity that is accumulated per unit length for a homogenous region of that value. Compositing is performed by approximating the continuously changing value through the volume by a large number of small homogeneous regions, where the opacity per unit length is transformed based on the size of these regions.

The ScalarOpacity and Color transfer functions are typically used to perform a simple classification of the data. Scalar values that are part of the background, or considered "noise" are mapped to an opacity of 0.0, eliminating them from contributing to the image. The remaining scalar values can be divided into different "materials" which have different opacities and colors. For example, data acquired from a CT scanner can often be categorized as air, soft tissue, or bone based on the density value contained in the data (**Figure 6–11**). The scalar values defined as air would be given an opacity of 0.0, the soft tissue scalar values might be given a light brown color and the bone values might be given a

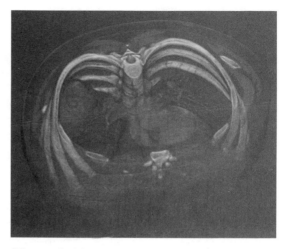

Figure 6–11 CT torso data classified using the ScalarOpacity, Color, and GradientOpacity transfer functions.

white color. By varying the opacity of these last two materials, you can visualize the skin surface or the bone surface, or potentially see the bone through the translucent skin. This process of determining the dividing line between materials in the data can be tedious, and in some cases not possible based on the raw input data values. For example, liver and kidney sample locations may have overlapping CT density values. In this case, a segmentation filter may need to be applied to the volume to either alter the data values so that materials can be classified solely on the basis of the scalar value, or to extract out one specific material type. These segmentation operations can be based on additional information such as location or a comparison to a reference volume.

Two examples of segmenting CT data in this manner are shown here, one for a torso (**Figure 6–11**) and the other for a head study (**Figure 6–12**). In both of these examples, the third transfer function maps the magnitude of the gradient of the scalar value to an opacity multiplier, and is used to enhance the contribution of transition regions of the volume. For example, a large gradient magnitude can be found where the scalar value transitions from air to soft tissue, or soft tissue to bone, while within the soft tissue and bone regions the magnitude remains relatively small. Below is a code fragment that defines a typical gradient opacity transfer function for 8-bit unsigned data.

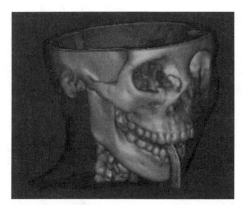

Figure 6–12 CT head data classified using the ScalarOpacity, Color, and GradientOpacity transfer functions.

```
vtkPiecewiseFunction gtfun
  gtfun AddPoint   0  0.0
  gtfun AddPoint   3  0.0
  gtfun AddPoint   6  1.0
  gtfun AddPoint 255  1.0
```

This function eliminates nearly homogeneous regions by defining an opacity multiplier of 0.0 for any gradient magnitude less than 3. This multiplier follows a linear ramp from 0.0 to 1.0 on gradient magnitudes between 3 and 6, and no change in the opacity value is performed on samples with magnitudes above 6. Noisier data may require a more aggressive edge detection (so the 3 and the 6 would be higher values).

There are a few methods in vtkVolumeProperty that relate to the color and opacity transfer functions. The SetColor() method accepts either a vtkPiecewiseFunction (if your color functions defines only greyscale values) or a vtkColorTransferFunction(). You can query the number of color channels with GetColorChannels() which will return 1 if a vtkPiecewiseFunction was set as the color, or 3 if a vtkColorTransferFunction was used to specify color. Once you know how many color channels are in use, you can call either GetGrayTransferFunction() or GetRGBTransferFunction() to get the appropriate function.

The SetScalarOpacity() method accepts a vtkPiecewiseFunction to define the scalar opacity transfer function, and there is a corresponding GetScalarOpacity() method that returns this function. Similarly, there are two methods for the gradient opacity transfer function: SetGradientOpacity() and GetGradientOpacity().

One other method in vtkVolumeProperty that can be used to control the color of a volume is SetRGBTextureCoefficient(). If a texture is defined in the volume mapper, and the volume mapper supports 3D texturing for the given rendering technique, then this coefficient will be considered when determining the color of a sample according to:

(color from scalar value) * (1 - RGBTextureCoefficient) +
          (color from texture) * (RGBTextureCoefficient)

Setting the coefficient to 0.0 will ignore the texture and use only the ScalarColor transfer function, while setting it to 1.0 will use only the texture. Applying a texture to a volume will be discussed in more detail later in this section.

Controlling Shading with a vtkVolumeProperty

Controlling shading of a volume with a volume property is similar to controlling the shading of a geometric actor with a property (see "Actor Properties" on page 58 and "Actor Color" on page 59). There is a flag for shading, and four basic parameters: the ambient coefficient, the diffuse coefficient, the specular coefficient and the specular power. Generally, the first three coefficients will sum to 1.0 but exceeding this value is often desirable in volume rendering to increase the brightness of a rendered volume. The exact interpretation of these parameters will depend on the illumination equation used by the specific volume rendering technique that is being used. In general, if the ambient term dominates then the volume will appear unshaded, if the diffuse term dominates then the volume will appear rough (like concrete) and if the specular term dominates then the volume will appear smooth (like glass). The specular power can be used to control how smooth the appearance is (such as brushed metal versus polished metal).

By default, shading is off. You must explicitly call ShadeOn() for the shading coefficients to affect the scene. Setting the shading flag off is generally the same as setting the ambient coefficient to 1.0, the diffuse coefficient to 0.0 and the specular coefficient to 0.0. Some volume rendering techniques, such as volume ray casting with a maximum intensity ray function, do not consider the shading coefficients regardless of the value of the shading flag.

The shaded appearance of a volume depends not only on the values of the shading coefficients in the vtkVolumeProperty, but also on the collection of light sources contained in the renderer, and their properties. The appearance of a rendered volume will depend on the number, position, and color of the light sources in the scene.

If possible, the volume rendering technique attempts to reproduce the lighting equations defined by OpenGL. Consider the following example, where the creation of the renderer, render window, and interactor is left out for clarity.

```
#Create a geometric sphere
vtkSphereSource sphere
   sphere SetRadius 20
   sphere SetCenter 70 25 25
   sphere SetThetaResolution 50
   sphere SetPhiResolution 50

vtkPolyDataMapper mapper
   mapper SetInput [sphere GetOutput]

vtkActor actor
   actor SetMapper mapper
   [actor GetProperty] SetColor 1 1 1
   [actor GetProperty] SetAmbient 0.01
   [actor GetProperty] SetDiffuse 0.7
   [actor GetProperty] SetSpecular 0.5
   [actor GetProperty] SetSpecularPower 70.0
```

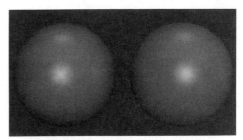

Figure 6–13 A geometric sphere
(right) and a volumetric sphere (left)
rendered with the same lighting
coefficients.

```
#Read in a volumetric sphere
vtkSLCReader reader
    reader SetFileName "$VTK_DATA_ROOT/Data/sphere.slc"

# Use this tfun for both opacity and color
vtkPiecewiseFunction opacityTransferFunction
    opacityTransferFunction AddSegment 0 1.0 255 1.0

# Make the volume property match the geometric one
vtkVolumeProperty volumeProperty
   volumeProperty SetColor opacityTransferFunction
   volumeProperty SetScalarOpacity tfun
   volumeProperty ShadeOn
   volumeProperty SetInterpolationTypeToLinear
   volumeProperty SetDiffuse 0.7
   volumeProperty SetAmbient 0.01
   volumeProperty SetSpecular 0.5
   volumeProperty SetSpecularPower 70.0

vtkVolumeRayCastCompositeFunction  compositeFunction
vtkVolumeRayCastMapper volumeMapper
   volumeMapper SetInput [reader GetOutput]
   volumeMapper SetVolumeRayCastFunction compositeFunction

vtkVolume volume
   volume SetMapper volumeMapper
   volume SetProperty volumeProperty
```

```
# Add both the geometric and volumetric spheres to the renderer
ren1 AddProp volume
ren1 AddProp actor

# Create a red, green, and blue light
vtkLight redlight
  redlight SetColor 1 0 0
  redlight SetPosition 1000 25 25
  redlight SetFocalPoint 25 25 25
  redlight SetIntensity 0.5

vtkLight greenlight
  greenlight SetColor 0 1 0
  greenlight SetPosition 25 1000 25
  greenlight SetFocalPoint 25 25 25
  greenlight SetIntensity 0.5

vtkLight bluelight
  bluelight SetColor 0 0 1
  bluelight SetPosition 25 25 1000
  bluelight SetFocalPoint 25 25 25
  bluelight SetIntensity 0.5

# Add the lights to the renderer
ren1 AddLight redlight
ren1 AddLight greenlight
ren1 AddLight bluelight

#Render it!
renWin Render
```

In the image shown for this example (**Figure 6–13**), the left sphere is the volumetric one rendered with volumetric ray casting, and the right sphere is the geometric one rendered with OpenGL. Since the vtkProperty used for the vtkActor, and the vtkVolumeProperty used for the vtkVolume were set up with the same ambient, diffuse, specular, and specular power values, and the color of both spheres is white, they have similar appearances.

Creating a vtkVolumeMapper

vtkVolumeMapper is an abstract superclass and is never created directly. Instead, you would create a mapper subclass of the specific type desired. Currently, the choices are vtkVolumeRayCastMapper, and vtkVolumeTextureMapper2D, or a vtkVolumeProMapper.

All volume mappers support the SetInput() method with an argument of a pointer to a vtkImageData object. Some rendering techniques support only certain types of input data. For example, the vtkVolumeRayCastMapper and the vtkVolumeTextureMapper2D both support only VTK_UNSIGNED_CHAR and VTK_UNSIGNED_SHORT data. The VolumePro mapper is even more restrictive in that it supports only 8 or 12 bit data, where the 12 bit data is represented as VTK_UNSIGNED_SHORT data with the significant bits either in the upper or lower 12 out of the 16 bits. (If your data is not of the types described above, you can use vtkImageShiftScale to scale the data to the right range and convert it to the right type.)

Be sure to set the input of the volume mapper before a volume that uses the volume mapper is rendered.

Cropping a Volume

Since volume rendered images of large, complex volumes can produce images that are difficult to interpret, it is often useful to view only a portion of the volume. The two techniques that can be used to limit the amount of data rendered are known as cropping and clipping.

Cropping is a method of defining visible regions of the volume using six planes—two along each of the major axes. These cropping planes are defined in data coordinates and are therefore dependent on the origin and spacing of the data, but are independent of any transformation applied to the volume. The most common way to use these six planes is to define a subvolume of interest as shown in the figure to the right.

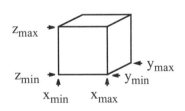

To crop a subvolume, you must turn cropping on, set the cropping region flags, and set the cropping region planes in the volume mapper as shown below.

```
set xmin 10.0
set xmax 50.0
set ymin 0.0
set ymax 33.0
```

```
set zmin 21.0
set zmax 47.0

vtkVolumeRayCastMapper mapper
  mapper CroppingOn
  mapper SetCroppingRegionPlanes $xmin $xmax $ymin $ymax $zmin $zmax
  mapper SetCroppingRegionFlagsToSubVolume
```

Note that the above example is shown for a vtkVolumeRayCastMapper, but it could have instead used any concrete volume mapper since the cropping methods are all defined in the superclass.

The six planes that are defined by the x_{min}, x_{max}, y_{min}, y_{max}, z_{min}, and z_{max} values break the volume into 27 regions (a 3x3 grid). The CroppingRegionFlags is a 27 bit number with one bit representing each of these regions, where a value of 1 indicates that data within that region is visible, and a value of 0 indicating that data within that region will be cropped. The region of the volume that is less than x_{min}, y_{min}, and z_{min} is represented by the first bit, with regions ordered along the x axis first, then the y axis and finally the z axis.

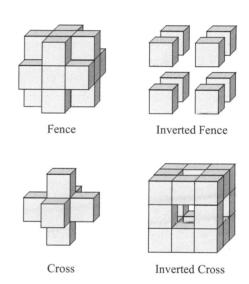

Fence   Inverted Fence

Cross   Inverted Cross

Figure 6–14 Cropping operations.

The SetCroppingRegionFlagsToSubVolume() method is a convenience method that sets the flags to 0x0002000—just the center region is visible. Although any 27 bit number can be used to define the cropping operation, in practice there are only a few that are used. Four additional convenience methods are provided for setting these flags: SetCroppingRegionFlagsToFence(), SetCroppingResgionFlagsToInvertedFence(), SetCroppingRegionFlagsToCross(), and SetCroppingRegionFlagsToInvertedCross(), as depicted in **Figure 6–14**.

Clipping a Volume

In addition to the cropping functionality supplied by
the vtkVolumeMapper, arbitrary clipping planes are
provided in the vtkAbstractMapper3D. For subclasses
of vtkAbstractMapper3D that use OpenGL to perform
the clipping in hardware such as vtkOpenGLPoly-
DataMapper, and vtkOpenGLVolumeTexture-
Mapper2D, an error message will be displayed if you
attempt to use more than six clipping planes. Software
rendering techniques such as vtkVolumeRayCast-
Mapper can support an arbitrary number of clipping
planes. The vtkVolumeProMapper does not support
these clipping planes directly, although the class does
contain methods for specifying one clipping box using
a plane and a thickness value.

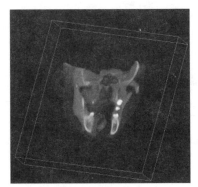

Figure 6–15 Clipping planes
are used to define a thick slab.

The clipping planes are specified by creating a vtkPlane, defining the plane parameters,
then adding this plane to the mapper using the AddClippingPlane() method. The most
common use of these arbitrary clipping planes in volume rendering is to specify two
planes parallel to each other in order to perform a thick reformatting operation. An example of this applied to CT data is shown in **Figure 6–15**.

Applying 3D Texture to a Volume

The volume mapper accepts data of the same type as Set-
Input() to the SetRGBTextureInput() method: a pointer
to a vtkImageData object. In the current implementation,
the texture input must have three components which represent R, G, and B, and each component must be an
unsigned char. Not all volume rendering techniques
make use of the RGBTextureInput. In the current implementation, the only volume rendering technique that
does make use of the texture is the vtkVolumeRayCast-
Mapper when a vtkVolumeRayCastIsosurfaceFunction
is used as the ray cast function. An example script is

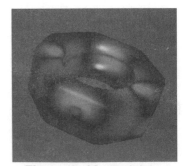

Figure 6–16 Applying
texture to a volume.

shown below (refer to **Figure 6–16**). Note that the creation of the renderer, render window, and interactor have been left out for clarity.

```
# A simple example of using a texture
# on a volume rendered with ray casting
# and an isosurface ray cast function.
# The texture data was created from two
# other volume data sets - with one data
# set duplicated to define R and B, and
# the other used to define G.

# Read the input data from disk
vtkSLCReader reader
    reader SetFileName "$VTK_DATA_ROOT/Data/nut.slc"

# Read the texture input from disk
vtkStructuredPointsReader rgbreader
    rgbreader SetFileName "$VTK_DATA_ROOT/Data/hipipTexture.vtk"

# Create transfer function for opacity - the surface is opaque
vtkPiecewiseFunction opacityTransferFunction
    opacityTransferFunction AddSegment 0 1.0 255 1.0

# Create the property - all color comes from the texture
vtkVolumeProperty volumeProperty
    volumeProperty SetScalarOpacity opacityTransferFunction
    volumeProperty ShadeOn
    volumeProperty SetInterpolationTypeToLinear
    volumeProperty SetRGBTextureCoefficient 1.0

# Create the isosurface function
vtkVolumeRayCastIsosurfaceFunction  isoFunction
    isoFunction SetIsoValue 128.0

# Create the mapper - set the input and texture
vtkVolumeRayCastMapper volumeMapper
    volumeMapper SetInput [reader GetOutput]
    volumeMapper SetRGBTextureInput [rgbreader GetOutput]
    volumeMapper SetVolumeRayCastFunction isoFunction

# Create the volume
vtkVolume volume
    volume SetMapper volumeMapper
    volume SetProperty volumeProperty
```

```
# Add the volume and render
ren1 AddProp volume
renWin Render
```

Controlling the Normal Encoding

The standard illumination equation relies on a surface normal in order to calculate the diffuse and specular components of shading. In volume rendering, the gradient at a location in the volumetric data is considered to point in the opposite direction of the "surface normal" at that location. A finite differences technique is typically used to estimate the gradient, but this tends to be an expensive calculation, and would make shaded volume rendering prohibitively slow if it had to be performed at every sample along every ray.

One way to avoid these expensive computations is to precompute the normals at the grid locations, and to use some form of interpolation in between. If done naively, this would require three floating point numbers per location, and we would still need to take a square root to determine the magnitude. Alternatively, we could store the magnitude so that each normal would require four floating point values. Since volumes tend to be quite large, this technique requires too much memory, so we must somehow quantize the normals into a smaller number of bytes.

In VTK we have chosen to quantize the normal direction into two byes, and the magnitude into one. The calculation of the normal is performed by a subclass of vtkEncodedGradientEstimator (currently only vtkFiniteDifferenceGradientEstimator) and the encoding of the direction into two bytes is performed by a subclass of vtkDirectionEncoder (currently only vtkRecursiveSphereDirectionEncoder). For mappers that use normal encoding (vtkVolumeRayCastMapper and vtkVolumeTextureMapper2D), these objects are created automatically so the typical user need not be concerned with these objects. In the case where one volume dataset is to be rendered by multiple mappers into the same image, it is often useful to create one gradient estimator to set in all the mappers. This will conserve space since otherwise there would be one copy of the normal volume per mapper. An example fragment of code is shown below:

```
# Create the gradient estimator
vtkFiniteDifferenceGradientEstimator GradientEstimator

# Create the first mapper
vtkVolumeRayCastMapper volumeMapper1
    volumeMapper1 SetGradientEstimator GradientEstimator
```

```
  volumeMapper1 SetInput [reader GetOutput]

# Create the second mapper
vtkVolumeRayCastMapper volumeMapper2
  volumeMapper2 SetGradientEstimator GradientEstimator
  volumeMapper2 SetInput [reader GetOutput]
```

If you set the gradient estimator to the same object in two different mappers, then it is important that these mappers have the same input. Otherwise, the gradient estimator will be out-of-date each time the mapper asks for the normals, and will regenerate them for each volume during every frame rendered. In the above example, the direction encoding objects were not explicitly created, therefore each gradient estimator created its own encoding object. Since this object does not have any significant storage requirements, this is generally an acceptable situation. Alternatively, one vtkRecursiveSphereDirectionEncoder could be created, and the SetDirectionEncoder() method would be used on each estimated to associate the encoder with the estimator.

Volumetric Ray Casting

The vtkVolumeRayCastMapper is a volume mapper that employs a software ray casting technique to perform volume rendering. It is generally the most accurate mapper, and also the slowest on most platforms. The ray caster is threaded to make use of multiple processors when available.

There are a few parameters that are specific to volume ray casting that have not yet been discussed. First, there is the ray cast function that must be set in the mapper. This is the object that does the actual work of considering the data values along the ray and determining a final RGBA value to return. Currently, there

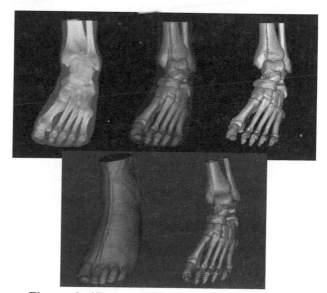

Figure 6–17 Volume rendering via ray casting.

are three supported subclasses of vtkVolumeRayCastFunction: the vtkVolumeRayCast-
IsosurfaceFunction that can be used to render isosurfaces within the volumetric data, the
vtkVolumeRayCastMIPFunction that can be used to generate maximum intensity projections of the volume, and vtkVolumeRayCastCompositeFunction that can be used to render
the volume with an alpha compositing technique. An example of the images that can be
generated using these different methods is **Figure 6–17**. The upper left image was generated using a maximum intensity projection. The other two upper images were generated
using compositing, while the lower two images were generated using an isosurface function. Note that it is not always easy to distinguish an image generated using a compositing
technique from one generated using an isosurface technique, especially when a sharp
opacity ramp is used.

Classify First

Interpolate First

Figure 6–18 The effect of
interpolation order in composite ray casting.

There are some parameters that can be set in each of the
ray cast functions that impact the rendering process. In
vtkVolumeRayCastIsosurfaceFunction, there is a Set-
IsoValue() method that can be used to set the value of the
rendered isosurface. In vtkVolumeRayCastMIPFunction,
you can call SetMaximizeMethodToScalarValue() (the
default) or SetMaximizeMethodToOpacity() to change
the behavior of the maximize operation. In the first case,
the scalar value is considered at each sample point along
the ray. The sample point with the largest scalar value is
selected, then this scalar value is passed through the color
and opacity transfer functions to produce a final ray value.
If the second method is called, the opacity of the sample is
computed at each step along the ray, and the sample with
the highest opacity value is selected.

In vtkVolumeRayCastCompositeFunction, you can call
SetCompositeMethodToInterpolateFirst() (the default) or
SetCompositeMethodToClassifyFirst() to change the
order of interpolation and classification (**Figure 6–18**).
This setting will only have an impact when trilinear interpolation is being used. In the first case, interpolation will
be performed to determine the scalar value at the sample
point, then this value will be used for classification (the
application of the color and opacity transfer functions). In the second case, classification is
done at the eight vertices of the cell containing the sample location, then the final RGBA
value is interpolated from the computed RGBA values at the vertex locations. Interpolat-

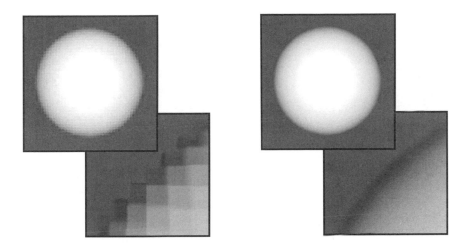

Figure 6–19 Different methods for interpolation. On the left, nearest neighbor interpolation. On the right, trilinear interpolation.

ing first generally produces "prettier" images as can be seen on the left where a geometric sphere is contained within a volumetric "distance to point" field, with the transfer functions defined to highlight three concentric spherical shells in the volume. The interpolate first method makes the underlying assumption that if two neighboring data points have values of 10 and 100, then a value of 50 exists somewhere between the two data points. In the case where material is being classified by scalar value, this may not be the case. For example, consider CT data where values below 20 are air (transparent), values from 20 to 80 are soft tissue, and values above 80 are bone. If interpolation is performed first, then bone can never be adjacent to air - there must always be soft tissue between the bone and air. This is not true inside the mouth where teeth meet air. If you render an image with interpolation performed first and a high enough sample rate, it will look like the teeth have a layer of skin on top of them.

The value of the interpolation type instance variable in the vtkVolumeProperty is important to ray casting. There are two options: SetInterpolationTypeToNearest() (the default) which will use a nearest neighbor approximation when sampling along the ray, and SetInterpolationTypeToLinear() which will use trilinear interpolation during sampling. Using the trilinear interpolation produces smoother images with less artifacts, but generally takes a bit longer. The difference in image quality obtained with these two methods is shown in **Figure 6–19**. A sphere is voxelized into a 50x50x50 voxel volume, and rendered using alpha compositing with nearest neighbor interpolation on the left and trilinear interpola-

Figure 6–20 The effects or varying sample distance along the ray. As the sample distance increases, sampling artifacts create the dramatic black and white banding. However, the cost of volume rendering increases inversely proportional to the sample size, i.e., the difference in rendering time for sample distance 0.1 is 20x faster than for 2.0.

Step Size = 0.1   Step Size = 1.0   Step Size = 2.0

tion on the right. In the image of the full sphere it may be difficult to distinguish between the two interpolation methods, but by zooming up on just a portion of the sphere it is easy to see the individual voxels in the left image.

Another parameter of vtkVolumeRayCastMapper that affects the image is the SampleDistance. This is the distance in world coordinates between sample points for ray functions that take samples. For example, the alpha compositing ray function performs a discrete approximation of the continuous volume rendering integral by sampling along the ray. The accuracy of the approximation increases with the number of samples taken, but unfortunately so does the rendering time. The maximum intensity ray function also takes samples to locate the maximum value. The isosurface ray function does not take samples but instead computes the exact location of the intersection according to the current interpolation function.

By default samples are taken 1 unit apart in world coordinates. In practice you should adjust this spacing based on the sample spacing of the 3D data being rendered, and the rate of change of not only the scalar values but also the color and opacity assigned to the scalar values through the transfer functions. An example is shown below of a voxelized vase with a 1x1x1 spacing between samples in the dataset. The scalar values vary smoothly in the data, but a sharp change has been introduced in the transfer functions by having the color change rapidly from black to white. You can clearly see artifacts of the "undersampling" of ray casting in the image created with a step size of 2.0. Even with a step size of 1.0 there are some artifacts since the color of the vase changes significantly within a world space distance of 1.0. If the sample distance is set to 0.1 the image appears smooth. Of course, this smooth image on the left takes nearly 20 times as long to generate as the one on the right.

2D Texture Mapping

As an alternative to ray casting, volume rendering can be performed by texture mapping the volume onto polygons, and projecting these with the graphics hardware. If your graphic board provides reasonable texture mapping acceleration, this method will be significantly faster than ray casting, but at the expense of accuracy since partial accumulation results are stored at the resolution of the framebuffer (usually 8 or less bits per component) rather than in floating point. To use 2D texture mapping, quads are generated along the axis of the volume which is most closely aligned with the viewing direction. As the viewing direction changes, the sample distance between quads will change, and at some point the set of quads will jump to a new axis which may cause temporal artifacts. Generally these artifacts will be most noticeable on small volumes. If 3D texture mapping is available, the polygons can be generated to always be perpendicular to the viewing direction, greatly reducing these artifacts. In this case, the polygons may be anything from 3 sided triangles to 6 sided hexagons. Unfortunately, 3D texture mapping is not yet widely supported across graphics cards.

The vtkVolumeTextureMapper is the superclass for volume mappers that employ hardware texture mapping as the rendering technique. Currently, the only concrete implementation is the vtkVolumeTextureMapper2D. Since this class requires access to the underlying graphics language, there is an automatically created graphics-specific object (vtkOpenGLVolumeTextureMapper2D) as well.

The current implementation of vtkVolumeTextureMapper2D supports only alpha compositing. Bilinear interpolation on the slice is used for texture mapping but since quads are only created on the data planes, there is no notion of interpolation between slices. Therefore, the value of the InterpolationType instance variable in the vtkVolumeProperty is ignored by this mapper.

Shading is supported in software for the texture mapping approach. If shading is turned off in the vtkVolumeProperty, then software shading calculations do not need to be performed, and therefore the performance of this mapper will be better than if shading is turned on.

VolumePro Rendering Hardware

Support has been included in VTK for the VolumePro rendering hardware. Both the VolumePro 500 and the VolumePro 1000 are supported in VTK 4.0 although the description in this chapter covers mainly the VolumePro 500. Please see the latest online documentation for a description of methods and functionality specific to the VolumePro 1000.

The version of this VolumePro 500 board implements a ray casting strategy to render volumes of up to 256x256x256 voxels (8 or 12 bits per voxel) at rates of 20 to 30 frames per second. Larger volumes can also be rendered, although at slower rates. For more information on the VolumePro product line, please visit the TeraRecon web site at http://www.terarecon.com.

In order to compile the vtkVolumeProMapper into VTK, you will need the header and library files for the board. Please visit the VTK web site at http://www.visualizationtoolkit.org in order to download the header and library files for the VolumePro 1000. If you are using the VolumePro 500, you will need to purchase the Software Development Kit from TeraRecon. To add this class to your VTK build you need to enable the `VTK_USE_VOLUMEPRO` option during setup.

If you are using a more recent version of VTK than the one that came on the CD-ROM with this book, please consult the instructions included in the comment block at the top of the file `VTK/Rendering/vtkVolumeProMapper.h` for the latest integration instructions.

Since all the work of volume rendering is performed on the special-purpose board, this is the simplest volume mapper class in VTK. The class essentially translates all the parameters of volume rendering that are stored in the vtkVolume, the vtkVolumeProperty, and the vtkVolumeMapper into vli (the library interface to the VolumePro board) classes and parameters. To create a mapper of this type, you would use the vtkVolumeProMapper class. This will automatically create the correct subclasses. Previously, the only supported version of the VolumePro hardware was the one based on the VG500 chip, so the New() method of vtkVolumeProMapper called the New() method of vtkVolumeProVG500Mapper. In addition, the results from the board are rendered to the graphics context by VTK using OpenGL, so a vtkOpenGLVolumeProVG500Mapper was the class that was finally created. In VTK 4.0, a choice will be made at either compile time (based on what headers and libraries are found) or at runtime (based on which driver is running) to select between the VolumePro 100 and VolumePro 500 versions of this class.

There are a few parameters that do not map well into vli. The arbitrary clipping planes defined in vtkAbstractMapper3D are not supported by the vtkVolumeProMapper, although thick slab clipping is supported as will be described later. The cropping region flags must be either set to off, subvolume, fence, inverted fence, cross, or inverted cross.

Specifying an arbitrary bit pattern that does not match one of these options is not supported by the vtkVolumeProMapper.

Two significant limitations of the VolumePro 500 version vtkVolumeProMapper is that it works only with parallel camera transformations, and geometry cannot be mixed within the volume. Undesirable results will occur if you attempt to use a perspective viewing transformation, or geometry is rendered within the volume. The VolumePro 1000 does support intermixed geometry although this feature may not make it into the VTK 4.0 release. Support for limited perspective projection may be added at some point for the VolumePro 1000 mapper, please check the online documentation for more details.

The VolumePro mapper does have some mapper-specific functionality. The hardware is based on a ray casting approach and supports three different ray functions. These can be selected by calling SetBlendModeToComposite(), SetBlendModeToMaximumIntensity(), or SetBlendModeToMinimumIntensity().

Since the VolumePro hardware does not support geometry that is intermixed with the volume, special functionality was added to support a 3D cursor. The following code fragment would set up a 3D cursor for a VolumePro mapper.

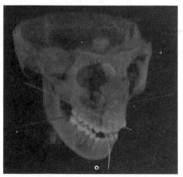

Figure 6–21 Defining a cursor in the VolumePro hardware.

```
vtkVolumeProMapper volumeMapper
   volumeMapper CursorOn
   volumeMapper SetCursorTypeToCrossHair
   volumeMapper SetCursorPosition 10 20 30
```

Alternatively, the cursor type could have been set to Plane, which would use three orthogonal planes instead of lines. By default the cursor type is CrossHair, and the x-axis line is drawn in red, the y-axis line is drawn in green, and the z-axis line is drawn in blue (**Figure 6–21**). When planes are used instead, the plane perpendicular to the x, y, or z axis is drawn in red, green, or blue, respectively. The cursor functionality is not supported in the VolumePro 1000 mapper since intermixed geometry is supported.

The VolumePro hardware supports supersampling in three dimensions by taking samples closer together along a ray, and casting more rays to generate an image. Supersampling can be turned on with the SuperSamplingOn() method, and the amount of supersampling can be controlled by SetSuperSamplingFactor(xfactor, yfactor, zfactor). Each factor should be a number between 0.125 and 1.0 representing the sampling distance along that axis, where a value of 1.0 would imply no supersampling and a value of 0.125 would imply an 8x supersampling. The supersampling factor for each axis will be rounded to the nearest $1/n$ where n is an integer between 1 and 8 inclusively.

As mentioned earlier, the vtkVolumeProMapper does not support the arbitrary clipping planes that are defined in the vtkAbstractMapper3D superclass. This mapper does support one arbitrarily-oriented thick cutting plane. There are several steps to setting up a thick cut plane, as shown in the code fragment below.

```
vtkVolumeProMapper volumeMapper
  volumeMapper CutPlaneOn
  volumeMapper SetCutPlaneEquation 0.5 0.3 0.8 3.4
  volumeMapper SetCutPlaneThickness 30
  volumeMapper SetCutPlaneFalloffDistance 4
```

As shown in this example, the cut plane must be turned on, the plane equation coefficients (A, B, C, D) must be specified where $Ax + By + Cz + D = 0$, and the thickness and opacity fall-off of the cut plane must be set. The opacity fall-off distance should be 0, 1, 2, 4, 8 or 16 and represents the distance in voxel from the cut plane during which opacity drops from completely opaque to completely transparent. A distance of 0 produces a sudden transition (similar to the arbitrary cut plane functionality supported in the other mappers) while a distance of 16 will produce a blurred or fuzzy cut.

There are three flags in the vtkVolumeProMapper that indicate what visualization parameters are modulated by the magnitude of the gradient of the scalar value. In order for the opacity to be modulated according to the GradientOpacityTransferFunction set in the vtkVolumeProperty as it is in other volume mappers, the GradientOpacityModulationOn() method must be called in the vtkVolumeProMapper. In addition, the diffuse and specular lighting calculation can be altered based on the gradient magnitude by calling Gradient-DiffuseModulationOn() and GradientSpecularModulationOn().

Speed vs. Accuracy Trade-offs

If you do not have a VolumePro volume rendering board, many fast CPUs, or high-end graphics hardware, you will probably not be satisfied with the rendering rates achieved when one or more volumes are rendered in a scene. It is often necessary to achieve a certain frame rate in order to effectively interact with the data, and it may be necessary to trade off accuracy in order to achieve speed. Fortunately, there are ways to do this for both ray casting and texture mapping approaches.

The support for achieving a desired frame rate for ray casting is available by default in VTK. You can set the desired update rate in the vtkRenderWindow, or the StillUpdateRate and the DesiredUpdateRate in the interactor if you are using one. Due to the fact that the time required for ray casting is mostly dependent on the size of the image, the ray caster mapper will automatically attempt to achieve the desired rendering rate by reducing the number of rays that it casts. By default, the automatic adjustment is on. In order to maintain interactivity, an abort check procedure should be specified in the render window so that the user will be able to interrupt the higher resolution image in order to interact with the data again.

There are limits on how blocky the image will become in order to achieve the desired update rate. By default, the adjustment will allow the image to become quite blocky, casting only 1 ray for every 10x10 neighborhood of pixels if necessary to achieve the desired update rate. Also by default the ray cast mapper will not cast more than 1 ray per pixel. These limits can be adjusted in the vtkVolumeRayCastMapper by setting the MinimumImageSampleDistance and MaximumImageSampleDistance. In addition AutoAdjustSampleDistances can be turned off, and the specified ImageSampleDistance will be used to represent the spacing between adjacent rays on the image plane. Results for one example are shown in **Figure 6–22**.

This technique of reducing the number of rays in order to achieve interactive frame rates can be quite effective. For example, consider the full resolution image shown on the left in **Figure 6–22**. This image may require 4 seconds to compute, which is much too slow for data interaction such as rotating or translating the data, or interactively adjusting the transfer function. If we instead subsample every other ray along each axis by setting the ImageSampleDistance to 2.0, we will get an image like the one shown in the middle in only about 1 second. Since this still may be too slow for effective interaction, we could subsample every fourth ray, and achieve rendering rates of nearly 4 frames per second with the image shown on the right. It may be blocky, but it is far easier to rotate a blocky volume at 4 frames per second than a full resolution volume at one frame every four seconds.

There are no built-in automatic techniques for trading off accuracy for speed in a texture mapping approach. This can be done by the user fairly easily by creating a lower resolution volume using vtkImageResample, and rendering this new volume instead. Since the speed of the texture mapping approach is highly dependent on the size of the volume, this will achieve similar results to reducing the number of rays in a ray casting approach.

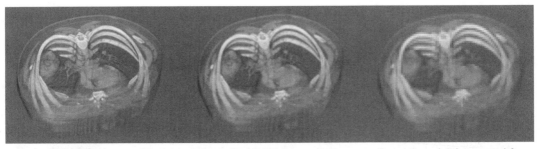

ImageSampleDistance = 1.0   ImageSampleDistance = 2.0   ImageSampleDistance = 4.0

Figure 6–22 The effect of changing the automatic scale lower limit on image quality.

Another option is to reduce the number of planes sampled through the volume. By default, the number of textured quads rendered will be equal to the number of samples along the major axis of the volume (as determined by the viewing direction). You may set the MaximumNumberOfPlanes instance variable to decrease the number of textured quads and therefore increase performance. The default value is 0 which implies no limit on the number of planes.

Using a vtkLODProp3D to Improve Performance

The vtkLODProp3D is a 3D prop that allows for the collection of multiple levels-of-detail and decides which to render for each frame based on the allocated rendering time of the prop (see "vtkLODProp3D" on page 64). The allocated rendering time of a prop is dependent on the desired update rate for the rendering window, the number of renderers in the render window, the number of props in the renderer, and any possible adjustment that a culler may have made based on screen coverage or other importance factors.

Using a vtkLODProp3D, it is possible to collect several rendering techniques into one prop, and allow the prop to decide which technique to use. Consider the following example of creating a vtkLODProp3D:

```
vtkImageResample resampler
  resampler SetAxisMagnificationFactor 0 0.5
  resampler SetAxisMagnificationFactor 1 0.5
  resampler SetAxisMagnificationFactor 2 0.5
```

```
vtkVolumeTextureMapper2D lowresMapper
  lowresMapper SetInput [resampler GetOutput]

vtkVolumeTextureMapper2D medresMapper
  medresMapper SetInput [reader GetOutput]

vtkVolumeRayCaster hiresMapper
  hiresMapper SetInput [reader GetOutput]

vtkLODProp3D volumeLOD
  volumeLOD AddLOD lowresMapper volumeProperty 0.0
  volumeLOD AddLOD medresMapper volumeProperty 0.0
  volumeLOD AddLOD hiresMapper volumeProperty 0.0
```

For clarity, many steps of reading the data and setting up visualization parameters have been left out of this example. At render time, one of the three levels-of-detail (LOD) for this prop will be selected based on the estimated time that it will take to render the LODs and the allocated time for this prop. In this case, all three levels-of-detail use the same property, but they could have used different properties if necessary. Also, in this case all three mappers are subclasses of vtkVolumeMapper, but we could add a bounding box representation as another level-of-detail, which would have a subclass of vtkMapper for the mapper, and a vtkProperty for the property parameter.

The last parameter of the AddLOD() method is an initial time to use for the estimated time required to render this level-of-detail. Setting this value to 0.0 requires that the LOD be rendered once before an estimated render time can be determined. When a vtkLODProp3D has to decide which LOD to render, it will choose one with 0.0 estimated render time if there are any. Otherwise, it will choose the LOD with the greatest time that does not exceed the allocated render time of the prop, if it can find such an LOD. Otherwise, it will choose the LOD with the lowest estimated render time. The time required to draw an LOD for the current frame replaces the estimated render time of that LOD for future frames.

Capabilities / Limitation of the Techniques

The following table (**Table 6–1**) indicates the level of support that the three different volume mappers provide for the features that have been discussed in this section. You may wish to refer to this table to choose the best volume rendering technique for you application.

Table 6-1 Features of the basic volume rendering mapper types supported in VTK.

Feature	Ray Casting	Texture Mapping	Volume-Pro
Alpha Blending / Compositing Projection	Yes	Yes	Yes
Maximum Intensity Projection	Yes	No	Yes
Minimum Intensity Projection	No[1]	No	Yes
Isosurface Projection	Yes	No	No
Parallel Viewing Transform	Yes	Yes	Yes
Perspective Viewing Transform	Yes	Yes	No
SuperSampling in XY	No	No	Yes
SuperSampling in Z	Yes[2]	No	Yes
InterpolationType in vtkVolumeProperty is Important	Yes	No	No
Arbitrary Clipping Planes	Yes	Yes[3]	Partial[4]
Cropping Regions	Yes	Yes	Partial[6]
Intermixed with Opaque Geometry in a Scene	Yes	Yes	Partial[7]
Intermixed with Other Volumes in a Scene	Partial[8]	Partial[8]	Partial[8]
3D Cursor	No[9]	No[9]	Yes[5,9]
Modulation of Opacity by Gradient Magnitude	Yes	Yes	Yes
Modulation of Specular Lighting by Gradient Magnitude	No	No	Yes
Modulation of Diffuse Lighting by Gradient Magnitude	No	No	Yes
Automatic Speed / Accuracy Trade-off	Yes	No	No
Multiprocessor Support	Yes	No	No
Classes Included in VTK by Default	Yes	Yes	No

1. Can be achieved by reversing the opacity ramp.
2. Not applicable for isosurface projections.
3. Limited by number supported in OpenGL.
4. Only 1 arbitrary cut plane with a thickness.
5. Only for VolumePro 500.
6. Only the basic region types.
7. No intersection geometry for VolumePro 500.
8. Volumes cannot intersect each other's bounds.
9. Use of intermixed opaque geometry

## Chapter 7

Building Models

We have seen how to use source objects (both readers and procedural objects) to create geometry (see "Creating Simple Models" on page 44). VTK provides several other techniques to generate more complex models. Three technique covered in this chapter are implicit modeling, extrusion, and surface reconstruction from unorganized points.

If you are working with data in a form that lacks topological or geometric structure, VTK can represent this information as field data (using class vtkDataObject), which can then be further manipulated to generate datasets that can be visualized with the techniques in this chapter (see "Working With Field Data" on page 194). For example, an n-dimensional financial record can be reduced to three dimensions by choosing three variables as independent variables. Then the techniques described here—Delaunay triangulation, Gaussian splatting, and surface reconstruction—can be used to create structure suitable for visualization by standard methods.

You may also wish to refer to the sections on clipping ("Clip Data" on page 111), and cutting ("Cutting" on page 96), and for alternative methods for modifying and creating geometry.

7.1 Implicit Modeling

Implicit modeling is a technique that employs 3D contouring (isosurface generation) to create polygonal surface meshes. The contouring is applied to a vtkImageData dataset (a regular volume) whose scalar values have been synthetically generated. These scalars are generated using convolution/sampling techniques in combination with boolean set operations. (Think of the convolution operation this way: the scalar field is defined as the distance between each point in the volume to a user-defined seed geometry such as a point, line, or polygon. Similarly, the sampling operation is an evaluation of an user-defined implicit function at each point in the volume.)

Figure 7–1 Implicit modeling from lines spelling the word "hello."

Defining Implicit Functions

Here's an example that uses some lines to generate a complex, polygonal surface. The lines are arranged to spell the word "HELLO" and serve as the generating seed geometry (**Figure 7–1**). (Tcl script taken from VTK/Examples/Modelling/Tcl/hello.tcl.)

```
# create lines
vtkPolyDataReader reader
    reader SetFileName "$VTK_DATA_ROOT/Data/hello.vtk"
vtkPolyDataMapper lineMapper
    lineMapper SetInput [reader GetOutput]
vtkActor lineActor
    lineActor SetMapper lineMapper
    eval [lineActor GetProperty] SetColor $red

# create implicit model
vtkImplicitModeller imp
    imp SetInput [reader GetOutput]
    imp SetSampleDimensions 110 40 20
    imp SetMaximumDistance 0.25
    imp SetModelBounds -1.0 10.0 -1.0 3.0 -1.0 1.0
vtkContourFilter contour
    contour SetInput [imp GetOutput]
    contour SetValue 0 0.25
vtkPolyDataMapper impMapper
    impMapper SetInput [contour GetOutput]
    impMapper ScalarVisibilityOff
vtkActor impActor;
    impActor SetMapper impMapper
    eval [impActor GetProperty] SetColor $peacock
    [impActor GetProperty] SetOpacity 0.5
```

What's happening in this script is that the lines that stroke out the word "hello" serve as the generating primitives. The vtkImplicitModeller class computes the distance from the lines (taking the closest distance to any line) to the points in the output structured points dataset, and assign this as the scalar to the dataset. The output is then fed to the vtkContourFilter which generates a polygonal isosurface. (The isosurface value is the distance from the generating primitives.)

There are a couple of important parameters in vtkImplicitModeller. The MaximumDistance instance variable controls how far from the generating primitives to carry the distance calculation. This instance variable, which is expressed as a fraction of the grid length, has a great affect on the speed of calculation: smaller values compute faster, but the isosurface may become choppy or break up if the values are too small. The SampleDimensions instance variable controls the resolution of the output structured points dataset, and ModelBounds controls the position and size of the dataset in space.

Sampling Implicit Functions

Another powerful modeling technique is the use of implicit functions. Implicit functions have the form

$$F(x,y,z) = \text{constant}$$

Spheres, cones, ellipsoids, planes, and many other useful geometric entities can be described with implicit functions. For example, a sphere S of radius R and centered at the origin can be described by the equation $F(x,y,z) = R^2 - x^2 - y^2 - z^2$. When $F(x,y,z)=0$, the equation describes S exactly. When $F(x,y,z) < 0$, we describe a sphere that lies inside the sphere S, and when $F(x,y,z) > 0$, we describe a sphere that lies outside the sphere S.

Figure 7–2 Implicit modeling using boolean combinations.

Besides modeling, implicit functions can also be combined using the set operations union, intersection, and difference. These operation allow you to create complex geometry using combinations of implicit functions. Here's an example script that creates an ice cream cone by using a sphere (ice cream), a cone intersected by two planes (to create a cone of finite extent), and another sphere to simulate the "bite" out of the ice cream. The script is taken from VTK/Examples/Modelling/Tcl/iceCream.tcl.

```
# create implicit function primitives
vtkCone cone
    cone SetAngle 20
vtkPlane vertPlane
    vertPlane SetOrigin .1 0 0
    vertPlane SetNormal -1 0 0
vtkPlane basePlane
    basePlane SetOrigin 1.2 0 0
    basePlane SetNormal 1 0 0
vtkSphere iceCream
    iceCream SetCenter 1.333 0 0
    iceCream SetRadius 0.5
vtkSphere bite
    bite SetCenter 1.5 0 0.5
    bite SetRadius 0.25

# combine primitives to build ice-cream cone
vtkImplicitBoolean theCone
theCone SetOperationTypeToIntersection
    theCone AddFunction cone
    theCone AddFunction vertPlane
    theCone AddFunction basePlane
vtkImplicitBoolean theCream
    theCream SetOperationTypeToDifference
    theCream AddFunction iceCream
    theCream AddFunction bite

# iso-surface to create geometry
vtkSampleFunction theConeSample
    theConeSample SetImplicitFunction theCone
    theConeSample SetModelBounds -1 1.5 -1.25 1.25 -1.25 1.25
    theConeSample SetSampleDimensions 60 60 60
    theConeSample ComputeNormalsOff
vtkContourFilter theConeSurface
    theConeSurface SetInput [theConeSample GetOutput]
    theConeSurface SetValue 0 0.0
vtkPolyDataMapper coneMapper
    coneMapper SetInput [theConeSurface GetOutput]
    coneMapper ScalarVisibilityOff
vtkActor coneActor
    coneActor SetMapper coneMapper
    eval [coneActor GetProperty] SetColor $chocolate
```

```
# iso-surface to create geometry
vtkSampleFunction theCreamSample
    theCreamSample SetImplicitFunction theCream
    theCreamSample SetModelBound 0 2.5 -1.25 1.25 -1.25 1.25
    theCreamSample SetSampleDimensions 60 60 60
    theCreamSample ComputeNormalsOff
vtkContourFilter theCreamSurface
    theCreamSurface SetInput [theCreamSample GetOutput]
    theCreamSurface SetValue 0 0.0
vtkPolyDataMapper creamMapper
    creamMapper SetInput [theCreamSurface GetOutput]
    creamMapper ScalarVisibilityOff
vtkActor creamActor
    creamActor SetMapper creamMapper
    eval [creamActor GetProperty] SetColor $mint
```

The class vtkSampleFunction and vtkContourFilter are the keys to building the polygonal geometry. vtkSampleFunction evaluates the implicit function (actually the boolean combination of implicit functions) to generate scalars across a volume (vtkImageData) dataset. vtkContourFilter is then used to generate an isosurface which approximates the implicit function. The accuracy of the approximation depends on the nature of the implicit function, as well as the resolution of the volume generated by vtkSampleFunction (the SetSampleDimensions() method).

A couple of usage notes. Boolean combinations can be nested to arbitrary depth. Just make sure the hierarchy does not contain self-referencing loops. Also, you may wish to use vtkDecimatePro to reduce the number of primitives output by the contour filter, since the number of triangles can be quite large. See "Decimation" on page 108 for more information.

7.2 Extrusion

Extrusion is a modeling technique that sweeps a generating object along a path to create a surface. For example, we can sweep a line in a direction perpendicular to it to create a plane.

The *Visualization Toolkit* offers two methods of extrusion: linear extrusion and rotational extrusion. In VTK, the generating object is a vtkPolyData

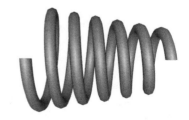

Figure 7–3 Rotational extrusion.

dataset. Lines, vertices, and "free edges" (edges used by one polygon), are used to generate the extruded surface. The vtkLinearExtrusionFilter sweeps the generating primitives along a straight line path; the vtkRotationalExtrusionFilter sweeps along a rotational path (translation during rotation is also possible).

In this example we will use an octagonal polygon (i.e., an approximation to a disk) to sweep out a combined rotational/translational path to model a "spring" (**Figure 7–3**). The filter extrudes its input (generating primitives) around the z axis, with the added capability of translating (during rotation) along the z axis, at the same time adjusting the sweep radius. By default, the instance variable Capping is on, so the extruded surface (a hollow tube) is capped by the generating primitive. Also, we must set the Resolution instance variable to generate a reasonable approximation. (The vtkPolyDataNormals filter is described in "Generate Surface Normals" on page 107.)

```
# create spring profile (a disk)
vtkPoints points
    points InsertPoint 0 1.0 0.0 0.0
    points InsertPoint 1 1.0732 0.0 -0.1768
    points InsertPoint 2 1.25 0.0 -0.25
    points InsertPoint 3 1.4268 0.0 -0.1768
    points InsertPoint 4 1.5 0.0 0.00
    points InsertPoint 5 1.4268 0.0 0.1768
    points InsertPoint 6 1.25 0.0 0.25
    points InsertPoint 7 1.0732 0.0 0.1768
vtkCellArray poly
    poly InsertNextCell 8;#number of points
    poly InsertCellPoint 0
    poly InsertCellPoint 1
    poly InsertCellPoint 2
    poly InsertCellPoint 3
    poly InsertCellPoint 4
    poly InsertCellPoint 5
    poly InsertCellPoint 6
    poly InsertCellPoint 7
vtkPolyData profile
    profile SetPoints points
    profile SetPolys poly

# extrude profile to make spring
vtkRotationalExtrusionFilter extrude
    extrude SetInput profile
    extrude SetResolution 360
    extrude SetTranslation 6
```

```
    extrude SetDeltaRadius 1.0
    extrude SetAngle 2160.0;#six revolutions

vtkPolyDataNormals normals
    normals SetInput [extrude GetOutput]
    normals SetFeatureAngle 60
vtkPolyDataMapper map
    map SetInput [normals GetOutput]
vtkActor spring
    spring SetMapper map
    [spring GetProperty] SetColor 0.6902 0.7686 0.8706
    [spring GetProperty] SetDiffuse 0.7
    [spring GetProperty] SetSpecular 0.4
    [spring GetProperty] SetSpecularPower 20
    [spring GetProperty] BackfaceCullingOn
```

The vtkLinearExtrusionFilter is similar, but simpler to use than vtkRotationalExtrusion-Filter. Linear extrusion can be performed along a user-specified vector (SetExtrusionType-ToVectorExtrusion()), towards a user-specified point (SetExtrusionTypeToPoint-Extrusion()), or the extrusion can be performed in the direction of the surface normals of the generating surface (SetExtrusionTypeToNormalExtrusion()).

7.3 Constructing Surfaces

Often we wish to construct a surface from a set of unstructured points or other data. The points may come from a laser digitizing system, or may be assembled from multi-variate data. In this section we examine techniques to build new surfaces from data of this form. You may also wish to refer to "Building Models" on page 165 for other methods to create surfaces from generating primitives (i.e., implicit modeling).

Delaunay Triangulation

The Delaunay triangulation is widely used in computational geometry. The basic application of the Delaunay triangulation is to create a simplicial mesh (i.e., triangles in 2D, tetrahedron in 3D) from a set of points. The resulting mesh can then be used in a variety of ways, including processing with standard visualization techniques. In VTK, there are two objects for creating Delaunay triangulations: vtkDelaunay2D and vtkDelaunay3D.

Note: Delaunay triangulation is numerically sensitive. The current version of vtkDelaunay3D may not be robust enough to reliably handle large numbers of points. This will be improved in the near future.

vtkDelaunay2D. The vtkDelaunay2D object takes vtkPointSet (or any of its subclasses) as input, and generates a vtkPolyData on output. Typically the output is a triangle mesh, but if you use a non-zero Alpha value it is possible to generate meshes consisting of triangles, lines, and vertices. (This parameter controls the "size" of output primitives. The size of the primitive is measured by a n-dimensional circumsphere; only those pieces of the mesh whose circumsphere is less than or equal to the alpha value are sent to the output. For example, if an edge of length L is less than 2*Alpha, the edge would be output).

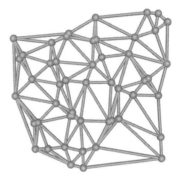

Figure 7–4 2D Delaunay triangulation.

In the following Tcl example we generate points using a random distribution in the $(0,1)$ x-y plane. (vtkDelaunay2D ignores the z-component during execution, although it does output the z value.) To create a nicer picture we use vtkTubeFilter and vtkGlyph3D to create tubes around mesh edges, and spheres around the mesh points. The script comes from `VTK/Examples/Modelling/Tcl/DelMesh.tcl`.

```
# create some points
vtkMath math
vtkPoints points
for {set i 0} {$i<50} {incr i 1} {
    eval points InsertPoint $i [math Random 0 1] \
                                [math Random 0 1] 0.0
}
vtkPolyData profile
    profile SetPoints points

# triangulate them
vtkDelaunay2D del
    del SetInput profile
    del SetTolerance 0.001
vtkPolyDataMapper mapMesh
    mapMesh SetInput [del GetOutput]
vtkActor meshActor
    meshActor SetMapper mapMesh
```

```
    eval [meshActor GetProperty] SetColor .1 .2 .4
vtkExtractEdges extract
    extract SetInput [del GetOutput]
vtkTubeFilter tubes
    tubes SetInput [extract GetOutput]
    tubes SetRadius 0.01
    tubes SetNumberOfSides 6
vtkPolyDataMapper mapEdges
    mapEdges SetInput [tubes GetOutput]
vtkActor edgeActor
    edgeActor SetMapper mapEdges
    eval [edgeActor GetProperty] SetColor $peacock
    [edgeActor GetProperty] SetSpecularColor 1 1 1
    [edgeActor GetProperty] SetSpecular 0.3
    [edgeActor GetProperty] SetSpecularPower 20
    [edgeActor GetProperty] SetAmbient 0.2
    [edgeActor GetProperty] SetDiffuse 0.8

vtkSphereSource ball
    ball SetRadius 0.025
    ball SetThetaResolution 12
    ball SetPhiResolution 12
vtkGlyph3D balls
    balls SetInput [del GetOutput]
    balls SetSource [ball GetOutput]
vtkPolyDataMapper mapBalls
    mapBalls SetInput [balls GetOutput]
vtkActor ballActor
    ballActor SetMapper mapBalls
    eval [ballActor GetProperty] SetColor $hot_pink
    [ballActor GetProperty] SetSpecularColor 1 1 1
    [ballActor GetProperty] SetSpecular 0.3
    [ballActor GetProperty] SetSpecularPower 20
    [ballActor GetProperty] SetAmbient 0.2
    [ballActor GetProperty] SetDiffuse 0.8
```

The Tolerance instance variable is used to determine whether points are coincident. Points located a distance Tolerance apart (or less) are considered coincident, and one of the points may be discarded. Tolerance is expressed as a fraction of the length of the diagonal of the bounding box of the input points.

Another useful feature of vtkDelaunay2D is the ability to define constraint edges and polygons. Normally, vtkDelaunay2D will generate a Delaunay triangulation of an input set of points to satisfy the circumsphere criterion. However, in many cases additional information specifying edges in the triangulation (constraint edges), or "holes" in the data (constraint polygons). By specifying constraint edges and polygons, vtkDelaunay2D can be used to generate sophisticated triangulations of points. The following example (taken from VTK/Examples/Modelling/Tcl/constrainedDelaunay.tcl) demonstrates this.

```
vtkPoints points
    points InsertPoint 0 1 4 0
    points InsertPoint 1 3 4 0
    points InsertPoint 2 7 4 0
    ...(more points defined)...
vtkCellArray polys
    polys InsertNextCell 12
    polys InsertCellPoint 0
    polys InsertCellPoint 1
    polys InsertCellPoint 2
    ...(a total of two polygons defined)...
vtkPolyData polyData
    polyData SetPoints points
    polyData SetPolys polys

# generate constrained triangulation
vtkDelaunay2D del
    del SetInput polyData
    del SetSource polyData
vtkPolyDataMapper mapMesh
    mapMesh SetInput [del GetOutput]
vtkActor meshActor
    meshActor SetMapper mapMesh

# tubes around mesh
vtkExtractEdges extract
    extract SetInput [del GetOutput]
vtkTubeFilter tubes
    tubes SetInput [extract GetOutput]
    tubes SetRadius 0.1
    tubes SetNumberOfSides 6
vtkPolyDataMapper mapEdges
    mapEdges SetInput [tubes GetOutput]
vtkActor edgeActor
    edgeActor SetMapper mapEdges
    eval [edgeActor GetProperty] SetColor $peacock
    [edgeActor GetProperty] SetSpecularColor 1 1 1
    [edgeActor GetProperty] SetSpecular 0.3
    [edgeActor GetProperty] SetSpecularPower 20
    [edgeActor GetProperty] SetAmbient 0.2
```

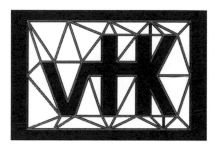   

Figure 7–5 Constrained Delaunay triangulation. On the left, constraint polygon defines a hole in the triangulation. On the right, constraint edges define fault lines in geological horizon.

```
[edgeActor GetProperty] SetDiffuse 0.8
```

In this example (resulting image shown in **Figure 7–5**(left), a second input to vtkDelaunay2D has been defined (with the SetSource() method). This input defines two polygons, one ordered counter-clockwise and defining the outer rectangular boundary, and the second clockwise-ordered polygon defining the "vtk" hole in the triangulation.

Using constraint edges is much simpler since the ordering of the edges is not important. Referring to the example VTK/Examples/Modelling/Tcl/faultLines.tcl, constraint edges (lines and polylines provided to the second input Source) are used to constrain the triangulation along a set of edges. (See **Figure 7–5**(right).)

vtkDelaunay3D. vtkDelaunay3D is similar to vtkDelaunay2D. The major difference is that the output of vtkDelaunay3D is an unstructured grid dataset (i.e., a tetrahedral mesh).

Figure 7–6 3D Delaunay triangulation with non-zero alpha.

```
vtkMath math
vtkPoints points
for {set i 0} {$i<25} {incr i 1} {
   eval points InsertPoint $i [math Random 0 1]\
           [math Random 0 1] [math Random 0 1]
}
vtkPolyData profile
    profile SetPoints points

# triangulate them
vtkDelaunay3D del
    del SetInput profile
```

```
    del BoundingTriangulationOn
    del SetTolerance 0.01
    del SetAlpha 0.2

vtkShrinkFilter shrink
    shrink SetInput [del GetOutput]
    shrink SetShrinkFactor 0.9
vtkDataSetMapper map
    map SetInput [shrink GetOutput]
vtkActor triangulation
    triangulation SetMapper map
    [triangulation GetProperty] SetColor 1 0 0
```

In this example (taken from VTK/Examples/Modelling/Tcl/Delaunay3D.tcl) we triangulate a random set of points in 3D space ranging between (0,1) along each of the coordinate axes. A non-zero Alpha is used, so the mesh consists of a collection of tetrahedra, triangles, lines, and points. The resulting tetrahedral mesh is shrunk with vtkShrinkFilter and mapped with vtkDataSetMapper.

Gaussian Splatting

Many times data has no inherent structure, or the dimension of the data is high relative to what 2D, 3D, or 4D (3D with animation) visualization techniques can represent. An example of one such data set is scalar values (i.e., temperature) located at random points in space from a thermocouple measuring system. Multidimensional financial data (i.e., many records each record having several variables), is another example. One of the simplest and most robust procedure that can used to treat such data is to resample the data on a volume (i.e., vtkImageData dataset) and then visualize the resampled dataset. In the following C++ example we show how to do this with multivariate financial data (VTK/Examples/ Modelling/Cxx/finance.cxx). (You may wish to refer to "Working With Field Data" on page 194 for an alternative way to work with this data.)

The data consists of an ASCII text file with 3188 financial records. Each record contains the following information: the time late in paying the loan (TIME_LATE); the monthly payment of the loan (MONTHLY_PAYMENT); the principal left on the loan (UNPAID_PRINCIPAL); the original amount of the loan (LOAN_AMOUNT); the interest rate on the loan (INTEREST_RATE); and the monthly income of the loanee (MONTHLY_INCOME).

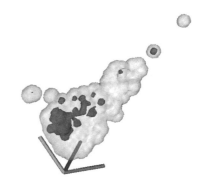

The purpose of the visualization is to understand the relationship of these variables to the variable of major concern: TIME_LATE. Building a mathematical model or understanding of this data helps finan-

Figure 7–7 Splatting data.

cial institutions make less risky loans. What we will do in the example is to show the late paying loans in context with the total loan population. We begin by choosing MONTHLY_PAYMENT as the *x*-axis, INTEREST_RATE as the *y*-axis, and LOAN_AMOUNT as the *z*-axis, and then choose TIME_LATE as the dependent variable (i.e., we reduce the dimensional of the data by selecting three variables and ignoring the others). The class vtkGaussianSplatter is used to take the reduced financial data and "splat" them using Gaussian ellipsoids into a vtkImageData dataset. Then vtkContourFilter is used to generate an isosurface. Note that the first instance of vtkGaussianSplatter splats the entire dataset without scaling the splats, while the second instance of vtkGaussianSplatter scales the splats according to the scalar value (which is TIME_LATE). The late loans are rendered red while the total population is rendered a translucent white color (see **Figure 7–7**). The C++ code is shown in the following.

```
main ()
{
  float bounds[6];
  int npts;
  vtkDataSet *dataSet;

  // read data
  dataSet = ReadFinancialData("MONTHLY_PAYMENT",
                              "INTEREST_RATE",
                              "LOAN_AMOUNT","TIME_LATE");
  if ( ! dataSet ) exit(0);

  // construct pipeline for original population
  vtkGaussianSplatter *popSplatter =
```

```
                                          vtkGaussianSplatter::New();
  popSplatter->SetInput(dataSet);
  popSplatter->SetSampleDimensions(50,50,50);
  popSplatter->SetRadius(0.05);
  popSplatter->ScalarWarpingOff();
vtkContourFilter *popSurface = vtkContourFilter::New();
  popSurface->SetInput(popSplatter->GetOutput());
  popSurface->SetValue(0,0.01);
vtkPolyDataMapper *popMapper = vtkPolyDataMapper::New();
  popMapper->SetInput(popSurface->GetOutput());
  popMapper->ScalarVisibilityOff();
vtkActor *popActor = vtkActor::New();
  popActor->SetMapper(popMapper);
  popActor->GetProperty()->SetOpacity(0.3);
  popActor->GetProperty()->SetColor(.9,.9,.9);

// construct pipeline for delinquent population
vtkGaussianSplatter *lateSplatter =
                                          vtkGaussianSplatter::New();
  lateSplatter->SetInput(dataSet);
  lateSplatter->SetSampleDimensions(50,50,50);
  lateSplatter->SetRadius(0.05);
  lateSplatter->SetScaleFactor(0.005);
vtkContourFilter *lateSurface = vtkContourFilter::New();
  lateSurface->SetInput(lateSplatter->GetOutput());
  lateSurface->SetValue(0,0.01);
vtkPolyDataMapper *lateMapper = vtkPolyDataMapper::New();
  lateMapper->SetInput(lateSurface->GetOutput());
  lateMapper->ScalarVisibilityOff();
vtkActor *lateActor = vtkActor::New();
  lateActor->SetMapper(lateMapper);
  lateActor->GetProperty()->SetColor(1.0,0.0,0.0);

// create axes
popSplatter->Update();
popSplatter->GetOutput()->GetBounds(bounds);
vtkAxes *axes = vtkAxes::New();
  axes->SetOrigin(bounds[0], bounds[2], bounds[4]);
  axes->SetScaleFactor(
                popSplatter->GetOutput()->GetLength()/5);
vtkTubeFilter *axesTubes = vtkTubeFilter::New();
  axesTubes->SetInput(axes->GetOutput());
  axesTubes->SetRadius(axes->GetScaleFactor()/25.0);
  axesTubes->SetNumberOfSides(6);
vtkPolyDataMapper *axesMapper = vtkPolyDataMapper::New();
  axesMapper->SetInput(axesTubes->GetOutput());
```

```
  vtkActor *axesActor = vtkActor::New();
    axesActor->SetMapper(axesMapper);

  // graphics stuff
  vtkRenderer *renderer = vtkRenderer::New();
  vtkRenderWindow *renWin = vtkRenderWindow::New();
    renWin->AddRenderer(renderer);
  vtkRenderWindowInteractor *iren =
                    vtkRenderWindowInteractor::New();
    iren->SetRenderWindow(renWin);

  // read data set up renderer
  renderer->AddActor(lateActor);
  renderer->AddActor(axesActor);
  renderer->AddActor(popActor);
  renderer->SetBackground(1,1,1);
  renWin->SetSize(500,500);

  // interact with data
  iren->Initialize();
  iren->Start();
...more stuff...
}
```

What's interesting about this example is that the majority of late payments occur in a region of a high interest rate (expected) and lower monthly payment amount. Therefore, it's the smaller loans with higher interest rates which are the problem in this data.

Another filter to resample data into a volume is vtkShepardMethod. You may wish to modify the previous C++ example to use this class.

Surfaces from Unorganized Points

In computer graphics applications, surfaces are often represented as three-dimensional unorganized points. Laser and
other digitizers are often the source of these point sets.
Reconstructing surfaces from point clouds is both computa-
tionally and algorithmically challenging. While the methods
described previously (Delaunay triangulation and Gaussian
splatting) may be used with varying levels of success to
reconstruct surfaces from point clouds, VTK has a class
designed specifically for this purpose.

Figure 7–8 Surface
reconstruction.

vtkSurfaceReconstructionFilter can be used to reconstruct
surfaces from point clouds. To use this filter, the filter takes
as input a dataset defining points assumed to lie on the surface of a 3D object. The following script (VTK/Examples/Modelling/Tcl/recon-
structSurface.tcl) shows how to use the filter. **Figure 7–8** shows the results.

```
vtkProgrammableSource pointSource
    pointSource SetExecuteMethod readPoints
proc readPoints {} {
    set output [pointSource GetPolyDataOutput]
    vtkPoints points
    $output SetPoints points
    set file [open "$VTK_DATA_ROOT/Data/cactus.3337.pts" r]
    while { [gets $file line] != -1 } {
       scan $line "%s" firstToken
       if { $firstToken == "p" } {
          scan $line "%s %f %f %f" firstToken x y z
          points InsertNextPoint $x $y $z
       }
    }
    points Delete; #okay, reference counting
}

# Construct the surface and create isosurface
vtkSurfaceReconstructionFilter surf
    surf SetInput [pointSource GetPolyDataOutput]
vtkContourFilter cf
    cf SetInput [surf GetOutput]
    cf SetValue 0 0.0
vtkReverseSense reverse
```

```
    reverse SetInput [cf GetOutput]
    reverse ReverseCellsOn
    reverse ReverseNormalsOn
vtkPolyDataMapper map
    map SetInput [reverse GetOutput]
    map ScalarVisibilityOff
vtkActor surfaceActor
    surfaceActor SetMapper map
```

The example begins by reading points from a file using vtkProgrammableSource filter (see "Programmable Filters" on page 292 for more information). The filter vtkSurfaceReconstructionFilter takes the points and generates a volumetric representation (similar to what vtkGaussianSplatter did in the previous section). The volume is contoured (with an isosurface value=0.0) to generate a surface and vertex normals. Because of the nature of the data, the vertex normals point inward so the filter vtkReverseSense is used to reverse the normals and polygon ordering (on some systems inward pointing normals will result in black surfaces).

The algorithm works reasonable well as long as long as the points are close enough together. The instance variable SampleSpacing can be set to control the dimensions of the output volume. If SampleSpacing is set less than zero, the algorithm makes a guess at the voxel size. The output volume bounds the input point cloud.

Part III

VTK Developer's Guide

## Chapter 8

Data Interface & Miscellaneous

In this chapter we briefly describe various ways to read, write, import, and export data. Readers ingest a single dataset, while importers create an entire scene, which may include one or more datasets, actors, lights, cameras, and so on. Writers output a single dataset to disk (or stream), and exporters output an entire scene. In some cases, you may want to interface to data that is not in standard VTK format, or in any other common format that VTK supports. In such circumstances, you may wish to treat data as field data, and convert it in the visualization pipeline into datasets that the standard visualization techniques can properly handle.

8.1 Readers

We saw in "Reader Source Object" on page 47 how to use a reader to bring data into the visualization pipeline. Using a similar approach, we can read many other types of data. Here's a list of the available readers:

Polygonal Data Readers

These readers produce a vtkPolyData as output.

- vtkBYUReader — read MOVIE.BYU files
- vtkMCubesReader — read binary marching cubes files
- vtkOBJReader — read Wavefront .obj files
- vtkPolyDataReader — read a VTK polygonal data files. See "VTK File Formats" on page 344 for information on VTK file formats.
- vtkPLYReader — read Stanford University PLY polygonal data files
- vtkSTLReader — read stereo-lithography files
- vtkUGFacetReader — read EDS Unigraphics facet files

Image and Volume Readers

These readers produce vtkImageData (or vtkStructuredPoints, now obsolete) as output.

- vtkBMPReader — read PC bitmap files
- vtkDEMReader — read digital elevation model files
- vtkJPEGReader — read JPEG files
- vtkImageReader — read various image files in various formats
- vtkPNMReader — read PNM (ppm, pgm, pbm) files
- vtkPNGReader — read Portable Network Graphics files
- vtkStructuredPointsReader — read VTK structured points data files. See "VTK File Formats" on page 344 for information on VTK file formats.
- vtkSLCReader — read SLC structured points files
- vtkTIFFReader — read files in TIFF format
- vtkVolumeReader — read image (volume) files
- vtkVolume16Reader — read 16-bit image (volume) files

Data Set Readers

These readers produce generic vtkDataSet as output. Typically, the reader requires an Update() invocation to determine what kind of concrete vtkDataSet subclass is created.

- vtkDataSetReader — read any VTK dataset file. See "VTK File Formats" on page 344 for information on VTK file formats.
- vtkGenericEnsightReader (and subclasses) — read Ensight files

Structured Grid Readers

These readers produce vtkStructuredGrid as output.

- vtkPLOT3DReader — read structured grid PLOT3D files
- vtkStructuredGridReader — read VTK structured grid data files. See "VTK File For-

mats" on page 344 for information on VTK file formats.

Rectilinear Grid Readers

These readers produce vtkRectilinearGrid as output.

*   vtkRectilinearGridReader — read VTK rectilinear grid data files. See "VTK File Formats" on page 344 for information on VTK file formats.

Unstructured Data Readers

These readers produce vtkUnstructuredGrid as output.

*   vtkUnstructuredGridReader — read VTK unstructured grid data files. See "VTK File Formats" on page 344 for information on VTK file formats.

8.2 Writers

Writers output datasets of various types to disk. Typically, a writer requires setting an input and specifying an output file name (sometimes multiple files) as shown in the following.

```
vtkPolyDataWriter writer
    writer SetInput [aFilter GetOutput]
    writer SetFileName "outFile.vtk"
    writer SetFileTypeToBinary
    writer Write
```

The VTK writers offer you the option of writing binary (SetFileTypeToBinary()) or ASCII (SetFileTypeToASCII()) files. (Note: binary files may not be transportable across computers. VTK takes care of swapping bytes, but does not handle transport between 64-bit and 32-bit computers.)

The following is a list of available writers.

Polygonal Data Writers

These writers require vtkPolyData as input.

- vtkBYUWriter — write MOVIE.BYU polygonal files
- vtkCGMWriter — write 2D polygonal data as a CGM file
- vtkIVWriter — write Inventor files
- vtkMCubesWriter — write triangles (polygonal data) in marching cubes format
- vtkPolyDataWriter — write a VTK vtkPolyData file. See "VTK File Formats" on page 344 for information on VTK file formats.
- vtkPLYWriter — write Stanford University PLY files
- vtkSTLWriter — write stereo-lithography files

Image and Volume Writers

These writers require vtkImageData as input.

- vtkBMPWriter — write PC bitmap files
- vtkJPEGWriter — write images in JPEG format
- vtkPNGWriter — write images in Portable Network Graphics format
- vtkPNMWriter — write images in PNM (ppm, pgm, pbm) format
- vtkPostScriptWriter — write images in PostScript format
- vtkStructuredPointsWriter — write a VTK vtkStructuredPoints file. See "VTK File Formats" on page 344 for information on VTK file formats.
- vtkTIFFWriter — write files in TIFF format

Structured Grid Writers

These writers require vtkStructuredGrid as input.

- vtkStructuredGridWriter — write a VTK vtkStructuredGrid file. See "VTK File Formats" on page 344 for information on VTK file formats.

Rectilinear Grid Writers

These writers require vtkRectilinearGrid as input.

- vtkRectilinearGridWriter — write a VTK vtkRectilinearGrid file. See "VTK File Formats" on page 344 for information on VTK file formats.

Unstructured Grid Writers

These writers require a vtkUnstructuredGrid as input.

- vtkUnstructuredGridWriter — write a VTK vtkUnstructuredGrid file. See "VTK File Formats" on page 344 for information on VTK file formats.

8.3 Importers

Importers accept data files that contain multiple datasets and/or the objects that compose a scene (i.e., lights, cameras, actors, properties, transformation matrices, etc.). Importers will either generate an instance of vtkRenderWindow and/or vtkRenderer, or you can specify them. If specified, the importer will create lights, cameras, actors, and so on, and place them into the specified instance(s). Otherwise, it will create instances of vtkRenderer and vtkRenderWindow, as necessary. The following example show how to use an instance of vtkImporter (in this case a vtk3DSImporter—imports 3D Studio files). This Tcl script was excerpted from VTK/Examples/IO/Tcl/flamingo.tcl (please see **Figure 8–1**).

Figure 8–1 Importing a file.

```
vtk3DSImporter importer
  importer ComputeNormalsOn
  importer SetFileName "$VTK_DATA_ROOT/Data/iflamigm.3ds"
  importer Read

set renWin [importer GetRenderWindow]
```

```
vtkRenderWindowInteractor iren
  iren SetRenderWindow $renWin
```

The *Visualization Toolkit* supports the following importers. (Note that the superclass vtkImporter is available for developing new subclasses.)

- vtk3DSImporter — import 3D Studio files
- vtkVRMLExporter — import VRML version 2.0 files

8.4 Exporters

Exporters output scenes in various formats. Instances of vtkExporter accept an instance of vtkRenderWindow, and write out the graphics objects supported by the exported format.

```
vtkRIBExporter exporter
    exporter SetRenderWindow renWin
    exporter SetFilePrefix "anExportedFile"
    exporter Write
```

The vtkRIBExporter shown above writes out multiple files in RenderMan format. The FilePrefix instance variable is used to write one or more files (geometry and texture map(s), if any).

The *Visualization Toolkit* supports the following exporters.

- vtkRIBExporter — export RenderMan files
- vtkIVExporter — export Inventor scene graph
- vtkOBJExporter — export a Wavefront .obj files
- vtkVRMLExporter — export VRML version 2.0 files

8.5 Creating Hardcopy

Creating informative pictures is a primary objective of VTK. And to document what you've done, saving pictures and series of pictures (i.e., animations) are important. This section describes various ways to create graphical output.

Saving Images

The simplest way to save images is to use the vtkWindowToImageFilter which grabs the output buffer of the render window and converts it into vtkImageData. This image can then be saved using one of the image writers (see "Writers" on page "Writers" on page 187 for more information). Here is an example

```
vtkWindowToImageFilter w2i
  w2i SetInput renWin

vtkJPEGWriter writer
  writer SetInput [w2i GetOutput]
  writer SetFileName "DelMesh.jpg"
  writer Write
```

Note that it is possible to use the off-screen mode of the render window when saving an image. The off-screen mode can be turned on by setting OffScreenRenderingOn() for the render window. Currently, this is supported on Windows and Mesa compiled with off-screen rendering support.

Saving Large (High-Resolution) Images

The images saved via screen capture or by saving the render window vary greatly in quality depending on the graphics hardware and screen resolution supported on your computer. To improve the quality of your images, there are two approaches that you can try. The first approach allows you to use the imaging pipeline to render pieces of your image and then combine them into a very high-resolution final image. We'll refer to this as piecemeal imaging. The second approach requires external software to perform high resolution rendering. We'll refer to this as the RenderMan solution.

Piecemeal Rendering. Often we want to save an image of resolution greater than the resolution of the computer hardware. For example, generating an image of 4000 x 4000 pixels is not possible (without tricks) on a computer system displaying 1280 x 1024 pixels. The *Visualization Toolkit* solves this problem with the class vtkRenderLargeImage. This class breaks up the rendering process into separate pieces, each piece containing just a portion of the final image. The pieces are assembled into a final image, which can be saved to file using one of the VTK image writers. Here's how it works (Tcl script taken from VTK/Examples/Rendering/Tcl/RenderLargeImage.tcl).

```
vtkRenderLargeImage renderLarge
  renderLarge SetInput ren
  renderLarge SetMagnification 4

vtkTIFFWriter writer
  writer SetInput [renderLarge GetOutput]
  writer SetFileName largeImage.tif
  writer Write
```

The Magnification instance variable (an integer value) controls how much to magnify the input renderer's current image. If the renderer's image size is (400,400) and the magnification factor is 5, the final image will be of resolution (2000,2000). In this example, the resulting image is written to a file with an instance of vtkPNMWriter. Of course, other writer types could be used.

RenderMan. RenderMan is a high-quality software rendering system currently sold by Pixar, the graphics animation house that created the famous *Toy Story* movie. Render-Man is a commercial package (retailing for about $5,000 at the time of this writing). Fortunately, there is at least one modestly priced (or free system if you're non-commercial) RenderMan compatible system that you can download and use: BMRT (Blue Moon Ray Tracer). BMRT is slower than RenderMan, but it also offers several features that Render-Man does not.

In an earlier section ("Exporters" on page 190) we saw how to export a RenderMan .rib file (and associated textures). You can adjust the size of the image RenderMan produces using the SetSize() method in the RIBExporter. This method adds a line to the rib file that causes RenderMan (or RenderMan compatible system such as BMRT) to create an output TIFF image of size (xres, yres) pixels.

8.6 Creating Animations (Using Splines)

Animations are simple to create in principle. A sequence of images is saved, using any of the methods described previously (see "Saving Images" on page 191), and the sequences are assembled into a final animation. The challenge of creating a good animation is controlling the motion or change in properties of objects and images to generate smooth, well-timed, and synchronized sequences. This is particularly hard when you combine images with sound.

Figure 8–2 A spline of a set of random points in 3D.

There are a couple of things you can do to simplify your task. First, if using sound, start by developing the sound track, and then plan and synchronize the animation around the track. You'll want a script detailing the start and duration of each sequence along with its relationship to the sound. Work hard on the timing of each sequence, make sure it's not too long or short, and that events don't happen too quickly or slowly. You might consider making sequences multiples of 30 frames (30 frames per second on video), or some multiple of your music beat. This greatly facilitates final editing.

VTK offers limited support for creating animations. Besides the image saving tools discussed previously, VTK supports splines for interpolating motion and other parameters. There are two types of interpolating 1D splines: vtkCardinalSpline and vtkKochanekSpline, both of subclass vtkSpline. (These splines differ in their basis functions. vtkKochenekSpline offers more control over the shape of the spline.) To define a spline, you create a sequence of independent/dependent variable pairs, and then optionally set end conditions and/or other spline parameters. To interpolate between points, the Evaluate() method is invoked as shown in the following example (taken from VTK/Examples/Rendering/Tcl/CSpline.tcl — see **Figure 8–2**).

```
set numberOfInputPoints 10

vtkCardinalSpline aSplineX
vtkCardinalSpline aSplineY
vtkCardinalSpline aSplineZ

vtkPoints inputPoints
for {set i 0} {$i < $numberOfInputPoints} {incr i 1} {
```

```
    set x   [math Random 0 1]
    set y   [math Random 0 1]
    set z   [math Random 0 1]
    aSplineX AddPoint $i $x
    aSplineY AddPoint $i $y
    aSplineZ AddPoint $i $z
    inputPoints InsertPoint $i $x $y $z
}
...more stuff...
# Interpolate x, y and z by using the three spline filters and
# create new points
for {set i 0} {$i< $numberOfOutputPoints} {incr i 1} {
    set t [expr ( $numberOfInputPoints - 1.0 ) / ( $numberOfOutputPoints -
1.0 ) * $i]
    points InsertPoint $i [aSplineX Evaluate $t] [aSplineY Evaluate $t]
[aSplineZ Evaluate $t]
}
```

Three separate splines are created, one each for the *x*, *y*, and *z* axes. Using these splines, a polyline is created by evaluating them at points along the range of the independent variable (which is the point id).

If you are using Tcl and would like to see an applications that employs splines to create animations, the example in VTK/Examples/Rendering/Tcl/keyBottle.tcl uses the Tcl script VTK/Examples/Rendering/Tcl/KeyFrame.tcl to create an animation sequence of camera motion (variations in camera azimuth).

8.7 Working With Field Data

Many times data is organized in a form different from that found in VTK. For example, your data may be tabular, or possibly even higher-dimensional. And sometimes you'd like to be able to rearrange your data, assigning some data as scalars, some as point coordinates, and some as other attribute data. In such situations VTK's field data, and the filters that allow you to manipulate field data, are essential.

To introduce this topic a concrete example is useful. In the previous chapter (see "Gaussian Splatting" on page 176) we saw an example that required writing custom code to read a tabular data file, extracting out specified data to form points and scalars (look at the function ReadFinancialData() found in VTK/Examples/Modelling/Cxx/

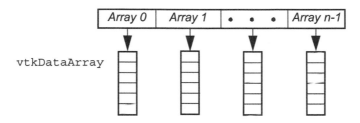

Figure 8–3 Structure of field data—an array of arrays. Each array may be of a different native data type and may have one or more components.

finance.cxx). While this works fine for this example, it does require a lot of work and is not very flexible. In the following example, we'll do the same thing using field data.

The data is in the following tabular format:

```
NUMBER_POINTS 3188
TIME_LATE
 29.14    0.00    0.00   11.71    0.00    0.00    0.00    0.00
  0.00   29.14    0.00    0.00    0.00    0.00    0.00    0.00
....
MONTHLY_PAYMENT
  7.26    5.27    8.01   16.84    8.21   15.75   10.62   15.47
  5.63    9.50   15.29   15.65   11.51   11.21   10.33   10.78
....
```

which repeats for the fields the time late in paying the loan (TIME_LATE); the monthly payment of the loan (MONTHLY_PAYMENT); the principal left on the loan (UNPAID_PRINCIPAL); the original amount of the loan (LOAN_AMOUNT); the interest rate on the loan (INTEREST_RATE); and the monthly income of the loanee (MONTHLY_INCOME). These six fields form a matrix of 3188 rows and 6 columns.

We start by parsing the data file. The class vtkProgrammableDataObjectSource is useful for defining special input methods without having to modify VTK. All we need to do is to define a function that parses the file and stuffs them into a VTK data object (recall that vtkDataObject is the most general form of data representation). Reading the data is the most challenging part of this example, which can be found in VTK/Examples/DataManipulation/Tcl/FinancialField.tcl.

```
set xAxis INTEREST_RATE
set yAxis MONTHLY_PAYMENT
```

```
set zAxis MONTHLY_INCOME
set scalar TIME_LATE

# Parse an ascii file and manually create a field. Then construct a
# dataset from the field.
vtkProgrammableDataObjectSource dos
    dos SetExecuteMethod parseFile

proc parseFile {} {
   global VTK_DATA_ROOT

   # Use Tcl to read an ascii file
   set file [open "$VTK_DATA_ROOT/Data/financial.txt" r]
   set line [gets $file]
   scan $line "%*s %d" numPts
   set numLines [expr (($numPts - 1) / 8) + 1 ]

   # Get the data object's field data and allocate
   # room for 4 fields
   set fieldData [[dos GetOutput] GetFieldData]
   $fieldData AllocateArrays 4

   # read TIME_LATE - dependent variable
   # search the file until an array called TIME_LATE is found
   while { [gets $file arrayName] == 0 } {}
   # Create the corresponding float array
   vtkFloatArray timeLate
   timeLate SetName TIME_LATE
   # Read the values
   for {set i 0} {$i < $numLines} {incr i} {
      set line [gets $file]
      set m [scan $line "%f %f %f %f %f %f %f %f" \
 v(0) v(1) v(2) v(3) v(4) v(5) v(6) v(7)]
      for {set j 0} {$j < $m} {incr j} {timeLate InsertNextValue $v($j)}
   }
   # Add the array
   $fieldData AddArray timeLate

   # MONTHLY_PAYMENT - independent variable
   while { [gets $file arrayName] == 0 } {}
   vtkFloatArray monthlyPayment
   monthlyPayment SetName MONTHLY_PAYMENT
   for {set i 0} {$i < $numLines} {incr i} {
      set line [gets $file]
      set m [scan $line "%f %f %f %f %f %f %f %f" \
 v(0) v(1) v(2) v(3) v(4) v(5) v(6) v(7)]
```

```
      for {set j 0} {$j < $m} {incr j} {monthlyPayment InsertNextValue
$v($j)}
   }
   $fieldData AddArray monthlyPayment

   # UNPAID_PRINCIPLE - skip
   while { [gets $file arrayName] == 0 } {}
   for {set i 0} {$i < $numLines} {incr i} {
      set line [gets $file]
   }

   # LOAN_AMOUNT - skip
   while { [gets $file arrayName] == 0 } {}
   for {set i 0} {$i < $numLines} {incr i} {
      set line [gets $file]
   }

   # INTEREST_RATE - independnet variable
   while { [gets $file arrayName] == 0 } {}
   vtkFloatArray interestRate
   interestRate SetName INTEREST_RATE
   for {set i 0} {$i < $numLines} {incr i} {
      set line [gets $file]
      set m [scan $line "%f %f %f %f %f %f %f %f" \
 v(0) v(1) v(2) v(3) v(4) v(5) v(6) v(7)]
      for {set j 0} {$j < $m} {incr j} {interestRate InsertNextValue $v($j)}
   }
   $fieldData AddArray interestRate

   # MONTHLY_INCOME - independent variable
   while { [gets $file arrayName] == 0 } {}
   vtkIntArray monthlyIncome
   monthlyIncome SetName MONTHLY_INCOME
   for {set i 0} {$i < $numLines} {incr i} {
      set line [gets $file]
      set m [scan $line "%d %d %d %d %d %d %d %d" \
 v(0) v(1) v(2) v(3) v(4) v(5) v(6) v(7)]
      for {set j 0} {$j < $m} {incr j} {monthlyIncome InsertNextValue $v($j)}
   }
   $fieldData AddArray  monthlyIncome
}
```

Now that we've read the data, we have to rearrange the field data contained by the output vtkDataObject into a form suitable for processing by the visualization pipeline (i.e., the vtkGaussianSplatter). This means creating a subclass of vtkDataSet, since vtkGaussian-

Splatter takes an instance of vtkDataSet as input. There are two steps required. First, the filter vtkDataObjectToDataSetFilter is used to convert the vtkDataObject to type vtk-DataSet. Then, vtkRearrangeFields and vtkAssignAttribute are used to move a field from the vtkDataObject to the vtkPointData of the newly created vtkDataSet and label it as the active scalar field.

```
vtkDataObjectToDataSetFilter do2ds
    do2ds SetInput [dos GetOutput]
    do2ds SetDataSetTypeToPolyData
    do2ds DefaultNormalizeOn
    do2ds SetPointComponent 0 $xAxis 0
    do2ds SetPointComponent 1 $yAxis 0
    do2ds SetPointComponent 2 $zAxis 0

vtkRearrangeFields rf
    rf SetInput [do2ds GetOutput]
    rf AddOperation MOVE $scalar DATA_OBJECT POINT_DATA

vtkAssignAttribute aa
    aa SetInput [rf GetOutput]
    aa Assign $scalar SCALARS POINT_DATA
    aa Update
```

There are several important notes here.

1. All filters pass their input vtkDataObject through to their output unless instructed otherwise (or unless they modify vtkDataObject). We will take advantage of this in the downstream filters.

2. vtkDataObjectToDataSetFilter is set up to create an instance of vtkPolyData as its output, with the three components of the field data serving as x, y, and z coordinates. In this case we use vtkPolyData because the data is unstructured and consists only of points.

3. The field values are normalized between $(0,1)$ because the axes' ranges are different enough that we create a better visualization by filling the entire space with data.

4. The filter vtkRearrangeFields copies/moves fields between vtkDataObject, vtkPoint-Data and vtkCellData. In this example, an operation to move the field called $scalar from the data object of the input to the point data of the output is assigned.

5. The filter vtkAssignAttribute labels fields as attributes. In this example, the field called $scalar (that is in the point data) is labeled as the active scalar field.

The Set___Component() methods are the key methods of vtkDataObjectToDataSetFilter. These methods refer to the data arrays in the field data by name and by component number. (Recall that a data array may have more than one component.) It is also possible to indicate a (min,max) tuple range from the data array, and to perform normalization. However, make sure that the number of tuples extracted matches the number of items in the dataset structure (e.g., the number of points or cells).

There are several related classes that do similar operations. These classes can be used to rearrange data arbitrarily to and from field data, into datasets, and into attribute data. These filters include:

- vtkDataObjectToDataSetFilter — Transform field data contained in a vtkDataObject to a subclass of vtkDataSet.

- vtkDataSetToDataObjectFilter — Transform vtkDataSet into vtkFieldData contained in a vtkDataObject.

- vtkRearrangeFields — Move/copy fields between field data, point data and cell data.

- vtkAssignAttribute — Labels a field as an attribute.

- vtkMergeFields — Merge multiple fields into one.

- vtkSplitField — Split a field into multiple single component fields.

- vtkDataObjectReader — Read a VTK formatted field data file. (See "Dataset Attribute Format" on page 351 for a description of the field data format.)

- vtkDataObjectWriter — Write a VTK formatted field data file. (See "Dataset Attribute Format" on page 351 for a description of the field data format.)

- vtkProgrammableDataObjectSource — Define a method to read data of arbitrary form and represent it as field data (i.e., place it in a vtkDataObject).

## Chapter 9

Contributing Code

The previous chapters (those found in Part II) offered an introduction to VTK via example. By now it should be apparent that VTK offers the functionality to create powerful graphics, imaging, and visualization applications. In addition, because you have access to the source code, you can extend VTK by adding your own classes. In Part III of the *User's Guide*, we show you how to extend VTK to suit the needs of your application. We begin in this chapter by introducing coding conventions that you may consider adopting—especially if you wish to contribute code to the VTK community. We also describe standard conventions and methods that your objects must implement to be incorporated into VTK. Later in Part III we discuss the implementation details of the process and data objects that make up VTK's visualization pipeline, as well as controlling the execution of the visualization pipeline, and describe how to interface VTK to various windowing systems.

9.1 Coding Considerations

If you develop your own filter or other addition to the *Visualization Toolkit*, we encourage you to contribute the source code. You will have to consider what it means to contribute code from a legal point of view, what coding styles and conventions to use, and how to go about contributing code.

Conditions on Contributing Code To VTK

When you contribute code to VTK, two things are bound to happen. First, many people will see the code—dissecting, improving, and modifying it; and second, you will in some sense "lose control" of the code due to the modifications that will inevitably occur to it. You will not want to release proprietary code or code you cannot relinquish control over (also, patented code is discouraged), and you'll want to carefully craft the code so that others can understand and improve it.

VTK's copyright is an open-source copyright (refer to any .cxx or .h file to see the copyright in its entirety). The copyright is stated as follows:

Conditions on the copyright are derived from the BSD license (see `www.open-source.org`) and places no constraints on modifying, copying, and redistributing source or binary code, with the exception of the four bulleted clauses, warranty, and indemnification clauses shown above. Other than respecting these four clauses, observing the usual indemnification clause, and commercial patent restriction on the handful of classes in the `VTK/Patented/` directory, you can use VTK in any way whatsoever, including in commercial application.

If these restrictions are acceptable, you can consider contributing code. However, you will need to meet other criteria before your code is accepted. These criteria are not formalized, but have to do with the usefulness, simplicity, and compatibility with the rest of the system. Important questions to ask are:

- Does the code meet the VTK coding standards (see next section)?

- Is the code documented and commented?

- Is the code general? Or is it specific to a narrow application?

- Does it require extensive modification to the system? (For example, modifications to widely-used object APIs.)

- Does the code duplicate existing functionality?

- Is the code robust?

- Does the code belong in a visualization toolkit?

If you can answer these questions favorably, chances are that the code is a good candidate for inclusion in VTK.

Coding Style

There are many useful coding styles, but we insist that you follow just one. We know this is a contentious issue, but we have found that it is very important to maintain a consistent style. Consistent style means that the code is easier to read, debug, maintain, test, and extend. It also means that the automated documentation facilities operate correctly. And these benefits are available to all users of VTK.

Here's a summary of the coding style. You may wish to examine VTK source code to see what it looks like.

- Variables, methods, and class names use changing capitalization to indicate separate words. Instance variables and methods always begin with a capital letter. Static variables are discouraged, but should also begin with a capital letter. Local variables begin with a lower-case letter. SetNumberOfPoints() or PickList are examples of a method name and instance variable.

- Class names are prefixed with `vtk` followed by the class name starting with a capital letter. For example, vtkActor or vtkPolyData are class names. The `vtk` prefix allows the VTK class library to be mixed with other libraries.

- Explicit `this->` pointers are used in methods. Examples include `this->Visibility` and `this->Property` and `this->Execute()`. We have found that the use of explicit `this->` pointers improves code understanding and readability.

- Variable, method, and class names should be spelled out. Abbreviations can be used, but the abbreviation should be entirely in capital letters. For example, vtkPolyData-ConnectivityFilter or vtkLODActor.

- Preprocessor variables are written in capital letters. These variables are the only one to use the underscore "_" to separate words. Preprocessor variables should also begin with VTK_ as in VTK_LARGE_FLOAT.

- Instance variables are typically protected or private class members. Access to instance variables is through Set/Get methods. Note that VTK provides Set/Get macros which should be used whenever possible (look in VTK/Common/vtkSet-Get.h for the implementation, and .h header files for example usage).

- The indentation style can be characterized as the "indented brace" style. Indentations are two spaces, and the curly brace (scope delimiter) is placed on the following line and indented along with the code (i.e., the curly brace lines up with the code).

- Use // to comment code. Methods are commented by adding // Description: followed by lines each beginning with //.

How To Contribute Code

Contributing code is fairly easy once you've created your class or classes following the coding convention described above. First, include the copyright notice in both the .cxx and .h source files. You may wish to place your name, organization, and or other identifying information in the "Thanks:" field of the copyright notice (see Vtk/Hybrid/vtkEarthSource.h for an example). Next, send e-mail to kitware@kitware.com with an explanation of what the code does, sample data (if needed), test code (in either C++, Tcl, or Python), and the source code (a single .h and .cxx file per class). Another method is to send the same information to the vtkusers mailing list (see "Additional Resources" on page 4 for information about joining the list). The advantage of sending contributed code to the mailing list is that users can take advantage of the code immediately.

There is no guarantee that contributed code will be incorporated into official VTK releases. This depends upon the quality, usefulness, and generality of the code as outlined in "Conditions on Contributing Code To VTK" on page 201.

(Note: skilled developers can obtain CVS write access and add their own code to the VTK code repository. Contact kitware@kitware.com for more information.)

9.2 Standard Methods: Creating and Deleting Objects

Almost every object in VTK responds to a set of standard methods. Many of these methods are implemented in vtkObject, from which most VTK classes are derived. However, subclasses typically require that you extend or implement the inherited methods for proper behavior. For example, the New() method should be implemented by every concrete (i.e., non-abstract, instantiable) class, while the Delete() is generally inherited from its superclass' vtkObject. Before you develop any code you should become familiar with these standard methods, and make sure your own classes support them.

`New()`
> This static class method is used to instantiate objects. We refer to this method as an "object factory" since it is used to create instances of a class. In VTK, every New() method should be paired with the Delete() method. (See also "Object Factories" on page 211.)

`instance = MakeObject()`
> This method is a virtual constructor. That is, invoking this method causes an object to create an instance of the same type as itself and then return a pointer to the new object.

`Delete()`
> Use this method to delete a VTK object created with the New() or MakeObject() method. Depending upon the nature of the object being deleted, this may or may not actually delete the object. For example, reference-counted objects will only be deleted if their reference count goes to zero.

`DebugOn()/DebugOff()`
> Turn debugging information on or off. These methods are inherited from vtkObject.

`Print()`
> Print out the object including superclass information. The Print() method, which is defined in vtkObject, requires implementation of a PrintSelf() method for each class. The PrintSelf() method is invoked in a chain, each subclass calling its superclass's PrintSelf() and then printing its own instance variables.

`PrintSelf(ostream, indent)`
> Each class should implement this method. The method invokes its parents PrintSelf(), followed by methods to print itself.

`name = GetClassName()`
> Return the name of the class as a character string. This method is used for debugging

information. (In vtk3.1, the macro vtkTypeMacro found in `vtkSetGet.h` defines this method.)

`flag = IsA(className)`
Return non-zero if the named class is a superclass of, or the same type of, this class. (In vtk3.1 and beyond, the macro vtkTypeMacro found in `vtkSetGet.h` defines this method.)

`<class> *ptr = <class>::SafeDownCast(vtkObject *o)`
This static class method is available in C++ for performing safe down casts (i.e., casting a general class to a more specialized class). If `ptr` is returned NULL, then the down cast failed, otherwise `ptr` points to an instance of the class `<class>`. For example, `ptr=vtkActor::SafeDownCast(prop)` will return non-NULL if prop is a vtkActor or a subclass of vtkActor. (In vtk3.1, the macro vtkTypeMacro found in `vtkSetGet.h` defines this method.)

`void Modified()`
This updates the internal modification time stamp for the object. The value is guaranteed to be unique and monotonically increasing.

`mtime = GetMTime()`
Return the last modification time of an object. Normally this method is inherited from vtkObject, however in some cases you'll want to overload it. See "Modified Time" on page 277 for more information.

The most important information you can take from this section is this: instances should be created with the New() method and destroyed with the Delete() method; and that for every New() there should be a Delete() method. For example, to create an instance of an actor:

```
vtkActor *anActor = vtkActor::New();
... (more stuff)
anActor->Delete();
```

The New() method is called an object factory: it's a class method used to create instances of the class. Typically, the New() method first asks the vtkObjectFactory to create an instance of the object, and if that fails, it simply invokes the C++ new operator as is shown in this excerpted code from `vtkSphereSource.cxx`:

```
vtkSphereSource* vtkSphereSource::New()
{
  // First try to create the object from the vtkObjectFactory
  vtkObject* ret = vtkObjectFactory::CreateInstance(
```

```
                                            "vtkSphereSource");
  if(ret)
    {
    return (vtkSphereSource*)ret;
    }
  // If the factory was unable to create the object, create it here.
  return new vtkSphereSource;
}
```

However, the New() method can be more complex, for example, to instantiate device-independent classes. For example, in vtkGraphicsFactory.cxx, the code used to instantiate a vtkActor looks like this:

```
  if(strcmp(vtkclassname, "vtkActor") == 0)
    {
    return vtkOpenGLActor::New();
    }
```

Here the New() method is used to create a device-*dependent* subclass of vtkActor (i.e., OpenGL), which is then returned as a pointer to a device-*independent* vtkActor. For example, depending on the compile-time flags (e.g., VTK_USE_OGLR) and possibly other information such as environment variables, different actor types corresponding to the rendering libraries (e.g., OpenGL, Mesa, and so on) are created transparently to the user. Using this mechanism we can create device-independent applications, or at run-time select different classes to use in the application. (See "Object Factories" on page 211 for more information.)

9.3 Copying Objects & Protected Methods

The constructor, destructor, operator=, and copy constructor methods are either protected or private members of most every VTK class. This means that for VTK class vtkX, the methods

- vtkX() — constructor
- ~vtkX() — destructor

are protected, and the methods

- operator=(const vtkX &) — equivalence operator, and
- vtkX(const vtkX &) — copy constructor

are private. In addition, the assignment operator and copy constructors should be declared only, and not implemented. This prevents the compiler from creating one automatically, and does not generate code that cannot be covered in the testing process. This means that you cannot use these methods in your application. (The reason for this is to prevent potentially dangerous misuse of these methods. For example, reference counting can be broken by using the constructor and destructor rather than the standard `New()` and `Delete()` methods described in the previous section.)

Since the copy constructor and operator= methods are private, other methods must be used to copy instances of an object. The methods to use are `DeepCopy()` and/or `Shallow-Copy()`. For example:

```
vtkActor *a1 = vtkActor::New();
vtkActor *a2 = vtkActor::New();
a2->ShallowCopy(a1);
```

A shallow copy is a copy of an object that copies references to objects (via reference counting) rather than the object themselves. For example, instances of the class `vtkActor` refer to a `vtkMapper` object (the mapper represents the geometry for the actor). In a shallow copy, replication of data is avoided, and just the reference to the `vtkMapper` is copied. However, any changes to the shared mapper indirectly affects all instances of `vtkActor` that refer to it. Alternatively, a `DeepCopy()` can be used to copy an instance, including any data it represents, without any references to other objects. Here's an examples:

```
vtkIntArray *ia1 = vtkIntArray::New();
vtkIntArray *ia2 = vtkIntArray::New();
ia1->DeepCopy(ia2);
```

In this example, the data in `ia2` is copied into `ia1`. From this point on, `ia1` and `ia2` can be modified without affecting each other.

At the current time, VTK does not support `DeepCopy()` and `ShallowCopy()` in all classes. This will be added in the future.

9.4 Writing A VTK Class: An Overview

In this section we give a broad overview of how to write a VTK class. If you are writing a new filter, you'll also want to refer to Chapter 12 "How To Write A Process Object" on page 275. If you want to extend the graphics subsystem, see Chapter 12 "Extending The Graphics System" on page 291. And of course, you should read the previous portion of this chapter.

Probably the hardest part about writing a VTK class is figuring out if you need it, and if so, where it fits into the system. These decisions come easier with experience. In the mean time, you probably want to start by working with other VTK developers, or posting to the vtkusers mailing list (see "Additional Resources" on page 4). If you determine that a class is needed, you'll want to look at the following issues.

Find A Similar Class

The best place to start is to find a class that does something similar to what you want to do. This will often guide the creation of the object API, and/or the selection of a superclass.

Identify A Superclass

Most classes should derive from vtkObject or one of vtkObject's descendants. Exceptions to this rule are few, since vtkObject implements important functionality such as reference counting, command/observer user methods, print methods, and debugging flags. All VTK classes use single inheritance. While this is a contentious issue, there are good reasons for this policy including Java support (Java allows only single inheritance) and simplification of the wrapping process as well as the code. You may wish to refer to the object diagrams found in "Object Diagrams" on page 321. These provide a succinct overview of many inheritance relationships found in VTK.

Single Class Per .h File

Classes in VTK are implemented one class per .h header file, along with any associated .cxx implementation file. There are some exceptions to this rule—for example, when you have to define internal helper classes. However, in these exceptions the helper class is not visible outside of the principle class. If it is, it should placed into its own .h/.cxx files.

Required Methods

Several methods and macros must be defined by every VTK class as follows. See "Standard Methods: Creating and Deleting Objects" on page 205 for a description of these methods.

- `New()` — Every non-abstract class (i.e., a class that does not implement a pure virtual function) must define the `New()` method.

- `vtkTypeMacro(className,superclassName)` — This macro is a convenient way to define methods used at run-time to determine the type of an instance, or to perform safe down casting. `vtkTypeMacro` is defined in the file `vtkSetGet.h`. The macro defines the methods GetClassName(), IsA(), and SafeDownCast().

- `PrintSelf()` — Print out instance variables in an intelligent manner.

- Constructor (must be `protected`)

- Destructor (must be `protected`)

- Copy Constructor (must be `private` and not implemented)

- `operator=` (must be `private` and not implemented)

The constructor, copy constructor, destructor, and `operator=` must not be public. The `New()` method should use the procedure outlined in "Object Factories" on page 211. Of course, depending upon the superclass(es) of your class, there may be additional methods to implement to satisfy the class API (i.e., fill in abstract virtual functions).

Document Code

The documentation of VTK classes depends upon proper use of documentation directives. Each `.h` class file should have a `// .NAME` description, which is a single-line description of what the class does. In addition, the header file should have a `// .SECTION Description` section, which is a multi-paragraph description (delimited with the C++ comment indicator `//`) giving detailed information about each class and how it works. Other possible information is contained in the `// .SECTION Caveats` section, which describes quirks and limitations of the class, and the `// .SECTION See Also` section, which refers to other, related classes.

Methods should also be documented. If a method satisfies a superclass API, or overloads a superclass method, you may not need to document the method. Those methods that you do document use the following construct:

```
// Description:
// This is a description...
```

Of course, you may want to embed other documentation, comments, etc. into the code to help other developers and users understand what you've done.

Use SetGet Macros

Whenever possible, use the `SetGet` macros found in `VTK/Common/SetGet.h` to define access methods to instance variables. Also, you'll want to use the debugging macros and additional `#defines` (e.g., `VTK_LARGE_FLOAT`) in your code, as necessary.

Add Class To VTK

Once you've created your class, you'll want to decide whether you want to incorporate it into the VTK build, or separate, in your own application. If you add your class to VTK, modify the `CMakeLists.txt` file in the appropriate subdirectory. You'll then have to re-run CMake (as described in "Running CMake" on page 15), and then recompile. You can add an entire new library by creating a file called `LocalUser.cmake` in the top level of your VTK source tree. This file is used only if it exits. You can put a CMake `SUBDIR` command into the file, telling CMake to go into the new library's directory. Inside the directory, you will need to create a new `CMakeLists.txt` file that contains CMake commands for building your library. If you are using one of the wrapped languages like Tcl, you can either add your library into the VTK executable with another `LocalUser.cmake` file in the `Wrapping/Tcl` directory, or you will have to build shared libraries, and load the new library at run time into the Tcl environment. To add classes that simply use VTK, see "C++" on page 30 for example `CMakeLists.txt` files.

9.5 Object Factories

VTK Version 3.0 and later has a potent capability that allows you to extend VTK at run time. Using *object factories*, you can replace a VTK object with one of your own creation.

For example, if you have special hardware, you create your own special high-performance filter at *run-time* by replacing object(s) in VTK with your own objects. So, if you wanted to replace the vtkImageFFT filter with a filter that performed FFT in hardware, or replace the cell vtkTetra with a high-performance, assembly code implementation, you could do this. Here are the benefits of using object factories.

- Allow sub-classes to be used in place of parent classes in existing code.

- Your application can dynamically load new object implementations.

- You can extend VTK at run-time.

- Proprietary extensions can be isolated from the public VTK builds.

- Removes the need for many #ifdefs in C++ code, for example, an OpenGL factory could replace all of the #ifdefs in vtkRenderer and vtkRenderWindow.

- An object factory can be used as a debugging aid. For example, a factory can be created that does nothing except track the invocation of New() for each class.

- Easier implementation of accelerated or alternative VTK objects on different hardware similar to the plug-in model of Netscape and Photoshop.

Overview

The key class when implementing an object factory is vtkObjectFactory. vtkObjectFactory maintains a list of "registered" factories. It also defines a static class method used to create VTK objects by string name—the method CreateInstance()—which takes as an argument a const char*. The create method iterates over the registered factories asking each one in turn to create the object. If the factory returns an object, that object is returned as the created instance. Thus, the first factory returning an object is the one used to create the object.

An example will help illustrate how the object factory is used. The New() method from the class vtkVertex is shown below.

```
vtkVertex* vtkVertex::New()
{
  // First try to create the object from the vtkObjectFactory
  vtkObject* ret = vtkObjectFactory::CreateInstance("vtkVertex");
  if(ret)
    {
    return (vtkVertex*)ret;
```

```
    }

    // If the factory was unable to create the object, then create it
    return new vtkVertex;
}
```

The implementation of this New() method is similar to most all other New() methods found in VTK. If the object factory does not return an instance of class vtkVertex, then the constructor for vtkVertex is used. Note that the factory must return an instance of a class that is a subclass of the invoking class (i.e., vtkVertex).

How To Write A Factory

The first thing you need to do is to create a subclass of vtkObjectFactory. You must implement two virtual functions in your factory: GetVTKSourceVersion() and GetDescription().

```
virtual const char* GetVTKSourceVersion();
virtual const char* GetDescription();
```

GetDescription() returns a string defining the functionality of the object factory. The method GetVTKSourceVersion() should return VTK_SOURCE_VERSION and NOT call vtkVersion::GetVTKSourceVersion(). You cannot call vtkVersion functions, because the version must be compiled into your factory, if you did call vtkVersion functions, it would just use the VTK version that the factory was loaded into and not the one it was built with. This method is used to check the version numbers of the factory and the objects it creates against the installed VTK. If the software versions are different, a warning will be produced and there's a good chance that a serious program error will follow.

There are two ways for a factory to create objects. The most convenient method is to use the protected method of vtkObjectFactory called RegisterOverride().

```
void RegisterOverride(const char* classOverride,
                      const char* overrideClassName,
                      const char* description,
                      int enableFlag,
                      CreateFunction createFunction);
```

This method should be called in your constructor once for each object your factory provides. The following are descriptions of the arguments:

- classOverride — This is the name of the class you are replacing.

- overrideClassName — This is the name of the class that will replace classOverride

- description — This is a text based description of what your replacement class does. This can be useful from a GUI if you want to select which object to use at run-time.

- enableFlag — This is a Boolean flag that should be 0 or 1. If it is 0, this override will not be used. Note, it is possible to change these flags at run-time from vtkObjectFactory class interface.

- createFunction — This is a pointer to a function that will create your class. The function must look like this:

```
vtkObject* createFunction();
```

You can write your own function or use the VTK_CREATE_FUNCTION macro provided in vtkObjectFactory.h.

The second way in which an object factory can create objects is the virtual function CreateObject():

```
virtual vtkObject* CreateObject(const char* vtkclassname);
```

The function should return NULL if your factory does not want to handle the class name it is being asked to create. It should return a sub-class of the named VTK class if it wants to override the class. Since the CreateObject() method returns a vtkObject* there is not much type safety other than the object must be a vtkObject, so be careful to only return sub-classes of the object to avoid run-time errors. A factory can handle as many objects as it wants. If many objects are to be created, it would be best to use a hash table to map from the string names to the object creation. The method should be as fast as possible since it may be invoked frequently. Also note that this method will not allow a GUI to selectively enable and disable individual objects like the RegisterOverride() method can.

How To Install A Factory

How factories are installed depends on whether they are compiled into your VTK library or application; or whether they are dynamically loaded DLLs or shared libraries. Compiled in factories need only call

```
vtkObjectFactory::RegisterFactory ( MyFactory::New() );
```

For dynamically loaded factories, a shared library or DLL must be created that contains the object factory subclass. The library should include the macro VTK_FACTORY_INTERFACE_IMPLEMENT(factoryName). This macro defines three external "C" linkage functions named vtkGetFactoryCompilerUsed(), vtkGetFactoryVersion(), and vtkLoad() that returns an instance of the factory provided by the library.

```
#define VTK_FACTORY_INTERFACE_IMPLEMENT(factoryName)   \
extern "C"                                             \
VTK_FACTORY_INTERFACE_EXPORT                           \
const char* vtkGetFactoryCompilerUsed()               \
{                                                      \
  return VTK_CXX_COMPILER;                             \
}                                                      \
extern "C"                                             \
VTK_FACTORY_INTERFACE_EXPORT                           \
const char* vtkGetFactoryVersion()                    \
{                                                      \
  return VTK_SOURCE_VERSION;                           \
}                                                      \
extern "C"                                             \
VTK_FACTORY_INTERFACE_EXPORT                           \
vtkObjectFactory* vtkLoad()                            \
{                                                      \
  return factoryName ::New();                          \
}
```

The library must then be put in the VTK_AUTOLOAD_PATH. This variable follows the convention of PATH on your machine using the separation delimiters ";" on Windows, and ":" on Unix. The first time the vtkObjectFactory is asked to create an object, it loads all shared libraries or DLLs in the VTK_AUTOLOAD_PATH. For each library in the path, vtkLoad() is called to create an instance of vtkObjectFactory. This is only done the first time to avoid performance problems. However, it is possible to re-check the path for new factories at run time by calling

```
vtkObjectFactory::ReHash();
```

(Note that the VTK class vtkDynamicLoader handles operating system independent loading of shared libraries or DLLs.)

Example Factory

Here is a simple factory that uses OLE automation on the Windows operating system to redirect all VTK debug output to a Microsoft Word document. To use this factory, just compile the code into a DLL, and put it in your VTK_AUTOLOAD_PATH.

```
#include "vtkOutputWindow.h"
#include "vtkObjectFactory.h"
#pragma warning (disable:4146)
#import "mso9.dll"
#pragma warning (default:4146)
#import "vbe6ext.olb"
#import "msword9.olb" rename("ExitWindows", "WordExitWindows")
// This class is exported from the vtkWordOutputWindow.dll
class vtkWordOutputWindow : public vtkOutputWindow {
public:
  vtkWordOutputWindow();
  virtual void DisplayText(const char*);
  virtual void PrintSelf(vtkOstream& os, vtkIndent indent);
  static vtkWordOutputWindow* New() { return new vtkWordOutputWindow;}
protected:
  Word::_ApplicationPtr m_pWord;
  Word::_DocumentPtr m_pDoc;
};

class vtkWordOutputWindowFactory : public vtkObjectFactory
{
public:
  vtkWordOutputWindowFactory();
  virtual const char* GetVTKSourceVersion();
  virtual const char* GetDescription();
};

// vtkWordOutputWindow.cpp : the entry point for the DLL application.
//
#include "vtkWordOutputWindow.h"
#include "vtkVersion.h"
BOOL APIENTRY DllMain( HANDLE hModule,
                       DWORD  ul_reason_for_call,
                       LPVOID lpReserved )
{
  if(ul_reason_for_call == DLL_PROCESS_ATTACH)
    {
    CoInitialize(NULL);
    }
```

```
      return TRUE;
}

void vtkWordOutputWindow::PrintSelf(vtkOstream& os, vtkIndent indent)
{
  vtkOutputWindow::PrintSelf(os, indent);
  os << indent <<  "vtkWordOutputWindow " << endl;
}

// This is the constructor of a class that has been exported.
// see vtkWordOutputWindow.h for the class definition
vtkWordOutputWindow::vtkWordOutputWindow()
{
   try
     {
     HRESULT hr = m_pWord.CreateInstance(__uuidof(Word::Application));
     if(hr != 0) throw _com_error(hr);

     m_pWord->Visible = VARIANT_TRUE;
     m_pDoc = m_pWord->Documents->Add();
     }
   catch (_com_error& ComError)
     {
     cerr << ComError.ErrorMessage() << endl;
     }
}

void vtkWordOutputWindow::DisplayText(const char* text)
{
  m_pDoc->Content->InsertAfter(text);
}

// Use the macro to create a function to return a vtkWordOutputWindow
VTK_CREATE_CREATE_FUNCTION(vtkWordOutputWindow);

// Register the one override in the constructor of the factory
vtkWordOutputWindowFactory::vtkWordOutputWindowFactory()
{
   this->RegisterOverride("vtkOutputWindow",
   "vtkWordOutputWindow",
   "OLE Word Window",
   1,
   vtkObjectFactoryCreatevtkWordOutputWindow);
}
```

```
// Methods to load and insure factory compatibility.
VTK_FACTORY_INTERFACE_IMPLEMENT(vtkWordOutputWindowFactory);

// return the version of VTK that the factory was built with
const char* vtkWordOutputWindowFactory::GetVTKSourceVersion()
{
  return VTK_SOURCE_VERSION;
}

// return a text description of the factory
const char* vtkWordOutputWindowFactory::GetDescription()
{
  return "vtk debug output to Word via OLE factory";
}
```

## Chapter 10

Managing Pipeline Execution

This chapter provides details of the VTK execution process. Understanding this process will help you to write new filters, and work with VTK's streaming functionality. The chapter begins by describing the pipeline execution process, and then follows that with a description of how to use streaming in an application.

10.1 The Execution Process

The *Visualization Toolkit* uses an implicit execution mechanism. That is, there is no central executive controlling the execution of the visualization pipeline. While this is unusual as compared to many visualization systems, it has several advantages. First, the method is relatively simple in principle—time stamps are used to determine when objects are out of date. Such objects execute as necessary to bring themselves, and the system, up to date. Second, implicit execution is natural for parallel processing because there is no centralized bottleneck preventing distribution across processors. And finally, without a central executive it is relatively straightforward to change the behavior of the execution process by controlling it in your own application. For example, you can make VTK look like a functional system (versus data flow) simply by invoking Update() on a single filter in response to a user input (e.g., a menu choice), as well as dynamically changing the input and output of each filter as necessary.

As we saw in the overview section (see "Pipeline Execution" on page 26), pipeline execution is initiated by a request for data. Typically the request is initiated when a subclass of vtkProp is rendered. The render request results in an Update() method being invoked on a mapper, which in turn forwards the method to its data object. The Update() method in vtk-DataObject consists of four separate steps as illustrated by the following.

```
void vtkDataObject::Update()
{
  this->UpdateInformation();
  this->PropagateUpdateExtent();
  this->TriggerAsynchronousUpdate();
  this->UpdateData();
}
```

Each of these methods is typically propagated recursively up the pipeline. In the first pass, the UpdateInformation() method travels up the pipeline (opposite the direction of data flow) and at least two important pieces of information come back down the pipeline—the WholeExtent (or MaximumNumberOfPieces) for each data object, and the PipelineM-Time. The whole extent refers to the entire data that is available for processing, and is expressed as a 6-vector $(x_{min}, x_{max}, y_{min}, y_{max}, z_{min}, z_{max})$ for structured data. The PipelineMTime is the maximum modified time (time stamp) found in the pipeline.

In the PropagateUpdateExtent() pass, each process object in the pipeline determines how much data it will produce (which will be at least as big as the requested update extent of the outputs) and how much input data it requires for execution.

In the TriggerAsynchronousUpdate() pass, ports are given an opportunity to begin a non-blocking update in another process. (A port is an object that transmits data across the network, or between processes. Ports are used in distributed, parallel applications.) If no ports exist in the pipeline then TriggerAsynchronousUpdate() propagates up and then back down the pipeline doing nothing.

The final stage is the UpdateData() pass where the actual execution of each source occurs on the way back up the pipeline via the process object Execute() method.

The reason for these methods, and the information they return, is probably somewhat of a mystery to you at this point. Besides the basic need to control the execution of filters, the execution process supports two other important features. First, it allows data to be *streamed*—that is, data can be divided into pieces (and processed piece-by-piece) to reduce memory consumption (see "Using Streaming" on page 232). Applications can also request just a piece of data. This can be useful when developing applications requiring high interactivity or when the user is only interested in a portion of the dataset. Second, the execution process supports asynchronous, distributed, parallel processing. Such a capability is necessary when visualizing large datasets and the problem must be distributed across many processors.

The next few sections will cover the execution process in more detail. This information is important if you plan to write your own process object. If you simply plan to make use of existing sources and filters, then these internal details are not necessary but they may help you better understand the behavior and capabilities of the pipeline execution model.

Overview and Terminology

As mentioned previously, each of the four stages of the Update() process may propagate recursively back up the pipeline. Of course, we do not want to execute process objects if it is not necessary, so we would like to terminate propagation when appropriate. In the first stage of the Update() process, the UpdateInformation() pass traverses up the entire pipeline since this is necessary for computing the PipelineMTime. In the other three stages, the data objects consult their PipelineMTime, their UpdateTime and whether or not their data has been released to determine whether they will need to be regenerated. The propagation continues through the data object only if regeneration of the data is necessary.

It is assumed that when the Update() method is called, the desired update extent has been set to something valid. If the update extent has not been set before the first call to UpdateInformation(), then the update extent is set to the whole extent of the data.

Data objects have two possible ways of storing extents. Which way the information is stored is indicated by the return value of GetExtentType() which may be VTK_PIECES_EXTENT or VTK_3D_EXTENT. Data objects that use pieces to define their extent store the MaximumNumberOfPieces that the data object can be broken into, the Piece out of how many NumberOfPieces that was created last time this data object was updated, and the UpdatePiece out of how many UpdateNumberOfPieces is being requested currently. If the UpdatePiece is -1 and the UpdateNumberOfPieces is 0, then no data is requested and the data object will remain empty after the update.

As mentioned previously, data objects that use 3D extents store all their extent information as six integers defining the $(x_{min}, x_{max}, y_{min}, y_{max}, z_{min}, z_{max})$ bounds of some structured data region. These data objects keep track of their WholeExtent which is the maximum size of the data, their Extent which is the size of the data last generated by an update, and their UpdateExtent which is the currently requested data size. The UpdateExtent must lie completely within the WholeExtent or must be a special invalid extent with $(x_{max} < x_{min})$ or $(y_{max} < y_{min})$ or $(z_{max} < z_{min})$. If this special extent is encountered during the UpdateInformation pass, then no data requested and the data object will remain empty after the update.

If Update() is called on a vtkProcessObject (or vtkSource) subclass instead of a vtk-DataObject subclass, the source simply calls the Update() method of its first output (as shown in the code following this paragraph). This way, the update extent of the first output can be considered. Please note that we will use the generic term "update extent" to refer to

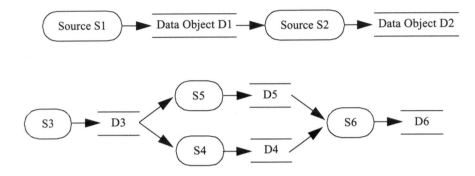

Figure 10–1 Two example pipeline configurations used to illustrate the ideas covered in this chapter. Here we are referring to process objects as "sources" of data.

either the UpdateExtent or the UpdatePiece depending on the actual data type of the data object.

```
void vtkSource::Update()
{
  if (this->GetOutput(0))
    {
    this->GetOutput(0)->Update();
    }
}
```

The two pipelines shown in **Figure 10–1** will be used to illustrate issues with the update mechanism. The first represents a simple case such as a reader providing data to a single filter. The second represents a slightly more complex case of a reader that provides data to two filters, which in turn provide their data to a two-input filter that produces one resulting output.

Looking at the example pipeline at the top of **Figure 10–1**, and assuming that it has not executed before (so all calls will propagate all the way up the pipeline), the high-level calls that would be made are illustrated by the following pseudo-code.

```
D2->Update()
  D2->UpdateInformation()
    S2->UpdateInformation();
      D1->UpdateInformation();
```

```
        S1->UpdateInformation();
  D2->PropagateUpdateExtent(D2);
    S2->PropagateUpdateExtent();
      D1->PropagateUpdateExtent(D1);
        S1->PropagateUpdateExtent();
  D2->TriggerAsynchronousUpdate();
    S2->TriggerAsynchronousUpdate();
      D1->TriggerAsynchronousUpdate();
        S1->TriggerAsynchronousUpdate();
  D2->UpdateData(D2);
    S2->UpdateData();
      D1->UpdateData(D1);
        S1->UpdateData();
```

Here we simply propagate each stage of the update independent of all the others. Looking at example pipeline B, we can see that this simple approach will not work in this case. The reason is that S4 might require a different input update extent than S5. If these stages are propagated independently, then when S4 goes to execute (within the UpdateData method), D3 will have the update extent that was requested by S5. Therefore, if a source has multiple inputs (as S6 does), then the update extent must be propagated again before calling either UpdateData() or TriggerAsynchronousUpdate().

The UpdateInformation() Pass

The UpdateInformation() method for vtkDataObject is shown in the following code. This method first calls UpdateInformation() on its source. After this, it checks if the update extent is invalid. If it is, then it sets the UpdatePiece to 0 and the UpdateNumberOfPieces to 1 in the case of data objects that use pieces for extent, or it copies the WholeExtent to the UpdateExtent in the case of data objects that use 3D extents.

```
void vtkDataObject::UpdateInformation()
{
  if (this->Source)
    {
    this->Source->UpdateInformation();
    }
  else
    {
    //If we don't have a source, then let's make our whole
    //extent equal to our extent.
    memcpy( this->WholeExtent, this->Extent, 6*sizeof(int) );
    //We also need to set the PipelineMTime to our MTime.
```

```
    this->PipelineMTime = this->GetMTime();
    }

  // Now we should know what our whole extent is. If our update extent
  // was not set yet, then set it to the whole extent.
  if(! this->UpdateExtenInitialized)
    {
    this->SetUpdateExtentToWholeExtent();
    this->UpdateExtentInitialized = 1;
    }
}
```

The UpdateInformation() method for vtkSource is shown in the code following this paragraph. To avoid infinite recursion, the first thing that is done for all update stages in vtk-Source is to check whether we are already updating. This would occur if there were a loop in the pipeline. If so, we set the PipelineMTime of our outputs to ensure we will execute, and then break the loop. Otherwise, we proceed to propagate the UpdateInformation() call to each of the inputs of this source. In addition, we compare the MTime of this vtkSource with the PipelineMTime of each input to find the largest value. This will be used to set the PipelineMTime of each of our outputs. If the PipelineMTime is larger than the InformationTime, the pipeline was modified since the last UpdateInformation pass, and the ExecuteInformation() method is called. The default implementation of ExecuteInformation() in vtkSource simply copies information from the first input to the outputs. Filters such as vtkImageClip that modify the WholeExtent, must implement their own version of ExecuteInformation(). A variable called locality is also computed in UpdateInformation(). This variable is used during the UpdateData() call to avoid serial execution of parallel pipelines.

```
void vtkSource::UpdateInformation()
{
  unsigned long t1, t2;
  int           idx;
  vtkDataObject *input;
  vtkDataObject *output;
  float         maxLocality = 0.0;
  float         locality;

  // Watch out for loops in the pipeline
  if ( this->Updating )
    {
    // Since we are in a loop, execute on every call to update.
    // We set the pipline mtimes of our outputs
    // to ensure the pipeline executes again.
```

```
   this->Modified();
   for (idx = 0; idx < this->NumberOfOutputs; ++idx)
     {
     output = this->GetOutput(idx);
     if (output)
       {
       output->SetPipelineMTime(this->GetMTime());
       }
     }
   return;
   }

// The MTime of this source will be used in determine the PipelineMTime
// for the outputs
t1 = this->GetMTime();

// Loop through the inputs
for (idx = 0; idx < this->NumberOfInputs; ++idx)
   {
   if (this->Inputs[idx] != NULL)
     {
     input = this->Inputs[idx];

     // Propagate the UpdateInformation call
     this->Updating = 1;
     input->UpdateInformation();
     this->Updating = 0;

     // Compute the max locality of the inputs.
     locality = input->GetLocality();
     if (locality > maxLocality)
       {
       maxLocality = locality;
       }

     // What is the PipelineMTime of this input? Compare this against
     // our current computation to find the largest one.
     t2 = input->GetPipelineMTime();

     if (t2 > t1)
       {
       t1 = t2;
       }
     }
   }
locality = maxLocality * 0.5;
```

```
  // Call ExecuteInformation for subclass specific information.
  // Since UpdateInformation propagates all the way up the pipeline,
  // we need to call ExecuteInformation only if necessary.
  if (t1 > this->InformationTime.GetMTime())
    {
    for (idx = 0; idx < this->NumberOfOutputs; ++idx)
      {
      output = this->GetOutput(idx);
      if (output)
        {
        output->SetPipelineMTime(t1);
        output->SetLocality(locality);
        }
      }

    this->ExecuteInformation();
    }
}
```

The PropagateUpdateExtent() Pass

The PropagateUpdateExtent() method for vtkDataObject is shown in the code following this paragraph. The first thing that happens is a check for an empty request. The call returns immediately if no data is requested. The next condition checks to see if the data object is already up to date. The UpdateTime is compared against the PipelineMTime, we check whether the data has been released, and we see if the update extent is already in the data object.

```
void vtkDataObject::PropagateUpdateExtent()
{
  if (this->UpdateExtentIsEmpty())
    {
    return;
    }

  // If we need to update due to PipelineMTime, or the fact that our
  // data was released, then propagate the update extent to the source
  // if there is one.
  if ( this->UpdateTime < this->PipelineMTime || this->DataReleased ||
       this->UpdateExtentIsOutsideOfTheExtent())
    {
    if (this->Source)
      {
```

```
      this->Source->PropagateUpdateExtent(this);
      }
    }

  // Check that the update extent lies within the whole extent
  this->VerifyUpdateExtent();
}
```

The next step in the PropagateUpdateExtent() method of vtkDataObject is to actually propagate the call to the source. This is done only if necessary according to the PipelineM-Time, or if the data has been released. After the propagation, we do some quick error checking to make sure the update extent has not been set to something that cannot be satis-fied. PropagateUpdateExtent() method for vtkSource is shown in the following code. As usual, the first step is to return if we detect that we are in a loop. The next step is to set the default value for RequestExactExtent. This flag is used as a part of structured data filters update extent. It indicates whether the filter is capable of handling more input than requested. In the next step, the subclass is asked how much input data is necessary to produce the output data. The default implementation is to ask for everything, although this is overridden in many subclasses. For example, vtkImageToImageFilter assumes that it needs the same input update extent as the output update extent. In the vtkImageSpatialFilter this is overridden again to add in the padding needed for execution. The final step in the PropagateUpdateExtent() method of vtkSource is to actually propagate the update extent.

```
void vtkSource::PropagateUpdateExtent(vtkDataObject *output)
{
  // Check flag to avoid executing forever if there is a loop.
  if (this->Updating)
    {
    return;
    }

  // Set the default value of RequestExactExtent.
  // This indicates that filters can handle more data than requested.
  for (idx = 0; idx < this->NumberOfInputs; ++idx)
    {
    if (this->Inputs[idx] != NULL)
      {
      this->Inputs[idx]->RequestExactExtentOff();
      }
    }

  // Give the subclass a chance to request a larger extent on
```

```
  // the inputs. This is necessary when, for example, a filter
  // requires more data at the "internal" boundaries to
  // produce the boundary values - such as an image filter that
  // derives a new pixel value by applying some operation to a
  // neighborhood of surrounding original values.
  this->ComputeInputUpdateExtents( output );

  // Now that we know the input update extent, propagate this
  // through all the inputs.
  this->Updating = 1;
  for (idx = 0; idx < this->NumberOfInputs; ++idx)
    {
    if (this->Inputs[idx] != NULL)
      {
      this->Inputs[idx]->PropagateUpdateExtent();
      }
    }
  this->Updating = 0;
}
```

The TriggerAsynchronousUpdate() Pass

The TriggerAsynchronousUpdate() method of vtkDataObject is shown in the following code. This method simply propagates the trigger method to its source depending on its PipelineMTime or if the data was released.

```
void vtkDataObject::TriggerAsynchronousUpdate()
{
  // If we need to update due to PipelineMTime, or the fact that our
  // data was released, then propagate the trigger to the source
  // if there is one.
  if ( this->UpdateTime < this->PipelineMTime || this->DataReleased )
    {
    if (this->Source)
      {
      this->Source->TriggerAsynchronousUpdate();
      }
    }
}
```

The TriggerAsynchronousUpdate() method of vtkSource is shown in the following code. After checking that we are not in a pipeline loop, the trigger is propagated to all inputs.

The TriggerAsynchronousUpdate() method will be overridden in the port objects to allow updates to begin in other processes without blocking until the data is requested.

```
void vtkSource::TriggerAsynchronousUpdate()
{
  // check flag to avoid executing forever if there is a loop
  if (this->Updating)
    {
    return;
    }
  // Propagate the trigger to all the inputs
  this->Updating = 1;
  for (int idx = 0; idx < this->NumberOfInputs; ++idx)
    {
    if (this->Inputs[idx] != NULL)
      {
      this->Inputs[idx]->TriggerAsynchronousUpdate();
      }
    }
  this->Updating = 0;
}
```

The UpdateData() Pass

The UpdateData() method of vtkDataObject is shown in the code following this paragraph. This method simply propagates the UpdateData() to the source if it is necessary according to the PipelineMTime or if the data was released.

```
void vtkDataObject::UpdateData()
{
  // If we need to update due to PipelineMTime, or the fact that our
  // data was released, then propagate the UpdateData to the source
  // if there is one.
  if ( this->UpdateTime < this->PipelineMTime || this->DataReleased )
    {
    if (this->Source)
      {
      this->Source->UpdateData(this);
      }
    }
}
```

The UpdateData() method of vtkSource is shown in the following code. This method begins by verifying that we are not in a pipeline loop. Then the UpdateData() method is propagated to all the inputs to make sure everything is up-to-date before this source executes. If there is only one input, then we simply need to propagate the UpdateData() call, but if we have more than one we must propagate the PropagateUpdateExtent() method before the UpdateData() method to ensure that all upstream data objects have the right update extent. The next step is to initialize all the outputs in preparation for execution. If there is a start method it is called, then execute is called, then the end method if there is one defined. The outputs are marked as up-to-date, and we release any inputs that require it. Finally, we update the InformationTime to indicate that we have updated this filter.

```
void vtkSource::UpdateData(vtkDataObject *output)
{
  int idx;
  // prevent chasing our tail
  if (this->Updating)
    {
    return;
    }
  // Propagate the update call - make sure everything we might rely on is
  // up-to-date
  // Must call PropagateUpdateExtent before UpdateData if multiple inputs
  // since they may lead back to the same data object.
  this->Updating = 1;
  if ( this->NumberOfInputs == 1 )
    {
    if (this->Inputs[0] != NULL)
      {
      this->Inputs[0]->UpdateData();
      }
    }
  else
    {
    for (idx = 0; idx < this->NumberOfInputs; ++idx)
      {
      if (this->Inputs[idx] != NULL)
       {
        this->Inputs[idx]->PropagateUpdateExtent();
        this->Inputs[idx]->UpdateData();
       }
      }
    }
  this->Updating = 0;
```

```
// Initialize all the outputs
for (idx = 0; idx < this->NumberOfOutputs; idx++)
  {
  if (this->Outputs[idx])
    {
    this->Outputs[idx]->Initialize();
    }
  }

// If there is a start method, call it
this->InvokeEvent(vtkCommand::StartEvent,NULL);
// Execute this object - we have not aborted yet, and our progress before
// we start to execute is 0.0.
this->AbortExecute = 0; this->Progress = 0.0;
this->Execute();
// If we ended due to aborting, push the progress up to 1.0 (since it
// probably didn't end there)
if ( !this->AbortExecute )
  {
  this->UpdateProgress(1.0);
  }
// Call the end method, if there is one
this->InvokeEvent(vtkCommand::EndEvent,NULL);
// Now we have to mark the data as up to data.
for (idx = 0; idx < this->NumberOfOutputs; ++idx)
  {
  if (this->Outputs[idx])
    {
    this->Outputs[idx]->DataHasBeenGenerated();
    }
  }

// Release any inputs if marked for release
for (idx = 0; idx < this->NumberOfInputs; ++idx)
  {
  if (this->Inputs[idx] != NULL)
    {
    if ( this->Inputs[idx]->ShouldIReleaseData() )
     {
     this->Inputs[idx]->ReleaseData();
     }
    }
  }

// Information gets invalidated as soon as Update is called,
// so validate it again here.
```

```
  this->InformationTime.Modified();
}
```

This description of the pipeline execution process may be useful when you wish to add a new process object or data object to the system. Refer to "How To Write A Graphics Filter" on page 280 for information about adding a filter to VTK.

10.2 Using Streaming

Visualization often involves working with large data. When data size becomes large, applications often become slow (due to excessive paging) or even fail, as virtual memory limits are exceeded. The *Visualization Toolkit* offers a technique to address this problem. This technique is referred to as *data streaming*. (Also see "The Execution Process" on page 219 for more details.)

In VTK, streaming is the process of separating large data into pieces, and then processing the dataset piece-by-piece. The advantage of streaming is that applications can avoid swapping or system failure due to memory constraints. On the other hand, streaming requires the ability to break data into pieces, adding complexity to the pipeline execution process as well as algorithms that process the data.

There are several other benefits to streaming. Streaming naturally lends itself to parallel processing, since streaming supports a parallel data model (i.e., process piece n of m total pieces). Streaming is also useful when supporting applications requiring high levels of interactivity since just a subset of the total data is required. It is easy to imagine an application that processes pieces ranked in order of importance, displays highest-ranked results first, and then allows the user to interact with the results, possibly interrupting data processing according to what is being visualized.

Streaming is a complex piece of functionality. The streaming mechanism has been reworked several times to insure that it is robust and easy to use. While this goal has been generally realized for certain types of data (e.g., vtkImageData—images and volumes), this is an ongoing research and implementation challenge in VTK. In particular, streaming implementations for unstructured data are currently under development, and you will likely see future changes.

The following C++ example demonstrates how to use streaming in the imaging pipeline. The example reads a volume of 256^2 x 93, magnifies the input data 3x3x1, computes the gradient, and then shrinks the result (the peak memory size is over 750 MByte without streaming).

The key step is the addition of the streamer object vtkImageDataStreamer. The streamer is told to divide its processing into 20 pieces. Its output update extent is separated into 20 non-overlapping pieces, and the input is updated on each piece separately. Exactly how the extent is divided can be controlled by using the vtkExtentTranslator class contained in the streamer. The vtkImageDataStreamer manages the pipeline execution so that the peak memory size does not exceed 40 megabytes.

```
#include "vtkImageViewer.h"
#include "vtkImageReader.h"
#include "vtkImageMagnify.h"
#include "vtkImageShrink3D.h"
#include "vtkImageGradient.h"
#include "vtkImageDataStreamer.h"
main ()
{
  int i, j;

  vtkImageReader *reader = vtkImageReader::New();
  reader->SetFilePrefix("$VTK_DATA_ROOT/Data/headsq/quarter");
  reader->SetDataByteOrderToLittleEndian();
  reader->SetDataExtent(0,255,0,255,1,93);
  reader->SetDataMask( 0x7fff);

  vtkImageMagnify *mag = vtkImageMagnify::New();
  mag->SetInput(reader->GetOutput());
  mag->SetMagnificationFactors(3,3,1);

  vtkImageGradient *grad = vtkImageGradient::New();
  grad->SetInput(mag->GetOutput());
  grad->SetDimensionality(3);

  vtkImageShrink3D *shrink = vtkImageShrink3D::New();
  shrink->SetInput(grad->GetOutput());
  shrink->SetShrinkFactors(3,3,1);

  vtkImageDataStreamer *ids = vtkImageDataStreamer::New();
  ids->SetInput(shrink->GetOutput());
  ids->SetNumberofStreamDivisions(20);
  ids->UpdateWholeExtent();

  vtkImageViewer *viewer = vtkImageViewer::New();
```

```
viewer->SetInput(ids->GetOutput());
viewer->SetColorLevel(0);
viewer->SetColorWindow(200);

// interact with data
for (j = 0; j < 10; j++)
  {
  for (i = 1; i < 93; i++)
    {
    viewer->SetZSlice(i);
    viewer->Render();
    }
  }

// Clean up
viewer->Delete();
reader->Delete();
grad->Delete();
shrink->Delete();
mag->Delete();
}
```

There are limits to what can be accomplished with streaming. As mentioned earlier, support for streaming unstructured data is minimal. Many algorithms, such as vtkImageAccumulate, cannot be streamed effectively because every output pixel requires a visit to every input pixcl. (Of course multipass algorithms are possible.) Some algorithms are written assuming that the entire input dataset is available. i.e., they have not been written with streaming in mind (e.g., such as volume rendering in Chapter 6).

## Chapter 11

Interfacing To VTK Data Objects

In this section we provide detailed information describing the interface to the many data objects in VTK. This ranges from datasets, which are processed by the filter objects in visualization pipelines, to data arrays, which are used represent a portion of a dataset (e.g., the scalar data).

To help you understand the relationship of data objects in VTK, refer to the object diagrams in **Figure 14–1** through **Figure 14–4**.

11.1 Data Arrays

Data arrays, implemented in the superclass vtk-DataArray and its many subclasses, are the foundation upon which many of the VTK data objects are built. Data arrays represent contiguous arrays of data in native type (e.g., char, int, float, etc.) and have the ability to manage internal memory by dynamic allocation. Data arrays are commonly used to represent geometry (vtkPoints manages an instance of vtkDataArray under the hood), attribute data (scalars, vectors, normals, tensors, texture coordinates) and field data. Data arrays also provide an interface to their internal data, which is based on a tuple abstraction (refer to **Figure 11–1**).

In the tuple abstraction, vtkDataArray represents data as an array of tuples, each tuple consisting of the same number of components and each of the same native data type. In implementation, the tuples are actually subarrays within a contiguous array of data, as shown in the figure.

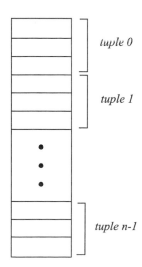

Figure 11–1 Data array structure. In this example, each tuple has three components.

The power of data arrays and the tuple abstraction is that data can be represented in native type, and visualization data can be represented as a tuple. For example, we can represent vector data of native type `float` by creating a vtkFloatArray (a subclass of vtkDataArray) of tuple size (i.e., number of components) equal to 3. In this case, the number of vectors is simply the number of tuples; or alternatively, the number of float values divided by the number of components (for a vector, the number of components is always three).

Methods

The following is a summary of the methods of vtkDataArray. Note that these are the methods required by all subclasses of vtkDataArray; there are several other methods specialized to each subclass. The special methods (which deal mainly with pointers and data specific information) for one subclass, vtkFloatArray, are shown immediately following the vtkDataArray method summary.

`dataArray = MakeObject()`
> Create an instance (`dataArray`) of the same type as the current data array. Also referred to as a "virtual" constructor.

`type = GetDataType()`
> Return the native type of data as an integer token (tokens are defined in `vtkSet-Get.h`). The possible types are VTK_VOID, VTK_BIT, VTK_CHAR, VTK_UNSIGNED_CHAR, VTK_SHORT, VTK_UNSIGNED_SHORT, VTK_INT, VTK_UNSIGNED_INT, VTK_LONG, VTK_UNSIGNED_LONG, VTK_FLOAT, and VTK_DOUBLE.

`SetNumberOfComponents(numComp)`
> Specify the number of components per tuple.

`GetNumberOfComponents()`
> Get the number of components per tuple.

`SetNumberOfTuples(number)`
> Set the number of tuples in the data array. This method allocates storage, and depends on prior invocation of the method SetNumberOfComponents() for proper allocation.

`numTuples = GetNumberOfTuples()`
> Return the number of tuples in the data array.

`tuple = GetTuple(i)`

Return a pointer to an array that represents a particular tuple in the data array. This method is not thread-safe, and data may be cast to a common type (i.e., `float`).

`GetTuple(i, tuple)`

Fill in a user-provided tuple (previously allocated) with data.

`SetTuple(i, tuple)`

Specify the tuple at array location `i`. This method does not do range checking, and is faster than methods that do (e.g., vtkInsertTuple()). You must invoke SetNumberOf-Tuples() prior to inserting data with this method.

`InsertTuple(i, tuple)`

Insert data at the tuple location `i`. This method performs range checking, and will allocate memory if necessary.

`i = InsertNextTuple(tuple)`

Insert data at the end of the data array, and return its position in the array. This method performs range checking, and will allocate memory if necessary.

`c = GetComponent(i, j)`

Get the component value as a `float` at tuple location i and component j (of the ith tuple).

`SetComponent(i, j, c)`

Set the jth component value at tuple location `i`. This method does not perform range checking, you must have previously allocated memory with the method SetNumber-OfTuples().

`InsertComponent(i, j, c)`

Insert the jth component value at tuple location `i`. This method performs range checking and will allocate memory as necessary.

`GetData(tupleMin, tupleMax, compMin, compMax, data)`

Extract a rectangular array of data (into `data`). The array `data` must have been pre-allocated. The rectangle is defined from the minimum and maximum ranges of the components and tuples.

`DeepCopy(dataArray)`

Perform a deep copy of another object. Deep copy means that the data is actually copied, not reference counted.

`ptr = GetVoidPointer(id)`

Return a pointer to the data as a `void *` pointer. This can be used, in conjunction with the method GetDataType(), to cast data to and from the appropriate type.

`Squeeze()`

Reclaim any unused memory the data array may have allocated. This method is typically used when you use Insert() methods and cannot exactly specify the amount of data at initial allocation.

`Reset()`

Modify the data array so it looks empty but retains allocated storage. Useful to avoid excessive allocation and deallocation.

`array = MakeObject()`

Create a data array of the same type as this one.

`range = GetRange(i)`

Return the range (min,max) of ith component. This method is not thread safe.

`GetRange(range, i)`

Fill in the minimum/maxmimum values of ith component in a user-provided array.

`CreateDefaultLookupTable()`

If no lookup table is specified, and a lookup table is needed, then a default table is created.

`SetLookupTable(lut)`

Specifiy a lookup table to use for mapping array values to colors.

`lut = GetLookupTable()`

Return the lookup table to use for mapping array values to colors.

`GetTuples(ids, array)`

Given a list of ids, fill user-provided array with tuples corresponding to those ids. For example, the ids might be the ids defining a cell and the return list is the cell scalars.

The following methods are from vtkFloatArray, which is a subclass of vtkDataArray. Note that there is overlap between the functionality available from the superclass vtkDataArray and its concrete subclasses. The is because the superclass provides some generic functionality useful for quick/compact coding, while the subclasses let you get at the data directly, which can be manipulated via pointer manipulation and/or templated functions.

`v = GetValue(i)`

Return the value at the ith data location in the array.

`SetNumberOfValues(number)`
Set the number of values in the array. This method performs memory allocation.

`SetValue(i, value)`
Set the value at the ith data location in the array. This method requires prior invocation of SetNumberOfValues() or WritePointer(). The method is faster than the insertion methods because no range checking is performed.

`InsertValue(i, f)`
Insert the value at the ith data location in the array. This method perform range checking and allocates memory as necessary.

`id = InsertNextValue(f)`
Insert the value f at the end of the data array, and return its position in the array. This method performs range checking, and will allocate memory if necessary.

`ptr = GetPointer(i)`
Return the pointer to the data array. The pointer is returned from the ith data location (usually i=0 and the method returns the pointer at the beginning of the array).

`ptr = WritePointer(i, number)`
Allocate memory and prepare the array for number direct writes starting at data location i. A pointer to the data starting at location i is returned.

`ptr = GetVoidPointer(id)`
Cast the data pointer to void *.

`SetArray(array, size, save)`
Directly set the data array from an outside source. This method is useful when you are interfacing to data and want to pass the data into VTK's pipeline. The save flag indicates whether the array passed in should be deleted when the data array is destructed. A value of one indicates that VTK should not delete the data array when it is done using it.

11.2 Datasets

Often times the hardest part about writing a filter is interfacing to the VTK data objects. Chances are that as a filter developer, you are intimately familiar with the algorithm. It's learning how to manipulate VTK datasets—reading the input and creating the output—that is the key to writing an efficient, robust, and useful filter. Probably the single most important step in learning how to manipulate datasets is understanding the data model.

Figure 11–2 summarizes the dataset types in VTK. If you're not familiar with these objects, you'll want to read *The Visualization Toolkit* text, and/or spend some quality time with the code to understand the data model. The following paragraphs highlight some of the important features of the data model.

One important aspect of VTK's data model is the relationship of the *structure* and *data attributes* of a dataset. Datasets are a subclass of vtkDataObject. The difference between the two classes is that datasets have topological and geometric structure while data objects represent a general field of data (see the "The Visualization Model" on page 23). The dataset structure consists of the geometric and topological relationship of points and cells to one another. The structure is the framework to which the dataset attributes are attached. The dataset attributes are information (such as scalars, vectors, tensors, normals, texture coordinates, and field data) that is associated with either the geometry (e.g., points) or topology (e.g., cells) of the dataset. When we refer to dataset type, we are actually referring to the structure of the dataset. The data attributes are assumed to be associated with the dataset, and are created and manipulated the same way no matter the type of dataset with which they are associated.

Another important feature of VTK's data model is the relationship of datasets to cells, and whether cells are represented implicitly or explicitly. A cell can be thought of as the atoms that form a dataset. Cells are a topological organization of the dataset points (*x-y-z* positions) into an ordered list, or connectivity array. For example, in a polygonal dataset (vtkPolyData), the polygons are the cells of the dataset, and each polygonal cell is represented as an ordered list of points (i.e., the vertices of the polygon). Some datasets represent points and cells explicitly (e.g., a list of points and cells in vtkPolyData), while others represent the points and cells implicitly (e.g., an image vtkImageData represented by its dimensions, spacing, and origin). Implicit representation means that we do not explicitly store point coordinates or cell connectivity. Instead, this information is derived as necessary. You may wish to refer to **Figure 14–15** to view the cell types found in VTK.

Assuming that you have a thorough understanding of VTK's data model, you'll need to know how to get data from the datasets, and how to create and put data into the datasets. These activities are dependent on the type of dataset—different datasets have different preferred ways to interface to them. Also, datasets can be accessed at different levels of abstraction corresponding to the inheritance hierarchy. For example, to get the coordinates of a point in a vtkPolyData, we can invoke the superclass method vtkDataSet::GetPoint(), or we can retrieve the points array in vtkPolyData with pts=vtkPolyData::GetPoints(), followed by access of the point coordinates pts->GetPoint(). Both approaches are valid, and

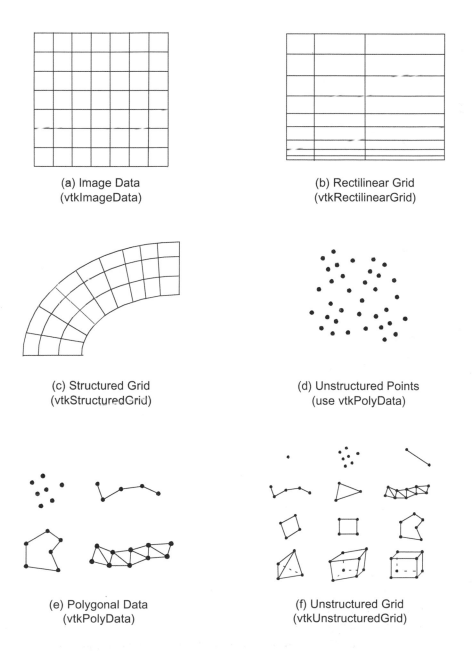

(a) Image Data
(vtkImageData)

(b) Rectilinear Grid
(vtkRectilinearGrid)

(c) Structured Grid
(vtkStructuredGrid)

(d) Unstructured Points
(use vtkPolyData)

(e) Polygonal Data
(vtkPolyData)

(f) Unstructured Grid
(vtkUnstructuredGrid)

Figure 11–2 Dataset types found in **VTK**. Note that unstructured points can be represented by either polygonal data or unstructured grids, so are not explicitly represented in the system.

both are used, depending on the circumstances. As a filter writer, you'll have to determine the correct level of abstraction by which to interface with the datasets.

Note: for the fasted access, you could get the pointer to the points array and then use templated methods to process the data. For example:

```
void *ptr = pts->GetData()->GetVoidPointer(0);
switch (pts->GetData()->GetDataType())
  case VTK_FLOAT:
    float *fptr = static_cast<float*>ptr;
    ...etc...
```

The next sections summarize how to manipulate the various types of datasets. You'll need this information if you're going to write a filter. Once you have understood the interface to the datasets, the actual construction of a graphics filter is relatively straightforward. As you read this material, you may wish to refer to the inheritance hierarchy (**Figure 14–3**). The summary information for each dataset is broken into three parts:

1. a general description of the dataset,

2. methods to create, manipulate, and extract information from the dataset,

3. and one or more examples demonstrating important concepts.

11.3 Interfacing To vtkDataSet

vtkDataSet is an abstract dataset type. Abstract objects provide an API to manipulate objects. Abstract objects cannot be (directly) instantiated; rather, they are used to manipulate concrete subclasses of the abstract object. In practice, abstract objects like vtkDataSet are used to create general filters that can manipulate any type of dataset.

Methods

vtkDataSet provides access methods that all other datasets inherit. This means that the methods described here can also be used by all other datasets since they are subclasses of vtkDataSet. Note that vtkDataSet is an abstract class typically used to refer to an underlying concrete class. Therefore, you must use the MakeObject() method to create an instance of the concrete class. This is almost always followed by the CopyStructure() method, which makes a copy of the geometric and topological structure of the dataset. (You may also wish to copy the dataset attributes, see "Interface To Field and Attribute Data" on page 270 for more information.)

```
dataSet = MakeObject()
```
Create an instance of the same type as the current dataset. Also referred to as a "virtual" constructor.

```
CopyStructure(dataSet)
```
Update the current structure definition (i.e., geometry and topology) with the supplied dataset. Note that copying is done using reference counting.

```
type = GetDataObjectType()
```
Return the type of data object (e.g., vtkDataObject, vtkPolyData, vtkImageData, vtkStructuredPoints, vtkStructuredGrid, vtkRectilinearGrid, or vtkUnstructuredGrid).

```
numPoints = GetNumberOfPoints()
```
Return the number of points in the dataset.

```
numCells = GetNumberOfCells()
```
Return the number of cells in the dataset.

```
x = GetPoint(ptId)
```
Given a point id, return a pointer to the *(x,y,z)* coordinates of the point.

```
GetPoint(ptId,x)
```
Given a point id, copy the *(x,y,z)* coordinates of the point into the array x provided. This is a thread-safe variant of the previous method.

```
cell = GetCell(cellId)
```
Given a cell id, return a pointer to a cell object.

```
GetCell(cellId, genericCell)
```
Given a cell id, return a cell in the user-provided instance of type vtkGenericCell. This is a thread-safe variant of the previous GetCell() method.

```
type = GetCellType(cellId)
```
Return the type of the cell given by cell id. The type is an integer flag defined in the include file vtkCellType.h.

```
GetCellTypes(types)
```
Generate a list of types of cells (supplied in types) that compose the dataset.

```
cells = GetPointCells(ptId)
```
Given a point id, return a list of cells that use this point.

`GetCellPoints(cellId, ptIds)`
Given a cell id, return the point ids (e.g., connectivity list) defining the cell.

`GetCellNeighbors(cellId, ptIds, neighbors)`
Given a cell id and a list of points composing a boundary face or edge of the cell, return the neighbor(s) of that cell sharing the points.

`pointId = FindPoint(x)`
Locate the closest point to the global coordinate x. Return the closest point or `-1` if the point x is outside of the dataset.

`foundCellId = FindCell(x, cell, cellId, tol2, subId, pcoords, weights)`
Given a coordinate value x, an initial search cell defined by `cell` and `cellId`, and a tolerance measure (squared), return the cell id and sub-id of the cell containing the point and its interpolation function weights. The initial search cell (if `cellId>=0`) is used to speed up the search process when the position x is known to be near the cell. If no cell is found, `foundCellId` < 0 is returned.

`cell = FindAndGetCell(x, cell, cellId, tol2, subId, pcoords, weights)`
This is a variation of the previous method (FindCell()) that returns a pointer to the cell instead of the cell id.

`pointData = GetPointData()`
Return a pointer to the object maintaining point attribute data. This includes scalars, vectors, normals, tensors, texture coordinates, and field data.

`cellData = GetCellData()`
Return a pointer to the object maintaining cell attribute data. This includes scalars, vectors, normals, tensors, texture coordinates, and field data.

`bounds = GetBounds()`
Get the bounding box of the dataset. The return value is an array of (xmin, xmax, ymin, ymax, zmin, zmax).

`GetBounds(bounds)`
Get the bounding box of the dataset. The return value is an array of (xmin, xmax, ymin, ymax, zmin, zmax). This is a thread-safe variant of the previous method.

`length = GetLength()`
Return the length of the diagonal of the bounding box of the dataset.

```
center = GetCenter()
```
Get the center of the bounding box of the dataset.

```
GetCenter(center)
```
Get the center of the bounding box of the dataset. (A thread safe variant of the previous method).

```
range = GetScalarRange()
```
A convenience method to return the (minimum, maximum) range of the scalar attribute data associated with the dataset.

```
GetScalarRange(range)
```
A thread-safe variant of the previous method.

```
Squeeze()
```
Reclaim any extra memory used to store data. Typically used after creating and inserting data into the dataset.

Example

Here's a typical example of using the vtkDataSet API. The code fragment is from vtk-ProbeFilter. vtkProbeFilter samples data attribute values from one dataset onto the points of another (the filter has two inputs). Please ignore the references to point data attributes for now; these methods will be explained in "Interface To Field and Attribute Data" on page 270.

```
numPts = input->GetNumberOfPoints();
pd = source->GetPointData();

// Allocate storage for output PointData
outPD = output->GetPointData();
outPD->InterpolateAllocate(pd);

// Use tolerance as a function of size of source data
tol2 = source->GetLength();
tol2 = tol2*tol2 / 1000.0;

// Loop over all input points, interpolating source data
for (ptId=0; ptId < numPts; ptId++)
  {
  // Get the xyz coordinate of the point in the input dataset
  x = input->GetPoint(ptId);
```

```
// Find the cell that contains xyz and get it
cell = source->FindAndGetCell(x,NULL,
                       -1,tol2,subId,pcoords,weights);
if (cell)
   {
   // Interpolate the point data
   outPD->InterpolatePoint(pd,ptId,
                           &(cell->PointIds),weights);
   }
else
   {
   outPD->NullPoint(ptId);
   }
}
delete [] weights;
```

The following example shows how to create a reference-counted copy of a dataset using the vtkDataSet API. Both the variables `newDataSet` and `dataSet` are pointers to vtk-DataSet.

```
newDataSet = dataSet->MakeObject();
newDataSet->CopyStructure(dataSet);
newDataSet->GetPointData()->PassData(
                           dataSet->GetPointData())
newDataSet->GetCellData()->PassData(
                           dataSet->GetCellData())
```

Now that we've covered the abstract API to vtkDataSet, we move to the concrete dataset types. Remember, every concrete subclass inherits the methods of its superclasses, including vtkDataSet.

11.4 Interface To vtkImageData

vtkImageData is a concrete dataset type representing a regular, *x-y-z* axis-aligned array of points. vtkImageData can represent 1D arrays, 2D images, and 3D volumes. Both the geometry and topology of the dataset structure are regular, and both are represented implicitly. A vtkImageData dataset is defined by data dimensions, interpoint spacing, and an origin of the lower-left corner of the dataset. If the dimension of the dataset is 2D, then we call vtkImageData dataset an image, and it is composed of vtkPixel cell types. If the dimension of the dataset is 3D, then we call vtkImageData dataset a volume, and it is composed of vtkVoxel cells.

Methods

`SetDimensions(i, j, k)`
Set the dimensions of the structured points dataset.

`SetDimensions(dim)`
An alternative form of the previous method where `dim` is an array of size 3.

`dims = GetDimensions()`
Return a pointer to an array of size 3 containing i-j-k dimensions of dataset.

`GetDimensions(dims)`
Thread-safe form of previous method.

`SetSpacing(sx, sy, sz)`
Set the spacing of the structured points dataset.

`SetSpacing(spacing)`
An alternative form of the previous method where `spacing` is an array of size 3.

`spacing = GetSpacing()`
Return a pointer to an array of size 3 containing i-j-k dimensions of dataset.

`GetSpacing(spacing)`
Thread-safe form of previous method.

`SetOrigin(x, y, z)`
Set the origin of the structured points dataset.

`SetOrigin(origin)`
An alternative form of the previous method where `origin` is an array of size 3.

`origin = GetOrigin()`
Return a pointer to an array of size 3 containing i-j-k dimensions of dataset.

`GetOrigin(origin)`
Thread-safe form of previous method.

`ComputeStructuredCoordinates(x, ijk, pcoords)`
Given a point x in the 3D modeling coordinate system, determine the structured coordinates i-j-k specifying which cell the point is in, as well as the parametric coordinates inside the cell.

`GetVoxelGradient(i, j, k, scalars, gradient)`
Given a cell specified by i-j-k structured coordinates, and the scalar data for the

structured points dataset, compute the gradient at each of the eight points defining the voxel.

GetPointGradient(i, j, k, scalars, gradient)
> Given a point specified by *i-j-k* structured coordinates, and the scalar data for the structured points dataset, compute the gradient at the point (an array of size 3).

d = GetDataDimension()
> Return the dimensionality of the dataset ranging from (0,3).

pointId = ComputePointId(int ijk[3])
> Given a point specified by *i-j-k* structured coordinates, return the point id.

cellId = ComputeCellId(int ijk[3])
> Given a cell specified by *i-j-k* structured coordinates, return the cell id of the point.

Examples

In this example, which is taken from the filter vtkExtractVOI, we subsample the input data to generate output data. In the initial portion of the filter (not shown), the dimensions, spacing, and origin of the output are determined and then set (shown). We then configure the output and copy the associated point attribute data.

```
output->SetDimensions(outDims);
output->SetSpacing(outAR);
output->SetOrigin(outOrigin);

// If output same as input, just pass data through
//
if ( outDims[0] == dims[0] && outDims[1] == dims[1] &&
outDims[2] == dims[2] &&
rate[0] == 1 && rate[1] == 1 && rate[2] == 1 )
  {
  output->GetPointData()->PassData(input->GetPointData());
  vtkDebugMacro(<<"Passed data through bacause input
                 and output are the same");
  return;
  }

// Allocate necessary objects
//
outPD->CopyAllocate(pd,outSize,outSize);
sliceSize = dims[0]*dims[1];
```

```
// Traverse input data and copy point attributes to output
//
newIdx = 0;
for ( k=voi[4]; k <= voi[5]; k += rate[2] )
  {
  kOffset = k * sliceSize;
  for ( j=voi[2]; j <= voi[3]; j += rate[1] )
    {
    jOffset = j * dims[0];
    for ( i=voi[0]; i <= voi[1]; i += rate[0] )
      {
      idx = i + jOffset + kOffset;
      outPD->CopyData(pd, idx, newIdx++);
      }
    }
  }
```

11.5 Interface To vtkPointSet

vtkPointSet is an abstract superclass for those classes that explicitly represent points (i.e., vtkPolyData, vtkStructuredGrid, vtkUnstructuredGrid). The basic function of vtkPointSet is to implement those vtkDataSet methods that access or manipulate points (e.g., Get-Point() or FindPoint()).

Methods

There are several access methods defined, but most overload vtkDataSet's API. Note that because this object is abstract, there are no direct creation methods. Refer to the vtk-DataSet::MakeObject() creation method (see vtkDataSet "Methods" on page 242 for more information).

```
numPoints = GetNumberOfPoints()
```
Return the number of points in the dataset.

```
points = GetPoints()
```
Return a pointer to an object of type vtkPoints. This class explicitly represents the points in the dataset.

SetPoints(points)

> Specify the explicit point representation for this object. The parameter `points` is an instance of vtkPoints.

Examples

Here's an example of a filter that exercises the vtkPointSet API. The following code is excerpted from vtkWarpVector.

```
inPts = input->GetPoints();
pd = input->GetPointData();
if ( !pd->GetVectors() || !inPts )
  {
  vtkErrorMacro(<<"No input data");
  return;
  }
inVectors = pd->GetVectors();
numPts = inPts->GetNumberOfPoints();
newPts = vtkPoints::New();
newPts->SetNumberOfPoints(numPts);

// Loop over all points, adjusting locations
//
for (ptId=0; ptId < numPts; ptId++)
  {
  x = inPts->GetPoint(ptId);
  v = inVectors->GetTuple(ptId);
  for (i=0; i<3; i++)
    {
    newX[i] = x[i] + this->ScaleFactor * v[i];
    }
  newPts->SetPoint(ptId, newX);
  }
```

The method to focus on is vtkPoint::GetPoints(), which returns a pointer to a vtkPoints instance (`inPts`). Also, notice that we use the invocation vtkPoints::GetPoint() to return the point coordinates of a particular point. We could replace this call with vtkPoint-Set::GetPoint() and achieve the same result.

11.6 Interface To vtkStructuredGrid

vtkStructuredGrid is a concrete dataset that represents information arranged on a topologically regular, but geometrically irregular, array of points. The cells are of type vtkHexahedron (in 3D) and of type vtkQuad (in 2D), and are represented implicitly with the Dimensions instance variable. The points are represented explicitly by the superclass vtkPointSet.

Methods

Most of vtkStructuredGrid's methods are inherited from it superclasses vtkPointSet and vtkDataSet.

```
SetDimensions(i, j, k)
```
Specify the *i-j-k* dimensions of the structured grid. The number of points for the grid, specified by the product $i*j*k$, must match the number of points returned from vtkPointSet::GetNumberOfPoints().

```
SetDimensions(dim)
```
An alternative form of the previous method. Dimensions are specified with an array of three integer values.

```
dims = GetDimensions()
```
Return a pointer to an array of size 3 containing *i-j-k* dimensions of dataset.

```
GetDimensions(dims)
```
Thread-safe form of the previous method.

```
dim = GetDataDimensions()
```
Return the dimension of the dataset, i.e., whether the dataset is 0, 1, 2, or 3-dimensional.

11.7 Interface To vtkRectilinearGrid

Description

vtkRectilinearGrid is a concrete dataset that represents information arranged on a topologically regular, and geometrically semi-regular, array of points. The points are defined by three vectors that contain coordinate values for the *x*, *y*, and *z* axes—thus the points are axis-aligned and only partially represented. The cells that make up vtkRectilinearGrid are implicitly represented and are of type vtkVoxel (3D) or vtkPixel (2D).

Creating a vtkRectilinearGrid requires specifying the dataset dimensions and three arrays defining the coordinates in the *x*, *y*, *z* directions (these arrays are represented by the XCoordinates, YCoordinates, and ZCoordinates instance variables). Make sure that the number of coordinate values is consistent with the dimensions specified.

Methods

The class vtkRectilinearGrid defines several methods beyond the inherited methods from vtkDataSet.

`SetDimensions(i, j, k)`
Set the dimensions of the rectilinear grid dataset. Note that the dimension values in the *x-y-z* directions must match the number of values found in the XCoordinates, YCoordinates, and ZCoordinates arrays.

`SetDimensions(dim)`
An alternative form of the previous method where dim is an array of size 3.

`dims = GetDimensions()`
Return a pointer to an array of size 3 containing *i-j-k* dimensions of dataset.

`GetDimensions(dims)`
Thread-safe form of previous method.

`ComputeStructuredCoordinates(x, ijk, pcoords)`
Given a point in the 3D modeling coordinate system, determine the structured coordinates *i-j-k* specifying which cell the point is in, as well as the parametric coordinates inside the cell.

`GetVoxelGradient(i, j, k, scalars, gradient);`
Given a cell specified by *i-j-k* structured coordinates, and the scalar data for the rectilinear grid dataset, compute the gradient at each of the eight points defining the voxel.

`GetPointGradient(i, j, k, scalars, gradient)`
Given a point specified by *i-j-k* structured coordinates, and the scalar data for the rectilinear grid dataset, compute the gradient at the point (an array of size 3).

```
d = GetDataDimension()
```
Return the dimensionality of the dataset ranging from (0,3).

```
pointId = ComputePointId(int ijk[3])
```
Given a point specified by *i-j-k* structured coordinates, return the point id of the point.

```
cellId = ComputeCellId(int ijk[3])
```
Given a cell specified by *i-j-k* structured coordinates, return the cell id of the point.

```
SetXCoordinates(xcoords)
```
Specify the array of values which define the *x* coordinate values. The array `xcoords` is of type vtkDataArray.

```
SetYCoordinates(ycoords)
```
Specify the array of values which define the *y* coordinate values. The array `ycoords` is of type vtkDataArray.

```
SetZCoordinates(zcoords)
```
Specify the array of values which define the *z* coordinate values.The array `zcoords` is of type vtkDataArray.

11.8 Interface To vtkPolyData

vtkPolyData is a concrete dataset type that represents rendering primitives such as vertices, lines, polygons, and triangle strips. The data is completely unstructured: points are represented in the superclass vtkPointSet, and the cells are represented using four instances of vtkCellArray, which is a connectivity list (**Figure 11–3**). The four vtkCellArrays represent vertices and polyvertices; lines and polylines; triangles, quads, and polygons; and triangle strips, respectively.

Because vtkPolyData is unstructured, cells and points must be explicitly represented. In order to support some of the required methods of its superclass vtkDataSet (mainly topological methods such as GetPointCells() and GetCellNeighbors()), vtkPolyData has a complex internal data structure as shown in **Figure 11–3**. Besides vtkPoints and the vtkCellArrays, the data structure consists of a list of cell types (vtkCellTypes) and cell links (vtkCellLinks). The cell types allows random access into the cells (note that the vtkCellArray cannot support random access) and the cell links supports topological operations by maintaining references to all cells that use a particular vertex (see *The Visualization Tool-*

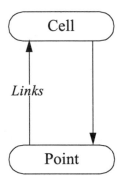

(a) Full unstructured data representation for vtkPolyData and vtkUnstructuredGrid. Cells refer to the points that define them; points refer to the cells that use them. This structure can be used to determine vertex, edge, and face neighbors and other topological information.

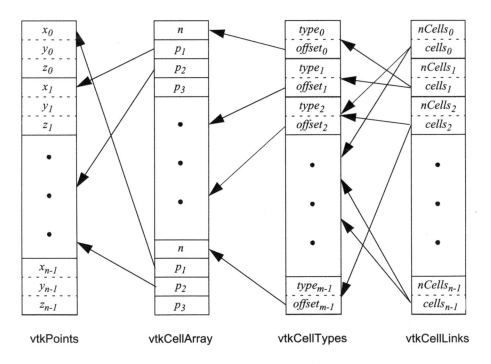

(b) Unstructured data is represented by points (geometry and position in 3D space), a cell array (cell connectivity), cell types (provides random access to cells), and cell links (provides topological information). The cell types and cell links arrays are only constructed if required.

Figure 11–3 Representing unstructured data. This structure is used to represent polygonal and unstructured grid datasets.

kit text for more information). Instances of these two classes vtkCellTypes and vtk-CellLinks are only instantiated if needed. That is, if random access to cells is required vtkCellTypes is instantiated; or if topological information is required, vtkCellLinks is instantiated.

While this structure is fairly complex, the good news is that for the most part the management of the internal structure is taken care of for you. Normally you'll never need to directly manipulate the structure as long as you use vtkDataSet's API to interface the information. In some cases, writing a filter or using some of the vtkPolyData or vtkUn-structuredGrid methods, you may have to explicitly create the cell types and/or cell links arrays using the BuildCells() and BuildLinks() methods. In rare cases you may want to directly manipulate the structure—deleting points or cells, and/or modifying the link array to reflect changing topology. Refer to section "Miscellaneous Interfaces" on page 264 for more information. Examples of code demonstrating the use these complex operators include the classes `Patented/vtkDecimate`, `Graphics/vtkDecimatePro`, and `Graphics/vtkDelaunay2D`.

Methods

The class vtkPolyData is fairly complex, overloading many of the methods inherited from its superclasses vtkDataSet and vtkPointSet. Most of the complexity is due to the definition of vertices, lines, polygons, and triangle strips in separate vtkCellArray's, and special (geometric) methods for operating on the mesh.

`SetVerts (verts)`
> Specify the list of vertices `verts`. The parameter `verts` is an instance of vtkCellArray. Note: the difference between vertices and points are that vertices are rendered, while points are not. Points define cell geometry, vertices represent a cell.

`verts = GetVerts()`
> Get the list of vertices. The list is an instance of vtkCellArray.

`SetLines (lines)`
> Specify the list of lines `lines`. The parameter `lines` is an instance of vtkCellArray.

`lines = GetLines()`
> Get the list of lines. The list is an instance of vtkCellArray.

SetPolys(polys)
> Specify the list of polygons `polys`. The parameter `polys` is an instance of vtkCellArray.

polys = GetPolys()
> Get the list of polygons. The list is an instance of vtkCellArray.

SetStrips(strips)
> Specify the list of triangle strips `strips`. The parameter `strips` is an instance of vtkCellArray.

strips = GetStrips()
> Get the list of triangle strips. The list is an instance of vtkCellArray.

numVerts = GetNumberOfVerts()
> Return the number of vertices.

numLines = GetNumberOfLines()
> Return the number of lines.

numPolys = GetNumberOfPolys()
> Return the number of polygons.

numStrips = GetNumberOfStrips()
> Return the number of triangle strips.

Allocate(numCells, extend)
> Perform initial memory allocation prior to invoking the InsertNextCell() methods (described in next two items). The parameter `numCells` is an estimate of the number of cells to be inserted; `extend` is the size to extend the internal structure (if needed).

cellId = InsertNextCell(type, npts, pts)
> Given a cell type `type`, number of points in the cell `npts`, and an integer list of point ids `pts`, insert a cell and return its cell id. See **Figure 14–15** for a definition of type values. Make sure to invoke Allocate() prior to invoking this method.

cellId = InsertNextCell(type, pts)
> Given a cell type `type` and instance of `vtkIdList`, `pts`, insert a cell and return its cell id. Make sure to invoke Allocate() prior to invoking this method.

Reset()
> Restores this instance of vtkPolyData to its initial condition without releasing allocated memory.

`BuildCells()`

> Build the internal vtkCellTypes array. This allows random access to cells (e.g., Get-Cell() and other special vtkPolyData methods). Normally you don't need to invoke this method unless you are doing specialized operations on vtkPolyData.

`BuildLinks()`

> Build the internal vtkCellLinks array. This enables access to topological information such as neighborhoods (e.g., vertex, edge, face neighbors). Normally you don't need to invoke this method unless you are doing special operations on vtkPolyData.

`GetPointCells(ptId, ncells, cells)`

> Given a point id `ptId`, return the number of cells using the point `ncells`, and an integer array of cell ids that use the point `cells`.

`GetCellEdgeNeighbors(cellId, p1, p2, cellIds)`

> Given a cell `cellId` and two points `p1` and `p2` forming an edge of the cell, fill in a user-supplied list of all cells using the edge (`p1`,`p2`).

`GetCellPoints(cellId, npts, pts)`

> Given a cell `cellId`, return the number of points `npts` and an integer list of point ids which define the cell connectivity. This is a specialized version of the method inherited from vtkUnstructuredGrid superclass' GetCellPoints(npts, ptIds).

`flag = IsTriangle(p1, p2, p3)`

> A special method meant for triangle meshes. Returns a 0/1 flag indicating whether the three points listed (`p1`,`p2`,`p3`) form a triangle in the mesh.

`flag = IsEdge(p1, p2)`

> Returns a 0/1 flag indicating whether the two points listed (`p1`,`p2`) forms a edge in the mesh.

`flag = IsPointUsedByCell(ptId,cellId)`

> Return a 0/1 flag indicating whether a particular point given by `ptId` is used by a particular cell `cellId`.

`ReplaceCell(cellId, npts, pts)`

> Redefine a cell `cellId` with a new connectivity list `pts`. Note that the number of points `npts` must be equal to the original number of points in the cell.

`ReplaceCellPoint(cellId, oldPtId, newPtId)`

> Redefine a cell's connectivity list by replacing one point id (`oldPtId`) with a new point id (`newPtId`).

`ReverseCell(cellId)`

> Reverse the order of the connectivity list definition for the cell `cellId`. For example, if a triangle is defined (p1,p2,p3), after invocation of this method it will be defined by the points (p3,p2,p1).

`DeletePoint(ptId)`

> Delete the point by removing all links from it to using cells. This method does not actually remove the point from the vtkPoints object.

`DeleteCell(cellId)`

> Delete a cell by marking its type as `VTK_NULL_ELEMENT`. This operator only modified the vtkCellTypes array, it does not actually remove the cell's connectivity from the vtkCellArray object.

`ptId = InsertNextLinkedPoint(x, numLinks)`

> If the instance of vtkCellLinks has been built, and you wish to insert a new point into the mesh, use this method. The parameter `numLinks` is the initial size of the list of cells using the point.

`cellId = InsertNextLinkedCell(type, npts, pts)`

> Insert a new cell into the vtkPolyData after the cell links and cell types structures have been built (i.e., BuildCells() and BuildLinks() have been invoked).

`ReplaceLinkedCell(cellId, npts, pts)`

> Replace one linked cell with another cell. Note that `npts` must be the same size for the replaced and replacing cell.

`RemoveCellReference(cellId)`

> Remove all references to the cell `cellId` from the cell links structure. This effectively topologically disconnects the cell from the data structure.

`AddCellReference(cellId)`

> Add references to the cell `cellId` into the cell links structure. That is, the links from all points are modified to reflect the use by the cell `cellId`.

`RemoveReferenceToCell(ptId,cellId)`

> Remove the reference from the links of `ptId` to the cell `cellId`.

`AddReferenceToCell(ptId,cellId)`

> Add a reference to the cell `cellId` into the point `ptId`'s link list.

`ResizeCellList(ptId, size)`

> Resize the link list for the point `ptId` and make it of size `size`.

11.9 Interface To vtkUnstructuredGrid

vtkUnstructuredGrid is a concrete dataset type that represents all possible combinations of VTK cells (i.e., all those shown on **Figure 14–15**). The data is completely unstructured. Points are represented by the superclass vtkPointSet, and cells are represented by a combinations of objects including vtkCellArray, vtkCellTypes, and vtkCellLinks. Typically, these objects (excluding vtkPoints) are used internally and you do not directly manipulate them. Refer to the previous section "Interface To vtkPolyData" on page 253 for additional information about the unstructured data structure in VTK. Also, see "Miscellaneous Interfaces" on page 264 for detailed interface information about vtkCellArray, vtkCellTypes, and vtkCellLinks.

Although vtkUnstructuredGrid and vtkPolyData are similar, there are substantial differences. vtkPolyData can only represent cells of topological dimension 2 or less (i.e., triangle strips, polygons, lines, vertices) while vtkUnstructuredGrid can represent cells of dimension 3 and less. Also, vtkUnstructuredGrid maintains an internal instance of vtkCellTypes to allow random access to its cells. vtkPolyData will instantiate vtkCellTypes only when random access is required. Finally, vtkUnstructuredGrid maintains a single internal instance of vtkCellArray to represent cell connectivity; vtkPolyData maintains four separate arrays corresponding to triangle strips, polygons, lines, and vertices.

Access Methods

`Allocate(numCells, extend)`
> Perform initial memory allocation prior to invoking the InsertNextCell() methods (described in the following two items). The parameter `numCells` is an estimate of the number of cells to be inserted; `extend` is the size to extend the internal structure (if needed).

`cellId = InsertNextCell(type, npts, pts)`
> Given a cell type `type`, number of points in the cell `npts`, and an integer list of point ids `pts`, insert a cell and return its cell id. See **Figure 14–15** for a definition of type values. Make sure to invoke Allocate() prior to invoking this method.

`cellId = InsertNextCell(type, ptIds)`
> Given a cell type `type` and instance of vtkIdList, `ptIds`, insert a cell and return its cell id. Make sure to invoke Allocate() prior to invoking this method.

Reset()
> Restores this instance of vtkUnstructuredGrid to its initial condition without releasing allocated memory.

SetCells(types, cells)
> This is a high performance method that allows you to define a set of cells all at once. You specify an integer list of cell types, `types`, followed by an instance of vtkCellArray.

cells = GetCells()
> Return a pointer to the cell connectivity list. The return value `cells` is of type vtkCellArray.

BuildLinks()
> Build the internal vtkCellLinks array. This enables access to topological information such as neighborhoods (e.g., vertex, edge, face neighbors). Normally you don't need to invoke this method unless you are doing specialized operations on vtkUnstructuredGrid.

GetCellPoints(cellId, npts, pts)
> Given a cell `cellId`, return the number of points `npts` and an integer list of point ids that define the cell connectivity. This is a specialized version of the method inherited from vtkUnstructuredGrid superclass' GetCellPoints(npts, ptIds).

ReplaceCell(cellId, npts, pts)
> Redefine the cell `cellId` with a new connectivity list `pts`. Note that the number of points `npts` must be equal to the original number of points in the cell.

cellId = InsertNextLinkedCell(type, npts, pts)
> Insert a new cell into the vtkUnstructuredGrid after the cell links structure has been built (i.e., the method BuildLinks() has been invoked).

RemoveReferenceToCell(ptId, cellId)
> Remove the reference from the links of `ptId` to the cell `cellId`.

AddReferenceToCell(ptId, cellId)
> Add a reference to the cell `cellId` into the point `ptId`'s link list.

ResizeCellList(ptId, size)
> Resize the link list for the point `ptId` and make it of size `size`.

11.10 Interface To Cells (Subclasses of vtkCell)

Cells are the atoms of datasets. They are used to perform local operations within the dataset such as interpolation, coordinate transformation and searching, and various geometric operations. Cells are often used as a "handle" into a dataset, returning local information necessary to the execution of an algorithm. To obtain a cell from a dataset, the method GetCell(int cellId) is used, and the returned cell can then be processed.

The class vtkCell represents data using an instance of vtkPoints and vtkIdList (representing point coordinates and point ids, respectively). These two instance variables are publicly accessible, one of the few exceptions in VTK where ivars are public. The following methods are available to all subclasses of vtkCell.

type = GetCellType()
> Return the type of the cell as defined in `vtkCellType.h`.

dim = GetCellDimension()
> Return the topological dimensional of the cell (0,1,2, or 3).

order = GetInterpolationOrder()
> Return the interpolation order of the cell. Usually linear (=1).

points = GetPoints()
> Get the point coordinates for the cell.

numPts = GetNumberOfPoints()
> Return the number of points in the cell.

numEdges = GetNumberOfEdges()
> Return the number of edges in the cell.

numFaces = GetNumberOfFaces()
> Return the number of faces in the cell.

ptIds = GetPointIds()
> Return the list of point ids defining the cell

id = GetPointId(ptId)
> For cell point i, return the actual point id.

edge = GetEdge(edgeId)
> Return the edge cell from the `edgeId` of the cell

```
cell = GetFace(faceId)
```
Return the face cell from the `faceId` of the cell.

```
status = CellBoundary(subId, pcoords[3], pts)
```
Given parametric coordinates of a point, return the closest cell boundary, and whether the point is inside or outside of the cell. The cell boundary is defined by a list of points (pts) that specify a face (3D cell), edge (2D cell), or vertex (1D cell). If the return value of the method is != 0, then the point is inside the cell.

```
status = EvaluatePosition(x[3], closestPoint[3], subId,
    pcoords[3], dist2, weights[])
```
Given a point x[3] return inside(=1) or outside(=0) cell; evaluate parametric coordinates, sub-cell id (!=0 only if cell is composite), distance squared of point x[3] to cell (in particular, the sub-cell indicated), closest point on cell to x[3], and interpolation weights in cell. (The number of weights is equal to the number of points defining the cell). Note: on rare occasions a -1 is returned from the method. This means that numerical error has occurred and all data returned from this method should be ignored.

```
EvaluateLocation(subId, pcoords[3], x[3], weights[])
```
Determine global coordinate (x[3]) from subId and parametric coordinates. Also returns interpolation weights. (The number of weights is equal to the number of points in the cell.)

```
Contour(value, cellScalars, locator, verts, lines, polys, inPd,
    outPd, inCd, cellId, outCd)
```
Generate contouring primitives. The scalar list `cellScalars` are scalar values at each cell point. The `locator` is essentially a points list that merges points as they are inserted (i.e., prevents duplicates). Contouring primitives can be vertices, lines, or polygons. It is possible to interpolate point data along the edge by providing input and output point data - if `outPd` is NULL, then no interpolation is performed. Also, if the output cell data (`outCd`) is non-NULL, the cell data from the contoured cell is passed to the generated contouring primitives.

```
Clip(value, cellScalars, locator, connectivity, inPd, outPd, inCd,
    cellId, outCd, insideOut)
```
Cut (or clip) the cell based on the input `cellScalars` and the specified value. The output of the clip operation will be one or more cells of the same topological dimension as the original cell. The flag `insideOut` controls what part of the cell is considered inside - normally cell points whose scalar value is greater than "value" are considered inside. If `insideOut` is on, this is reversed. Also, if the output cell data

is non-NULL, the cell data from the clipped cell is passed to the generated contouring primitives.

status = IntersectWithLine(p1[3], p2[3], tol, t, x[3], pcoords[3], subId)
Intersect with the ray defined by p1 and p2. Return parametric coordinates (both line and cell). A non-zero return value indicates that an intersection has occurred. You can specify a tolerance tol on the intersection operation.

status = Triangulate(index, ptIds, pts)
Generate simplices of the appropriate dimension that approximate the geometry of this cell. 3D cells will generate tetrahedra,; 2D cells triangles; and so on. If triangulation failure occurs, a zero is returned.

Derivatives(subId, pcoords[3], values, dim, derivs)
Compute the derivatives of the values given for this cell.

GetBounds(bounds[6])
Set the $(x_{min}, x_{max}, y_{min}, y_{max}, z_{min}, z_{max})$ bounding box values of the cell.

bounds = GetBounds()
Return a pointer to the bounds of the cell.

length2 = GetLength2()
Return the length squared of the cell (the length is the diagonal of the cell's bounding box).

status = GetParametricCenter(pcoords[3])
Return the parametric coordinates of the center of the cell. If the cell is a composite cell, the particular subId that the center is in is returned.

status = HitBBox(bounds[6], origin[3], dir[3], coord[3], t)
Return non-zero value if cell bounding box is hit by ray starting at origin and in direction of dir. Intersection point and parametric coordinate of intersection are returned (valid intersection when $0 <= t <= 1$).

void ShallowCopy(cell)
Perform shallow (reference counted) copy of the cell.

void DeepCopy(cell)
Perform deep (copy of all data) copy of the cell.

11.11 Miscellaneous Interfaces

We saw earlier that some dataset types required instantiation and manipulation of component objects. For example, vtkStructuredGrid requires the creation of an instance of vtk-Points to define its point locations, and vtkPolyData requires the instantiation of vtkCellArray to define cell connectivity. In this section we describe the interface to these supporting objects. You may want to refer to **Figure 11–3** for additional information describing the relationship of these objects.

vtkPoints

vtkPoints represents *x-y-z* point coordinate information. Instances of vtkPoints are used to explicitly represent points. vtkPoints depends on an internal instance of vtkDataArray, thereby supporting data of different native types (i.e., int, float, etc.) The methods for creating and manipulating vtkPoints are shown below.

num = GetNumberOfPoints()
> Return the number of points in the array.

x = GetPoint(int id)
> Return a pointer to an array of three floats: the *x-y-z* coordinate position. This method is not thread safe.

GetPoint(id, x)
> Given a point is id, fill in a user-provided float array of length 3 with the *x-y-z* coordinate position.

SetNumberOfPoints(number)
> Specify the number of points in the array, allocating memory if necessary. Use this method in conjunction with SetPoint() to put data into the vtkPoints array.

SetPoint(id, x)
> Directly set the point coordinate x at the location id specified. Range checking is not performed and as a result, is faster than the insertion methods. Make sure SetNumberOfPoints() is invoked prior to suing this method.

InsertPoint(id, x)
> Insert the point coordinate x at the location id specified. Range checking is performed and memory allocated as necessary.

`InsertPoint(id, x, y, z)`
> Insert the point coordinate (x,y,z) at the location `id` specified. Range checking is performed and memory allocated as necessary.

`pointId = InsertNextPoint(x)`
> Insert the point coordinate x at the end of the array returning its point id. Range checking is performed and memory allocated as necessary.

`pointId = InsertNextPoint(x, y, z)`
> Insert the point coordinate (x,y,z) at the end of the array returning its point id. Range checking is performed and memory allocated as necessary.

`GetPoints(ptIds, pts)`
> Given a list of points `ptIds`, fill-in a user-provided vtkPoints instance with corresponding coordinate values.

`bounds = GetBounds()`
> Return a pointer to an array of size 6 containing the (x_{min},x_{max}, y_{min},y_{max}, z_{min},z_{max}) bounds of the points. This method id not thread-safe.

`GetBounds(bounds)`
> Fill in a user-provided array of size 6 with the (x_{min},x_{max}, y_{min},y_{max}, z_{min},z_{max}) bounds of the points.

vtkCellArray

vtkCellArray represents the topology (i.e., connectivity) information of cells. The connectivity of a cell is defined by an ordered integer list of point ids. In addition, cells are defined by a `type` flag, indicating what type of cell they are (see **Figure 14–15** for more information about type flags). The methods for creating and manipulating vtkCellArrays are shown below.

`Allocate(size, extend)`
> Perform initial memory allocation prior to invoking the InsertNextCell() methods. The parameter `numCells` is an estimate of the number of cells to be inserted; `extend` is the size to extend the internal structure (if needed).

`Initialize()`
> Change the object to its original state, releasing memory that may have been allocated.

`size = EstimateSize(numCells, PtsPerCell)`

Estimate the size of the data to insert based on the number of cells, and the expected number of points per cell. This method returns an estimate; use it in conjunction with the Allocate() method to obtain initial memory allocation.

`void InitTraversal()`

Initialize the traversal of the connectivity array. Used in conjunction with GetNext-Cell().

`nonEmpty = GetNextCell(npts, pts)`

Get the next cell in the list, returning the number of points `npts` and an integer array of point ids `pts`. If the list is empty, return 0; non-zero otherwise.

`size = GetSize()`

Return the allocated size of the list.

`numEntries = GetNumberOfConnectivityEntries()`

Return the total number of entries in the list. This `size` parameter represents the total number of integer values required to represent the connectivity list.

`GetCell(loc, npts, pts)`

A special method to return the cell at location offset `loc`. This method is typically used by unstructured data for random access into the cell array. Note that `loc` is not the same as a cell id, it is a offset into the cell array.

`cellId = InsertNextCell(cell)`

Insert a cell into the array. The parameter `cell` is of type vtkCell. Return the cell id.

`cellId = InsertNextCell(npts, pts)`

Insert a cell into the array by specifying the number of points `npts` and an integer list of cell ids. Return the cell id.

`cellId = InsertNextCell(pts)`

Insert a cell into the array by supplying an id list (vtkIdList). Return the cell id.

`cellId = InsertNextCell(npts)`

Insert a cell into the cell array by specifying the number of cell points. This method is generally followed by multiple invocations of InsertCellPoint() to define the cell points, and possibly UpdateCellCount() to specify the final number of points.

`InsertCellPoint(id)`

Insert a cell point into the cell array. This method requires prior invocation of Insert-NextCell(npts).

UpdateCellCount (npts)

Specify the final number of points defining a cell after invoking InsertNextCell(npts) and InsertCellPoint(). This method allows you to adjust the number of points after estimating an initial point count with InsertNextCell(npts).

location = GetInsertLocation (npts)

Return the current insertion location in the cell array. The insertion location is used by methods such as InsertNextCell(). The location is an offset into the cell array.

location = GetTraversalLocation (npts)

Return the current traversal location in the cell array. The insertion location is used by methods such as GetCell(). The location is an offset into the cell array.

ReverseCell (loc)

Reverse the order of the connectivity list definition for the cell cellId. For example, if a triangle is defined (p1,p2,p3), after invocation of this method it will be defined by the points (p3,p2,p1).

ReplaceCell (loc, npts, pts)

Redefine the cell at offset location loc with a new connectivity list pts. Note that the number of points npts must be equal to the original number of points in the cell array.

GetMaxCellSize ()

Return the maximum length of any cell in the cell array connectivity list.

ptr = GetPointer ()

Return an integer pointer to the cell array. The structure of the data in the returned data is then number of points in a cell, followed by its connectivity list, which repeats for each cell: (npts, p_0, p_1, p_2, ..., p_{npts-1}; npts, p_0, p_1, p_2, ..., p_{npts-1}, ...).

ptr = WritePointer (ncells, size)

Allocate memory for a cell array with ncells cells and of size specified. The size includes the connectivity entries as well as the count for each cell.

Reset ()

Restore the object to its initial state with the exception that previously allocated memory is not released.

Squeeze ()

Recover any unused space in the array.

vtkCellTypes

The class vtkCellTypes provides random access to cells. Instances of vtkCellTypes are always associated with one or more instances of vtkCellArray, which actually defines the connectivity list for the cells. The information contained in the vtkCellTypes is a type specified (an integer flag as defined in **Figure 14–15**) and a location offset, which an integer value representing offset into the associated vtkCellArray.

`Allocate(size, extend)`
> Perform initial memory allocation prior to invoking the InsertNextCell() methods. The parameter `size` is an estimate of the number of cells to be inserted; `extend` is the size to extend the internal structure (if needed).

`cellId = InsertCell(id, type, loc)`
> Given a cell type `type` and its location offset in an associated vtkCellArray, insert the cell type at the location (`id`) specified and return its cell id.

`cellId = InsertNextCell(type, loc)`
> Given a cell type `type` and its location offset in an associated vtkCellArray, insert the cell type at the end of the array and return its cell id.

`DeleteCell(cellId)`
> Delete a cell by marking its type as VTK_NULL_ELEMENT.

`numTypes = GetNumberOfTypes()`
> Return the number of different types of cells in the vtkCellTypes array. Used to determine whether the array contains a homogeneous set of cells.

`IsType(type)`
> Return 1 if type specified is contained in the vtkCellTypes array, or zero otherwise.

`cellId = InsertNextType(type)`
> Insert the next type into the list.

`type = GetCellType(id)`
> Return the type of the cell give by `id`.

`loc = GetCellLocation(id)`
> Get the offset location into an associated vtkCellArray instance for the cell given by id.

`cell_s = GetCell(id)`
> Return a pointer to a structure containing the cell type and offset location for the given cell `id`.

`Squeeze()`
> Recover any unused space in the array.

`Reset()`
> Restore the object to its initialize state with the exception that previously allocated memory is not released.

vtkCellLinks

The class vtkCellLinks provides topological information describing the use of points by cells. Think of the vtkCellLinks object as a list of lists of cells using a particular point. (See **Figure 11–3**.) This information is used to derive secondary topological information such as face, edge, and vertex neighbors. Instances of vtkCellLinks are always associated with a vtkPoints instance, and access to the cells is through vtkCellTypes and vtkCellArray objects.

`link_s = GetLink(ptId)`
> Return a pointer to a structure containing the number of cells using the point `pointId`, as well as a pointer to a list of cells using the point.

`ncells = GetNcells(pointId)`
> Return the number of cells using the point `pointId`.

`BuildLinks(dataset)`
> Given a pointer to a VTK dataset, build the link topological structure.

`cellList = GetCells(ptId)`
> Return a pointer to the list of cells using the point `ptId`.

`ptId = InsertNextPoint(numLinks)`
> Allocate (if necessary) and insert space for a link at the end of the cell links array.

`InsertNextCellReference(ptId, cellId)`
> Insert a reference to the cell `cellId` for the point `ptId`. This implies that `cellId` uses the point `ptId` in its definition.

`DeletePoint(ptId)`
> Delete the point by removing all links from it to using cells. This method does not actually remove the point from the vtkPoints object.

`RemoveCellReference(cellId, ptId)`
> Remove all references to the cell `cellId` from the point `ptId`'s list of using cells.

`AddCellReference(cellId, ptId)`
> Add a reference to the cell `cellId` to the point `ptId`'s list of using cells.

`ResizeCellList(ptId, size)`
> Allocate (if necessary) and resize the list of cells using the point `ptId` to the size given.

`Squeeze()`
> Recover any unused space in the array.

`Reset()`
> Restore the object to its initial state with the exception that previously allocated memory is not released.

11.12 Interface To Field and Attribute Data

The previous section described how to create, access, and generate the structure of datasets. In this section we describe a class and its methods used to manage the processing of dataset attributes (scalars, vectors, tensors, normals, and texture coordinates) and field data as the filter executes. vtkDataSetAttributes and vtkFieldData are used for this purpose. They provide a number of convenience methods for copying, interpolating, and passing data from a filter's input to its output.

vtkFieldData Methods

As of VTK 4.0, vtkFieldData is the superclass of vtkDataSetAttributes (and therefore of vtkPointData and vtkCellData which inherit from vtkDataSetAttributes). Therefore, all fields and attributes (scalars, vectors, normals, tensors, texture coordinates) are stored in the field data and can be easily interchanged (see "Working With Field Data" on page 194 for more information on manipulating fields). It is now possible to associate a field (vtkDataArray) to, for example, vtkPointData and label it as the active vector array afterwards.

`PassData(fromData)`
> Copy the field data from the input (fromData) to the output. Reference counting is used, and the copy flags (e.g., CopyFieldOn/Off) are used to control which fields are copied.

`num = GetNumberOfArrays()`
> Get the number of arrays currently in the field data.

`array = GetArray(index)`
> Given an index, return the corresponding array.

`array = GetArray(name)`
> Given a name, return the corresponding array.

`AddArray(array)`
> Add a field (vtkDataArray).

`RemoveArray(name)`
> Remove the array with the given name.

`DeepCopy(data)`
> Copy the instance data. Performs a deep copy, which means duplicating allocated memory.

`ShallowCopy(data)`
> Copy the instance data. Performs a shallow copy, which means reference counting underlying data objects.

`Squeeze()`
> Recover an extra space used by the attribute data.

`mtime = GetMTime()`
> Return the modified time of this object by examining its own modified time as well as the modified time of the associated fields (arrays).

`CopyFieldOn/Off(name)`
> These methods are used to control the copying and interpolation of individual fields from the input to the output. If off, the field with the given name is not copied or interpolated.

vtkDataSetAttributes Methods

Recall that there are two types of attributes: those associated with the points of the dataset (vtkPointData) and those associated with the cells of the dataset (vtkCellData). Both of these classes are subclasses of vtkDataSetAttributes (which is a subclass of vtkFieldData) and have nearly identical interfaces The following methods are defined by vtkDataSetAttributes and are common to both vtkPointData and vtkCellData. Remember: all datasets have attribute data (both cell and point), so all datasets' attribute data respond to these methods.

PassData(fromData)
> Copy the attribute data from the input (fromData) to the output attribute data. Reference counting is used, and the copy flags (e.g., CopyScalars) are used to control which attribute data is copied.

CopyAllocate(fromData, size, extend)
> Allocate memory and initialize the copy process. The copy process involves copying data on an item by item basis (e.g., point by point or cell by cell). The initial allocated size of each vtkAttributeData object is given by size, if the objects must be dynamically resized during the copy process, then the objects are extended by extend.

CopyData(fromData, fromId, toId)
> Copy the input attribute data (fromData) at location fromId to location toId in the output attribute data.

InterpolateAllocate(fromData, size, extend)
> Allocate memory and initialize the interpolate process. The interpolation process involves interpolating data across a cell or cell topological feature (e.g., an edge). The initial allocated size of each vtkAttributeData object is given by size, if the objects must be dynamically resized during the interpolate process, then the objects are extended by extend.

InterpolatePoint(fromData, toId, Ids, weights)
> Interpolate from the dataset attributes given (fromData) to the point specified (toId). The interpolation is performed by summing the product of the attribute values given at each point in the list Ids with the interpolation weights provided.

InterpolateEdge(fromData, toId, id1, id2, t)
> Similar to the previous method, except that the interpolation is performed between id1 and id2 using the parametric coordinate t.

`DeepCopy(data)`
    Copy the instance data. Performs a deep copy, which means duplicating allocated memory.

`ShallowCopy(data)`
    Copy the instance data. Performs a shallow copy, which means reference counting underlying data objects.

`Squeeze()`
    Recover an extra space used by the attribute data.

`mtime = GetMTime()`
    Return the modified time of this object by examining its own modified time as well as the modified time of the associated attribute data.

`SetScalars(scalars)`
    Specify the scalar (vtkDataArray) attribute data.

`scalars = GetScalars()`
    Retrieve the scalar (vtkDataArray) attribute data.

`SetVectors(vectors)`
    Specify the vector (vtkDataArray) attribute data.

`vectors = GetVectors()`
    Retrieve the vector (vtkDataArray) attribute data.

`SetTensors(tensors)`
    Specify the tensor (vtkDataArray) attribute data.

`tensors = GetTensors()`
    Retrieve the tensor (vtkDataArray) attribute data

`SetNormals(normals)`
    Specify the normal (vtkDataArray) attribute data.

`normals = GetNormals()`
    Retrieve the normal (vtkDataArray) attribute data.

`SetTCoords(tcoords)`
    Specify the texture coordinate (vtkDataArray) attribute data.

`tcoords = GetTCoords()`
    Retrieve the texture coordinate (vtkDataArray) attribute data.

`CopyScalarsOn/Off()`

These methods are used to control the copying and interpolation of scalar data from the input to the output. If off, scalar data is not copied or interpolated.

`CopyVectorsOn/Off()`

These methods are used to control the copying and interpolation of vector data from the input to the output. If off, vector data is not copied or interpolated.

`CopyTensorsOn/Off()`

These methods are used to control the copying and interpolation of tensor data from the input to the output. If off, tensor data is not copied or interpolated.

`CopyNormalsOn/Off()`

These methods are used to control the copying and interpolation of normal data from the input to the output. If off, normal data is not copied or interpolated.

`CopyTCoordsOn/Off()`

These methods are used to control the copying and interpolation of texture coordinate data from the input to the output. If off, texture coordinate data is not copied or interpolated.

`CopyAllOn/Off()`

These convenience methods set all the copy flags on or off at the same time.

## Chapter 12

How To Write A Process Object

This section describes how to create your own process object in VTK. Process objects are objects that ingest data (sources), operate on data to generate new data (filters), and interface the data to graphics systems and/or other systems (mappers). (Process objects are also referred to generically as filters.) You may want to review "The Visualization Model" on page 23 for information about the graphics pipeline.

12.1 Overview

If you have an algorithm or process that you wish to implement as a VTK filter, there are several issues to consider.

1. Is the object to be a source, filter, or mapper? Does it ingest data and/or generate data?

2. What type (i.e., dataset type) does it accept as input? What type of dataset does it generate (if any)? This information will help you decide what superclass to derive your filter from.

3. How many inputs and outputs does it have? Multiple inputs and/or outputs often require special treatment since convenience superclasses often do not exist. For example, you may have to write methods similar to SetInput() or GetOutput() to accept extra inputs or retrieve the extra outputs.

4. Is the process object to be written for generality or for performance? High-performing filters are often much faster but are usually limited in the type of data they can accept. General filters treat a variety of data and are therefore of wider applicability.

5. Is there a similar object in the system that can serve as a superclass or be expanded to accommodate the new functionality? It's best to try and consolidate similar functionality, if appropriate.

There are several other basic concepts that we address in the following sections.

Never Modify Input Data

One of the most important guidelines for any filter writer is to never modify the input to the filter. The reason for this is simple: the proper execution of the pipeline requires that filters create and modify their own output. Remember, other filters may be using the input data as well; if you modify a filters input, you can be potentially corrupt the data with respect to other filters that use it, or the filter that created it.

Reference Count Data

If the input data to a filter is sent to the output of the filter unchanged, make sure that you use reference counting. Do not copy data, the memory cost can be quite high for large visualization data. Typically, if you use Get__() and Set__() methods to get and set data, reference counting is taken care of for you. You also may wish to use specialized methods for passing data through a filter, see "Interface To Field and Attribute Data" on page 270 for more information.

Use Debug Macros

Filters should provide debugging information when the object's Debug flag is set. This is conveniently done using VTK's debug macros defined in `VTK/Common/vtkSetGet.h`. At a minimum, a filter should report the initiation of execution similar to the following (from `VTK/Graphics/vtkContourFilter.cxx`):

```
vtkDebugMacro(<< "Executing contour filter");
```

You may also wish to provide other information as the filter executes, for example, a summary of execution (again from `vtkContourFilter.cxx`):

```
vtkDebugMacro(<<"Created: "
          << newPts->GetNumberOfPoints() << " points, "
          << newVerts->GetNumberOfCells() << " verts, "
          << newLines->GetNumberOfCells() << " lines, "
          << newPolys->GetNumberOfCells() << " triangles");
```

Do not place debugging macros in the inner portions of a loop, since the macro invokes an `if` check that may affect performance. Also, if debugging is turned on in an inner loop, too much information will be output to be meaningfully interpreted.

Reclaim/Delete Allocated Memory

One common mistake that filter writers make is introducing memory leaks or using excessive memory. Memory leaks can be avoided by pairing New() and Delete() methods for all VTK objects, and `new` and `delete` methods for all native or non-VTK objects. (See "Standard Methods: Creating and Deleting Objects" on page 205.)

Another way to reduce memory usage is to use the Squeeze() methods that all data objects support. This method reclaims excess memory that an object may be using. Use the Squeeze() method whenever the size of the data object can only be estimated.

Modified Time

One of the trickiest parts of writing a filter is making sure that its modified time is properly managed. As you may recall, modified time is an internal time stamp that each object maintains in response to changes in its internal state. Typically, modified time changes when a Set__() method is invoked. For example, the method vtkTubeFilter::SetNumberOfSides(num) causes the vtkTubeFilter's modified time to change when this method is invoked, as long as num is different than the tube filter's original instance variable value.

Normally, the modified time of a filter is maintained without requiring intervention. For example, if you use the vtkSet/Get macros defined in `VTK/Common/vtkSetGet.h` to get and set instance variable values, modified time is properly managed, and the inherited method vtkObject::GetMTime() returns the correct value. However, if you define your own Set__() methods, or include methods that modify the internal state of the object, you will have to invoke Modified() (i.e., change the internal modified time) on the filter as appropriate. And, if your object definition includes references to other objects, the correct modified time of the filter includes both the filter and objects it depends on. This requires overloading the GetMTime() method.

vtkCutter is an example of a filter demonstrating this behavior. This filter makes reference to another object, (i.e., the CutFunction), an instance of vtkImplicitFunction. When the implicit function definition changes, we expect the cutter to reexecute. Thus, the GetMTime() method of the filter must reflect this by considering the modified time of the implicit function, and the GetMTime() method inherited from its superclass vtkObject must be overloaded. The implementation of vtkCutter::GetMTime() method is as follows. It's actually more complicated than suggested here because vtkCutter depends on two other objects: vtkLocator and vtkContourValues as shown.

```
unsigned long vtkCutter::GetMTime()
{
  unsigned long mTime=this->vtkDataSetFilter::GetMTime();
  unsigned long
      contourValuesMTime=this->ContourValues->GetMTime();
  unsigned long time;

  mTime = ( contourValuesMTime > mTime ?
                              contourValuesMTime : mTime );
  if ( this->CutFunction != NULL )
    {
    time = this->CutFunction->GetMTime();
    mTime = ( time > mTime ? time : mTime );
    }
  if ( this->Locator != NULL )
    {
    time = this->Locator->GetMTime();
    mTime = ( time > mTime ? time : mTime );
    }
  return mTime;
}
```

The class vtkLocator is used to merge coincident points as the filter executes; while vtkContourValues is a helper class used to generate contour values for those functions using isosurfacing as part of their execution process. The GetMTime() method must check all objects that vtkCutter depends on, returning the largest modified time it finds.

Although the use of modified time and the implicit execution model of the VTK visualization pipeline is simple, there is one common source of confusion. That is, you must distinguish between a filter's modified time and its dependency on the data stream. Remember, filters will execute either when they are modified (the modified time changes), or the input to the filter changes (dependency on data stream). Modified time only reflects changes to a filter or dependencies on other objects independent of the data stream.

ProgressEvent and AbortExecute

The ProgressEvent is invoked at regular intervals during the execution of a source, filter, or mapper object (i.e., any process object). Progress user methods typically perform such functions as updating an application user interface (e.g., imagine manipulating a progress bar in the GUI). (See "General Guidelines for GUI Interaction" on page 305 and "User Methods, Observers, and Commands" on page 28 for more information.)

A progress user method is created by invoking AddObserver() with an event type of vtk-Command::ProgressEvent. When the progress method is invoked, the filter also sets the current progress value (a decimal fraction between (0,1) retrieved with the GetProgress() method). The progress method can be used in combination with the vtkProcessObject's invocation of StartEvent and EndEvent. For example, Examples/Tutorial/Step2 shows how to use these methods. Here's a code fragment to show how it works.

```
vtkDecimatePro deci
    deci AddObserver StartEvent {StartProgress deci "Decimating..."}
    deci AddObserver ProgressEvent {ShowProgress deci "Decimating..."}
    deci AddObserver EndEvent EndProgress
```

Not all filters invoke ProgressEvents or invoke them infrequently (depending on the filter implementation). Also, the progress value may not be a true measure of the actual work done by the filter. It is difficult to measure progress in some filters and/or the filter implementor will often choose to update the filter at key points in the algorithm (e.g., after building internal data structures, reading in a piece of data, etc.).

Related to progress methods is the concept of a flag that is used to stop execution of a filter. This flag, defined in vtkProcessObject, is called the AbortExecute flag. When set, some filters will terminate their execution, sending to their output some portion of the result of their execution (maybe even nothing). Typically, the flag is set during invocation of a ProgressEvent and is used to prematurely terminate execution of a filter when it is taking too long or the application is attempting to keep up with user input events. Not all filters support the AbortExecute flag. Check the source code to be sure which ones support the flag. (Most do, and those that don't will in the near future.)

An example use of progress user methods and the abort flag is shown in the following code fragment taken from VTK/Graphics/vtkDecimatePro.cxx:

```
for ( ptId=0; ptId < npts && !abort ; ptId++ )
  {
  if ( ! (ptId % 10000) )
    {
    vtkDebugMacro(<<"Inserting vertex #" << ptId);
    this->UpdateProgress (0.25*ptId/npts);//25% inserting
    if (this->GetAbortExecute())
      {
      abort = 1;
      break;
      }
    }
  }
```

```
this->Insert(ptId);
}
```

Note that the filter implementor made some arbitrary decisions: the progress methods are invoked every 10,000 points; and the portion of the Execute() method shown is assumed to take approximately 25% of the total execution time. Also, some debug output is combined with the execution of the progress method, as well as a status check on the abort flag. This points out an important guideline: as a filter implementor you do not want to invoke progress methods too often because they can affect overall performance.

12.2 How To Write A Graphics Filter

In "Interfacing To VTK Data Objects" on page 235 we dealt at length with the methods used to create, manipulate, and access VTK datasets and other data objects. With this background, the actual procedure to write a filter is relatively straightforward. The idea is simple: we access information from the input dataset, configure the output dataset, and implement in the body of the filter a method that generates data and sends it to the output. However, many complications can creep in due to multiple inputs and/or outputs, instance variables referenced by the filter, unusual combinations of input and output data, and the desire to stream data.

The instructions written here assume that you'll be implementing the filter in C++. However, you may want to investigate writing a programmable filter, which lets you implement filters in other languages and at run-time (i.e., no compiling, linking, or rebuilding libraries required). See "Programmable Filters" on page 292 for more information.

Overview

Besides the general considerations outlined in the "Overview" on page 275, you must make several design decisions when writing a filter in the graphics pipeline.

1. which superclass to derive from,

2. how to properly manage modified time including overloading the GetMTime() method and invoking Modified(), as appropriate,

3. whether to overload methods defined by the pipeline execution process,

4. creation of an Execute() method,

5. whether to support Progress() and Abort() methods,

6. and any instance variables, structures, or methods required by the filter implementation.

The proper derivation from a superclass is a function of whether the filter is a source, filter, or mapper object; how many inputs and outputs the class has; and the type(s) of input and output data (see "The Visualization Model" on page 23 for more information about sources, filters, and mappers). Many objects require only a single input and output, these can derive much of their implementation from the convenience superclasses provided by VTK, and do not need to overload the pipeline execution or GetMTime() methods. These classes we call simple filters and are described in "Simple Filters" on page 281. Filters that are not simple filters are termed complex filters and are described in "Complex Filters and Pipeline Execution" on page 286.

Simple Filters

Simple filters are filters that manifest typical behavior. This means that they have one input and/or output, support common combinations of input and output data types, and do not require overloading the GetMTime() method. If you are writing a simple filter, generally all you'll need to do is follow the coding conventions outlined in Chapter 9 "Contributing Code" on page 201, create an Execute() method and any other supporting methods or functions internal to the filter. The most difficult task you'll face (for simple filters) is finding the correct superclass to inherit from. Of course, the algorithm may be difficult to implement as well.

Here are some candidate abstract superclasses to inherit from. These classes provide control of input and output, as well as the appropriate Update() method. Typically the choice of superclass is made from the type of input/output data, and the type of process object (source, filter, mapper).

If you are writing a source object, consider deriving from these classes. The abstract superclasses are used by both reader and procedural source objects.

- vtkPolyDataSource — read data from a file or procedurally generate vtkPolyData

- vtkStructuredPointsSource — read data from a file and or procedurally generate vtkStructuredPoints

- vtkRectilinearGridSource — read data from a file and or procedurally generate vtkRectilinearGrid

- vtkStructuredGridSource — read data from a file and or procedurally generate vtkStructuredGrid

- vtkUnstructuredGridSource — read data from a file and or procedurally generate vtkUnstructuredGrid

If you are writing a filter object, consider deriving from the classes listed in the following. The names of these abstract classes clearly identify the input and output data types of the filter.

- vtkDataSetToPolyDataFilter

- vtkDataSetToStructuredGridFilter

- vtkDataSetToStructuredPointsFilter

- vtkDataSetToUnstructuredGridFilter

- vtkPolyDataToPolyDataFilter

- vtkRectilinearGridToPolyDataFilter

- vtkStructuredGridToPolyDataFilter

- vtkStructuredGridToStructuredGridFilter

- vtkStructuredPointsToPolyDataFilter

- vtkStructuredPointsToUnstructuredGridFilter

If you are writing a mapper object, consider deriving from the classes listed in the following. Mappers generally are not simple process objects, with the exceptions of writers. And even these require writing a WriteData() method as well as a SetInput() method. You'll also have to provide instance variables to handle output file names, and methods to manipulate them.

- vtkWriter — specify abstract interface for writer objects

Once you've chosen the correct superclass, you'll want to implement the Execute() method. The execute method should access the appropriate input data, perform error checking if necessary, implement an algorithm (i.e., generate data objects), and send the data objects to the output.

Here's a full example from vtkShrinkFilter. vtkShrinkFilter shrinks cells towards their geometric center. It takes generic vtkDataSet for input and generate vtkUnstructuredGrid as output. Thus we can subclass from the abstract superclass vtkDataSetToUnstructuredGridFilter as shown in the following (from VTK/Graphics/vtkShrinkFilter.h):

```
#ifndef __vtkShrinkFilter_h
#define __vtkShrinkFilter_h

#include "vtkDataSetToUnstructuredGridFilter.h"

class VTK_GRAPHICS_EXPORT vtkShrinkFilter : public
                          vtkDataSetToUnstructuredGridFilter
{
public:
  static vtkShrinkFilter *New();
  vtkTypeMacro(vtkShrinkFilter,
                    vtkDataSetToUnstructuredGridFilter);
  void PrintSelf(ostream& os, vtkIndent indent);
  // Description:
  // Set the fraction of shrink for each cell.
  vtkSetClampMacro(ShrinkFactor,float,0.0,1.0);
  // Description:
  // Get the fraction of shrink for each cell.
  vtkGetMacro(ShrinkFactor,float);
protected:
  vtkShrinkFilter();
  ~vtkShrinkFilter() {};

  void Execute();
  float ShrinkFactor;

private:
  vtkShrinkFilter(const vtkShrinkFilter&);
  void operator=(const vtkShrinkFilter&);
};
#endif
```

To complete the definition of the class, we need only to implement the PrintSelf() and Execute() methods. The Execute() method (excerpted from the VTK/Graphics/vtkShrinkFilter.cxx file) is shown in the following. (Note: VTK_GRAPHICS_EXPORT is a #define macro that is used by some compilers to export symbols.)

```
void vtkShrinkFilter::Execute()
```

```
{
vtkPoints *newPts;
  int i, j, cellId, numCells, numPts;
  int oldId, newId, numIds;
  float center[3], *p, pt[3];
  vtkPointData *pd, *outPD;;
  vtkIdList *ptIds, *newPtIds;
  vtkDataSet *input= this->GetInput();
  vtkUnstructuredGrid *output = this->GetOutput();
```

We continue by accessing the input data and performing error checking. Note the use of the debug macro:

```
vtkDebugMacro(<<"Shrinking cells");
numCells=input->GetNumberOfCells();
numPts = input->GetNumberOfPoints();
if (numCells < 1 || numPts < 1)
  {
  vtkErrorMacro(<<"No data to shrink!");
  return;
  }
```

The input and output to the filter is guaranteed to be non-NULL in the Execute() method. Next, we instantiate and allocate some data objects.

```
ptIds = vtkIdList::New();
ptIds->Allocate(VTK_CELL_SIZE);
newPtIds = vtkIdList::New();
newPtIds->Allocate(VTK_CELL_SIZE);

output->Allocate(numCells);
newPts = vtkPoints::New();
newPts->Allocate(numPts*8,numPts);
pd = input->GetPointData();
outPD = output->GetPointData();
outPD->CopyAllocate(pd,numPts*8,numPts);
```

We've estimated the size of the allocated object (i.e., numPts*8) because we don't know the exact size of the resulting output data (or at least we don't want to do the work necessary to find the exact size). Next, we implement the algorithm proper (shrink cells towards their center). If any of these data object methods are unfamiliar to you, see "Interfacing To VTK Data Objects" on page 235.

```
for (cellId=0; cellId < numCells; cellId++)
```

```
{
input->GetCellPoints(cellId,ptIds);
numIds = ptIds->GetNumberOfIds();
// get the center of the cell
center[0] = center[1] = center[2] = 0.0;
for (i=0; i < numIds; i++)
  {
  p = input->GetPoint(ptIds->GetId(i));
  for (j=0; j < 3; j++) center[j] += p[j];
  }
for (j=0; j<3; j++) center[j] /= numIds;
// Create new points and cells
newPtIds->Reset();
for (i=0; i < numIds; i++)
  {
  p = input->GetPoint(ptIds->GetId(i));
  for (j=0; j < 3; j++)
    pt[j] = center[j] + this->ShrinkFactor*(p[j] -
                                         center[j]);
  oldId = ptIds->GetId(i);
  newId = newPts->InsertNextPoint(pt);
  newPtIds->InsertId(i,newId);
  outPD->CopyData(pd, oldId, newId);
  }
output->InsertNextCell(input->GetCellType(cellId),
                       newPtIds);
}
```

Finally, we pass through any cell attribute data (because the cells didn't change, only their defining points), set the point coordinates data, and use the Squeeze() method to reclaim memory. Also, we use the Delete() method on the points. (In this case the points don't actually get deleted because their reference count is non-zero. The output data references them.)

```
output->GetCellData()->PassData(input->GetCellData());
output->SetPoints(newPts);
output->Squeeze();
newPts->Delete();
ptIds->Delete();
newPtIds->Delete();
newPts->Delete();
}
```

Complex Filters and Pipeline Execution

Complex filters are non-simple filters that cannot derive their implementation from one of the convenience classes listed in "Simple Filters" on page 281. Typically these classes have more than one input and/or output, have unusual combinations of input and output data, and/or need to overload methods defined in the pipeline execution process. Creating a complex filter means that you'll have to create methods to set the input, define internal data objects (and methods to access them) to represent the output, and/or you'll have to overload one or more methods defined in "The Execution Process" on page 219.

The best place to begin this discussion is to look at what a simple filter does. A simple filter like vtkShrinkPolyData derives from the superclass vtkPolyDataToPolyDataFilter. This class in turn derives from the superclasses vtkPolyDataSource, vtkSource, and vtkProcessObject. These classes perform the following functions.

- vtkProcessObject are expected to invoke the StartEvent, ProgressEvent, and EndEvent events; so it defines and interfaces with the AbortExecute and Progress instance variables. It also defines the Inputs instance variable, which is a list of inputs to the filter. There are also special methods for setting and managing the inputs.

- vtkSource defines the API for and implements the pipeline execution process; and interfaces with the vtkDataObject ReleaseData flags. It also creates the protected instance variable Outputs, which is a list of outputs of the filter. The execution time of the filter is tracked with the InformationTime instance variable.

- vtkPolyDataSource defines the GetOutput() method as a method that returns a pointer to a vtkPolyData.

- vtkPolyDataToPolyDataFilter defines the SetInput() method to accept a pointer to vtkPolyData.

- And finally, vtkShrinkPolyData overloads the Execute() method to actually do something useful.

Hopefully it's a little clearer why filters with multiple inputs and/or outputs, or with unusual combinations of input and output types, require special treatment. As you can see, there are several assumptions about the number of inputs and the combination of input and output. If you do wish to write a complex filter, what you need to do is provide the functionality contained in this combination of objects. The best way to see how it's done is to look at an example. We'll look at the class vtkExtractVectorComponents.

The functionality of the class vtkExtractVectorComponents is to extract the *x-y-z* vector components of the input vector field into three separate outputs, one for each component. The structure of each output is the same, but the scalar data is changed. The class header file looks like the following (VTK/Graphics/vtkExtractVectorComponents.h).

```
#ifndef __vtkExtractVectorComponents_h
#define __vtkExtractVectorComponents_h
#include "vtkSource.h"
#include "vtkDataSet.h"

class VTK_GRAPHICS_EXPORT vtkExtractVectorComponents :
                  public vtkSource
{
public:
  static vtkExtractVectorComponents *New();
  vtkTypeMacro(vtkExtractVectorComponents,vtkSource);
  void PrintSelf(ostream& os, vtkIndent indent);

  virtual void SetInput(vtkDataSet *input);
  vtkDataSet *GetInput();

  vtkDataSet *GetVxComponent();
  vtkDataSet *GetVyComponent();
  vtkDataSet *GetVzComponent();
  vtkDataSet *GetOutput(int i=0);

  vtkSetMacro(ExtractToFieldData, int);
  vtkGetMacro(ExtractToFieldData, int);
  vtkBooleanMacro(ExtractToFieldData, int);

protected:
  vtkExtractVectorComponents();
  ~vtkExtractVectorComponents();

  void Execute();
  int ExtractToFieldData;

private:
  vtkExtractVectorComponents(const vtkExtractVectorComponents&);
  void operator=(const vtkExtractVectorComponents&);

};
#endif
```

This example demonstrates several important concepts. First, notice that we're inheriting from vtkSource, since no convenience superclass is available. And second, we have to define SetInput() and several methods to get the output of the filter (i.e., GetVxComponent(), GetVyComponent(), GetVzComponent(), and GetOutput()).

The SetInput() method is most instructive:

```
void vtkExtractVectorComponents::SetInput(vtkDataSet *input)
{
  if (this->NumberOfInputs > 0 && this->Inputs[0] == input )
    {
    return;
    }
  this->vtkProcessObject::SetNthInput(0, input);
  if ( input == NULL )
    {
    return;
    }
  if (this->NumberOfOutputs < 3)
    {
    this->SetNthOutput(0,input->MakeObject());
    this->Outputs[0]->Delete();
    this->SetNthOutput(1,input->MakeObject());
    this->Outputs[1]->Delete();
    this->SetNthOutput(2,input->MakeObject());
    this->Outputs[2]->Delete();
    return;
    }
  // since the input has changed we might need to create a new output
  if (strcmp(this->Outputs[0]->GetClassName(),
                                     input->GetClassName()))
    {
    this->SetNthOutput(0,input->MakeObject());
    this->Outputs[0]->Delete();
    this->SetNthOutput(1,input->MakeObject());
    this->Outputs[1]->Delete();
    this->SetNthOutput(2,input->MakeObject());
    this->Outputs[2]->Delete();
    vtkWarningMacro(<<" a new output had to be created since the input type
changed.");
    }
}
```

As you can see, the filter takes advantage of superclass methods to set the inputs and outputs. One of the unusual behaviors of this filter is that setting the input causes the outputs (there are three) to be generated. The MakeObject() method is used, which is called a virtual constructor because it creates an object as the same type as the invoking object.

Abstract Graphics Filters

There are a number of VTK filters that generate abstract dataset output types such as vtkDataSet or vtkPointSet. Since abstract dataset types cannot be instantiated (due to the presence of pure virtual functions), you may be wondering how this is possible, or why such filters are even useful. The answers are that 1) we make a reference-counted copy of the input dataset's structure and place it in the output, and 2) many filters manipulate attribute data (e.g., scalars or vectors) and do not modify the dataset structure. Thus, filters that can pass the structure through (independent of input type) and modify or generate attribute data are valuable additions to the toolkit.

There are two superclasses to use if you want to create abstract graphics filters. These are

* vtkDataSetToDataSetFilter — input any dataset type and output the same dataset type, and

* vtkPointSetToPointSetFilter — input any dataset of type vtkPointSet (i.e., datasets that explicitly represent their points) and output a vtkPointSet.

Writing filters of this type are quite simple as shown in the following example. Here we'll show how vtkElevationFilter is implemented, a subclass of vtkDataSetToDataSetFilter. The header .h file is as follows (and is found in Graphics/vtkElevationFilter.h).

```
class VTK_GRAPHICS_EXPORT vtkElevationFilter : public
                                    vtkDataSetToDataSetFilter
{
public:
  static vtkElevationFilter *New();
  vtkTypeMacro(vtkElevationFilter,vtkDataSetToDataSetFilter);
  void PrintSelf(ostream& os, vtkIndent indent);

  // Description:
  // Define one end of the line (small scalar values).
  vtkSetVector3Macro(LowPoint,float);
  vtkGetVectorMacro(LowPoint,float,3);
```

```
  // Description:
  // Define other end of the line (large scalar values).
  vtkSetVector3Macro(HighPoint,float);
  vtkGetVectorMacro(HighPoint,float,3);

  // Description:
  // Specify range to map scalars into.
  vtkSetVector2Macro(ScalarRange,float);
  vtkGetVectorMacro(ScalarRange,float,2);
protected:
  vtkElevationFilter();
  ~vtkElevationFilter() {};

  void Execute();
  float LowPoint[3];
  float HighPoint[3];
  float ScalarRange[2];

private:
  vtkElevationFilter(const vtkElevationFilter&); //not implemented
  void operator=(const vtkElevationFilter&); //not implemented
};
```

Note that we only have to implement the usual class methods, as well as the Execute()
method. The body of the Execute() method appears as follows.

```
void vtkElevationFilter::Execute()
{
  int i, j, numPts;
  vtkFloatArray *newScalars;
  float l, *x, s, v[3];
  float diffVector[3], diffScalar;
  vtkDataSet *input = this->GetInput();

  // Initialize
  vtkDebugMacro(<<"Generating elevation scalars!");

  // First, copy the input to the output as a starting point
  this->GetOutput()->CopyStructure( input );
  if ( ((numPts=input->GetNumberOfPoints()) < 1) )
    {
    vtkErrorMacro(<< "No input!");
    return;
    }
```

```
// Allocate
newScalars = vtkFloatArray::New();
newScalars->SetNumberOfTuples(numPts);

// Set up 1D parametric system
bounds = input->GetBounds();
for (i=0; i<3; i++)
    {diffVector[i] = this->HighPoint[i] - this->LowPoint[i];}
if ( (l = vtkMath::Dot(diffVector,diffVector)) == 0.0)
  {
  vtkErrorMacro(<< this << ": Bad vector, using (0,0,1)\n");
  diffVector[0] = diffVector[1] = 0.0; diffVector[2] = 1.0;
  l = 1.0;
  }

// Compute parametric coordinate and map into scalar range
diffScalar = this->ScalarRange[1] - this->ScalarRange[0];
for (i=0; i<numPts; i++)
  {
  if ( ! (i % 10000) )
    {
    this->UpdateProgress ((float)i/numPts);
    if (this->GetAbortExecute())
      {
      break;
      }
    }
  x = input->GetPoint(i);
  for (j=0; j<3; j++)
    {
    v[j] = x[j] - this->LowPoint[j];
    }
  s = vtkMath::Dot(v,diffVector) / l;
  s = (s < 0.0 ? 0.0 : s > 1.0 ? 1.0 : s);
  newScalars->SetValue(i,this->ScalarRange[0]+s*diffScalar);
  }
// Update output
  this->GetOutput()->GetPointData()->CopyScalarsOff();
  this->GetOutput()->GetPointData()->PassData(input->GetPointData());
  this->GetOutput()->GetCellData()->PassData(input->GetCellData());
  newScalars->SetName("Elevation");
  this->GetOutput()->GetPointData()->SetScalars(newScalars);
  newScalars->Delete();
}
```

Note that the filter only computes scalar data and then passes it to the output. The actual generation of the output structure is done using the CopyStructure() method. This method makes a reference-counted copy of the input data topological/geometric structure.

vtkPointSetToPointSetFilter works in a similar fashion, except that the point coordinates are modified or generated and sent to the output. See vtkTransformFilter if you'd like to see a concrete example of vtkPointSetToPointSetFilter.

If you desire to write a filter that modifies attribute data, or modifies point positions without changing the number of points or cells, these abstract filters should be used.

Programmable Filters

An alternative to developing a filter in C++ is to use programmable process objects. These objects allow you to create a function that is invoked during the execution of the process object (i.e., during the Execute() method). The advantage of programmable filters is that you do not have to rebuild the VTK libraries, or even use C++. In fact, you can use the supported interpreted languages Tcl, Java, and Python to create a filter!

Programmable sources and filters are process objects that enable you to create new filters at run-time. There is no need to create a C++ class or rebuild object libraries. Programmable objects take care of the overhead of hooking into the visualization pipeline (i.e., managing modified time checking, properly invoking the Update() and Execute() methods, and providing methods for setting input and/or getting filter output), requiring only that you write the body of the filter's Execute() method.

The new objects are vtkProgrammableSource, vtkProgrammableFilter, and vtkProgrammableAttributeDataFilter. vtkProgrammableSource is a source object that supports and can generate an output of any of the VTK dataset types. vtkProgrammableFilter allows you to set input and retrieve output of any dataset type (e.g., GetPolyDataOutput()). The filter vtkProgrammableAttributeDataFilter allows one or more inputs of the same or different types, and can generate an output of any dataset type.

An example will clarify the application of these filters. This excerpted code is from VTK/ Examples/Modelling/Tcl/expCos.tcl.

```
vtkProgrammableFilter besselF
   besselF SetInput [transF GetOutput]
   besselF SetExecuteMethod bessel
```

```
proc bessel {} {
    set input [besselF GetPolyDataInput]
    set numPts [$input GetNumberOfPoints]
    vtkPoints newPts
    vtkFloatArray derivs
    for {set i 0} {$i < $numPts} {incr i} {
        set x [$input GetPoint $i]
        set x0 [lindex $x 0]
        set x1 [lindex $x 1]
        set r [expr sqrt($x0*$x0 + $x1*$x1)]
        set x2 [expr exp(-$r) * cos(10.0*$r)]
        set deriv [expr -exp(-$r) * (cos(10.0*$r) + 10.0*sin(10.0*$r))]
        newPts InsertPoint $i $x0 $x1 $x2
        eval derivs InsertValue $i $deriv
    }
    [besselF GetPolyDataOutput] CopyStructure $input
    [besselF GetPolyDataOutput] SetPoints newPts
    [[besselF GetPolyDataOutput] GetPointData] SetScalars derivs
    newPts Delete; #reference counting - it's ok
    derivs Delete
}

# warp plane
vtkWarpScalar warp
    warp SetInput [besselF GetPolyDataOutput]
    warp XYPlaneOn
    warp SetScaleFactor 0.5
```

This example instantiates a vtkProgrammableFilter and then the Tcl proc bessel() serves as the function to compute the Bessel functions and derivatives. Note that bessel() works directly with the output of the filter obtained with the method GetPoly-DataOutput(). This is because the output of besselF can be of any VTK supported dataset type, and we have to indicate to objects working with the output which type to use.

Overloading Pipeline Execution Methods

Probably the most difficult task you can undertake when writing a new filter is to overload one or more of the pipeline execution methods described in "The Execution Process" on page 219. The difficulty of this task lies in understanding how the pipeline execution process works. Do this only if you need your filter to stream.

There are relatively few methods that you need to consider overloading. These methods are described here, with a general description of what you must do and how they affect the execution process.

ExecuteInformation(). This method gives the subclass a chance to configure the output. For example, the WholeExtent, spacing, origin, scalar type, and number of components can be modified. By default, vtkSource simply copies the basic extent information from the first input to all its outputs. If this is not the correct behavior for your filter, then you must overload this method.

EnlargeOutputUpdateExtents(). This method gives the subclass a chance to indicate that it will provide more data than required for the output. This can happen, for example, when the filter can only produce the whole output. Although this is being called for a specific output which is passed in as a parameter, the source may need to enlarge all outputs. The default implementation is to do nothing (do not enlarge the output). If your filter requires the output update extent to be larger than requested (for example, your filter can only produce the whole output), then you must overload this method.

ComputeInputUpdateExtents(). This method gives the subclass a chance to request a larger extent on the inputs. This is necessary when, for example, a filter requires more data at the "internal" boundaries to produce the boundary values—such as an image filter that derives a new pixel value by applying some operation to a kernel of surrounding input values. The default implementation is to require the entire input in order to generate the output. This is overridden, for example, in vtkImageToImageFilter to request the same input update extent as the output update extent. It is redefined again in vtkImageSpatial-Filter in order to request a slightly larger input update extent due to the additional pixels required according to the kernel size of the filter. You should carefully look up the hierarchy for your filter too see if the default implementation is the correct one.

Execute(). The Execute() method almost always has to be overloaded. The major exception to this rule are imaging filters (see "How To Write An Imaging Filter" on page 295). Most imaging filters are derived from vtkImageToImageFilter that implements an Execute() method that in turn invokes ThreadedExecute(). ThreadedExecute() is a special version of Execute() that supports multithreading.

12.3 How To Write An Imaging Filter

The graphics pipeline and the imaging pipeline share a unified execution process with the release of version VTK 3.1 and later. If you understand the pipeline execution process described previously, you understand it for imaging filters as well. However, there remains several important difference between imaging filters and other types of filters.

1. Imaging algorithms are typically local in nature, and the input and output type is the same.

2. Most imaging filters only process scalar data attributes (of one to four components). Other information, such as vectors, normals, etc., is not processed.

3. Imaging filters use templated functions to implement their Execute() method.

4. Almost all imaging filters have been written to stream data.

5. Almost all imaging filters are multi-threaded.

These difference gives rise to code different than we have seen previously. The code is typically more complex (e.g., multithreaded and streaming) but better performing (localized algorithms and templated functions).

Implementing An Imaging Filter

To demonstrate creation of an imaging filter, let's consider an image filter that performs a simple scale and shift operation on each input pixel. The filter—vtkImageShiftScale—is a subclass of vtkImageToImageFilter, as are most imaging filters.

```
#include "vtkImageToImageFilter.h"
class VTK_IMAGING_EXPORT vtkImageShiftScale : public vtkImageToImageFilter
{
public:
  static vtkImageShiftScale *New();
  vtkTypeMacro(vtkImageShiftScale,vtkImageToImageFilter);
  void PrintSelf(ostream& os, vtkIndent indent);

  // Description:
  // Set/Get the shift value.
  vtkSetMacro(Shift,float);
  vtkGetMacro(Shift,float);

  // Description:
```

```
  // Set/Get the scale value.
  vtkSetMacro(Scale,float);
  vtkGetMacro(Scale,float);

  // Description:
  // Set the desired output scalar type. The result of the shift
  // and scale operations is cast to the type specified.
  vtkSetMacro(OutputScalarType, int);
  vtkGetMacro(OutputScalarType, int);
  void SetOutputScalarTypeToDouble()
    {this->SetOutputScalarType(VTK_DOUBLE);}
  void SetOutputScalarTypeToFloat()
    {this->SetOutputScalarType(VTK_FLOAT);}
  void SetOutputScalarTypeToLong()
    {this->SetOutputScalarType(VTK_LONG);}
  void SetOutputScalarTypeToUnsignedLong()
    {this->SetOutputScalarType(VTK_UNSIGNED_LONG);};
  void SetOutputScalarTypeToInt()
    {this->SetOutputScalarType(VTK_INT);}
  void SetOutputScalarTypeToUnsignedInt()
    {this->SetOutputScalarType(VTK_UNSIGNED_INT);}
  void SetOutputScalarTypeToShort()
    {this->SetOutputScalarType(VTK_SHORT);}
  void SetOutputScalarTypeToUnsignedShort()
    {this->SetOutputScalarType(VTK_UNSIGNED_SHORT);}
  void SetOutputScalarTypeToChar()
    {this->SetOutputScalarType(VTK_CHAR);}
  void SetOutputScalarTypeToUnsignedChar()
    {this->SetOutputScalarType(VTK_UNSIGNED_CHAR);}

  // Description:
  // When the ClampOverflow flag is on, the data is thresholded so
  // that the output value does not exceed the max or min of the
  // data type. By defualt, ClampOverflow is off.
  vtkSetMacro(ClampOverflow, int);
  vtkGetMacro(ClampOverflow, int);
  vtkBooleanMacro(ClampOverflow, int);

protected:
  vtkImageShiftScale();
  ~vtkImageShiftScale() {};

  float Shift;
  float Scale;
  int OutputScalarType;
  int ClampOverflow;
```

```
  void ExecuteInformation(vtkImageData *inData,
                          vtkImageData *outData);
  void ExecuteInformation(){
      this->vtkImageToImageFilter::ExecuteInformation();};
  void ThreadedExecute(vtkImageData *inData, vtkImageData *outData,
      int extent[6], int id);

private:
  vtkImageShiftScale(const vtkImageShiftScale&);
  void operator=(const vtkImageShiftScale&);
};
```

As you can see from the header file, this class is implemented similar to other VTK filter classes. The major differences are the extra protected methods ExecuteInformation() and ThreadedExecute(). These methods are required to support streaming and multithreading, as we'll see shortly.

Inside the C++ file VTK/Imaging/vtkImageShiftScale.cxx, there are some other important differences from what we've seen before. First, the ThreadedExecute() method:

```
void vtkImageShiftScale::ThreadedExecute(vtkImageData *inData,
 vtkImageData *outData,
 int outExt[6], int id)
{
  void *inPtr = inData->GetScalarPointerForExtent(outExt);

  switch (inData->GetScalarType())
    {
    vtkTemplateMacro6(vtkImageShiftScaleExecute1, this,
                      inData, (VTK_TT*)(inPtr), outData, outExt, id);
    default:
      vtkErrorMacro(<< "Execute: Unknown ScalarType");
      return;
    }
}
```

The ThreadedExecute() method is actually invoked by the superclass vtkImageToImage-Filter in its Execute() method. ThreadedExecute() is meant to process the filter in multiple threads (i.e., a shared memory implementation).

An important feature of this code is the switch statement. This code switches on the input data type and invokes a templated function. This templated function, vtkImageShiftScaleExecute1(), in turn invokes another templated function vtkImage-ShiftScaleExecute() (switched on output data type). The double template is necessary because the input and output types may be different.

```
template <class T>
static void vtkImageShiftScaleExecute1(vtkImageShiftScale *self,
      vtkImageData *inData, T *inPtr,
      vtkImageData *outData,
      int outExt[6], int id)
{
  void *outPtr = outData->GetScalarPointerForExtent(outExt);

  switch (outData->GetScalarType())
    {
vtkTemplateMacro7(vtkImageShiftScaleExecute, self, inData, inPtr,
      outData, (VTK_TT*)(outPtr),outExt, id);
    default:
    vtkGenericWarningMacro("Execute: Unknown input ScalarType");
    return;
    }
}
```

The templated functions used here are not declared in the header file since it will only be used by this one class. It is not a class method either, just a simple C++ templated function. It should always appear in the source code before it is used. So typically the templated execute function comes right before the Execute() (or ThreadedExecute()) method discussed previously. The template keyword before the function definition indicates that it is a templated function, and that it is templated over the type T. You can think of T as a string that gets replaced by int, short, float, etc. at compile time. Notice that T is used as the data type for inPtr and outPtr. Since this is a function instead of a method, it doesn't have access to the this pointer and its associated instance variables. So we pass in the this pointer as a variable called self. Self can then be used to access the values of the class as is done on the first line of the function. Here we obtain the value of Scale from the instance and place it into a local variable called scale. The remaining lines declare some local variables that will be used to move through the data.

Finally, the actual work of the algorithm is performed in the vtkImageShiftScaleExecute() method: Note the use of AbortExecute instance variable and the UpdateProgress() method as we saw in previous implementations of filters.

```
template <class IT, class OT>
static void vtkImageShiftScaleExecute(vtkImageShiftScale *self,
```

```
      vtkImageData *inData, IT *inPtr,
      vtkImageData *outData, OT *outPtr,
      int outExt[6], int id)
{
  float typeMin, typeMax, val;
  int clamp;
  float shift = self->GetShift();
  float scale = self->GetScale();
  int idxR, idxY, idxZ;
  int maxY, maxZ;
  int inIncX, inIncY, inIncZ;
  int outIncX, outIncY, outIncZ;
  int rowLength;
  unsigned long count = 0;
  unsigned long target;
  // for preventing overflow
  typeMin = outData->GetScalarTypeMin();
  typeMax = outData->GetScalarTypeMax();
  clamp = self->GetClampOverflow();

  // find the region to loop over
  rowLength = (outExt[1] - outExt[0]+1)*
              inData->GetNumberOfScalarComponents();
  maxY = outExt[3] - outExt[2];
  maxZ = outExt[5] - outExt[4];
  target = (unsigned long)((maxZ+1)*(maxY+1)/50.0);
  target++;

  // Get increments to march through data
  inData->GetContinuousIncrements(outExt, inIncX, inIncY, inIncZ);
  outData->GetContinuousIncrements(outExt, outIncX,
                                   outIncY, outIncZ);
  // Loop through ouput pixels
  for (idxZ = 0; idxZ <= maxZ; idxZ++)
    {
    for (idxY = 0; !self->AbortExecute && idxY <= maxY; idxY++)
      {
      if (!id)
        {
        if (!(count%target))
          {
          self->UpdateProgress(count/(50.0*target));
          }
        count++;
        }
      if (clamp) // put the test for clamp to avoid the innermost loop
```

```
    {
    for (idxR = 0; idxR < rowLength; idxR++)
      {
      // Pixel operation
      val = ((float)(*inPtr) + shift) * scale;
      if (val > typeMax)
        {
        val = typeMax;
        }
      if (val < typeMin)
        {
        val = typeMin;
        }
      *outPtr = (OT)(val);
      outPtr++;
      inPtr++;
      }

  else
    {
    for (idxR = 0; idxR < rowLength; idxR++)
      {
      // Pixel operation
      *outPtr = (OT)(((float)(*inPtr) + shift) * scale);
      outPtr++;
      inPtr++;
      }
    }
  outPtr += outIncY;
  inPtr += inIncY;
  }
outPtr += outIncZ;
inPtr += inIncZ;
  }
}
```

Initially we computes the length of a row of pixels. This is just the number of pixels multiplied by the number of components per pixel (e.g. three for RGB, one for grayscale). The second and third lines compute the y and z dimensions. The next two lines get the continuous increments for the inData and outData. There are two types of increments that can be used to step through the data: regular and continuous. The regular increments specify how many units in memory you need to move in order to navigate though the image. The regular x increment specifies how many units to move to go from one pixel to the next. The regular y and z increments do the same for rows and slices, respectively. For example, if `foo` was a pointer to a pixel in the image and you wanted to get the value of the pixel one row above `foo`, it would be `* (foo + yInc)`.

Continuous increments are retrieved using the following method invocations:

```
inData->GetContinuousIncrements(outExt, inIncX, inIncY, inIncZ);
outData->GetContinuousIncrements(outExt, outIncX,
                                 outIncY, outIncZ);
```

Continuous increments are a convenience that makes it easier to loop through the data in the current extent. The *y* and *z* continuous increments are the only values that get used. The *y* continuous increment indicates how many units in memory must be moved past to get from the end of one row to the beginning of the next. If the UpdateExtent matches the data's Extent that value will be zero. But when working on a sub-portion of the image, it may have a non zero value. The same idea applies for the *z* continuous increment. It indicates how many units in memory need to be skipped to get from the end of one slice to the beginning of the next.

Another important feature of this filter is that the ExecuteInformation() is overloaded.

```
void vtkImageShiftScale::ExecuteInformation(vtkImageData *inData,
    vtkImageData *outData)
{
  this->vtkImageToImageFilter::ExecuteInformation(inData,
                                                  outData );
  if (this->OutputScalarType != -1)
    {
    outData->SetScalarType(this->OutputScalarType);
    }
}
```

The purpose of this method is to overload the default superclass behavior that sets the output type to the same as the input type. In this particular filter, the user may optionally set the output type to a different type, hence the need for the method overload.

We hope that this chapter helps you write your own filters in VTK. You may wish to build on the information given here by studying the source code in other filters. It's particularly helpful if you can find an algorithm that you understand, and then look to see how VTK implements it.

## Chapter 13

Integrating With The Windowing System

At some point in your use of VTK you will probably want to modify the default interaction behavior (in vtkRenderWindowInteractor) or add a graphical user interface (GUI) to your VTK based application. This section will explain how to do this for many common user interface toolkits. Up-to-date and new examples might be found in the VTK/Examples/GUI source directory. Begin by reading the next section on changing interaction style. Then (to embed VTK into a GUI) look at "General Guidelines for GUI Interaction" on page 305 and then only the subsection appropriate to your user interface. If you are using a GUI other than the ones covered here, read the subsections that are similar to your GUI.

13.1 vtkRenderWindow Interaction Style

The class vtkRenderWindowInteractor is used to capture mouse and keyboard events in the render window, and then dispatches these events to another class—the interactor style. Therefore, to add a new style of interaction to VTK, you need to derive a new class from vtkInteractorStyle. For example, the class vtkInteractorStyleTrackball implements the trackball style interaction described in "vtkRenderWindowInteractor" on page 48. vtkInteractorStyleJoystickActor or vtkInteractorStyleJoystickCamera implements the joystick interaction style described in the same section. Another option is to use the class vtkInteractorStyleUser. This class allows users to define a new interactor style without subclassing.

Basically, the way this works as follows. vtkRenderWindowInteractor intercepts events occurring in the vtkRenderWindow with which it is associated. Recall that on instantiation, vtkRenderWindowInteractor actually instantiates a device/windowing-specific implementation—either vtkXRenderWindowInteractor (Unix) or vtkWin32RenderWindowInteractor (Windows). The event intercepts are enabled when the vtkRenderWindowInteractor::Start() method is called. These events are in turn forwarded to the vtkRenderWindowInteractor::InteractorStyle instance. The interactor style processes the events as appropriate.

Here is a list of the available interactor styles with a brief description of what each one does.

- vtkInteractorStyleJoystickActor — implements joystick style for actor manipulation.
- vtkInteractorStyleJoystickCamera — implements joystick style for camera manipulation.
- vtkInteractorStyleTrackballActor — implements trackball style for actor manipulation.
- vtkInteractorStyleTrackballCamera — implements trackball style for camera manipulation.
- vtkInteractorStyleSwitch — manages the switching between trackball and joystick mode, and camera and object (actor) mode. It does this by intersection keystrokes and internally switching to one of the modes listed above.
- vtkInteractorStyleTrackball — a legacy class, this interactor style combines both the actor and camera trackball modes.
- vtkInteractorStyleFlight — a special class that allows the user to "fly-through" complex scenes.
- vtkInteractorStyleImage — a specially designed interactor style for images. This class performs window and level adjustment via mouse motion, as well as pan and dolly constrained to the x-y plane.
- vtkInteractorStyleUnicam — single button camera manipulation. Rotation, zoom, and pan can all be performed with the one mouse button.

If one of these interactor style does not suit your needs, you can create your own interactor style. To create your own, subclass from vtkInteractorStyle. This means overriding the following methods (as described in vtkInteractorStyle.h):

```
// Description:
// Generic event bindings must be overridden in subclasses
virtual void OnMouseMove    (int ctrl, int shift, int X, int Y);
virtual void OnLeftButtonDown(int ctrl, int shift, int X, int Y);
virtual void OnLeftButtonUp  (int ctrl, int shift, int X, int Y);
virtual void OnMiddleButtonDown(int ctrl, int shift, int X, int Y);
virtual void OnMiddleButtonUp  (int ctrl, int shift, int X, int Y);
virtual void OnRightButtonDown(int ctrl, int shift, int X, int Y);
virtual void OnRightButtonUp  (int ctrl, int shift, int X, int Y);
```

```
// Description:
// OnChar implements keyboard functions, but subclasses can override this
// behavior
virtual void OnChar(int ctrl, int shift, char keycode, int repeatcount);
virtual void OnKeyDown(int ctrl, int shift, char keycode,
                       int repeatcount);
virtual void OnKeyUp(int ctrl, int shift, char keycode, int repeatcount);
virtual void OnKeyPress(int ctrl, int shift, char keycode,
                        char *keysym, int repeatcount);
virtual void OnKeyRelease(int ctrl, int shift, char keycode,
                          char *keysym,int repeatcount);

// Description:
// These are more esoteric events, but are useful in some cases.
virtual void OnConfigure(int width, int height);
virtual void OnEnter(int ctrl, int shift, int x, int y);
virtual void OnLeave(int ctrl, int shift, int x, int y);
```

Then to use the interactor style, associate it with vtkRenderWindowInteractor via the SetInteractorStyle() method.

13.2 General Guidelines for GUI Interaction

For the most part VTK has been designed to isolate the functional objects from the user interface. This has been done for portability and flexibility. But sooner or later you will need to create a user interface, so we have provided a number of hooks to help in this process. These hooks are called *user methods* and they are discussed in Chapter 3 (see "User Methods, Observers, and Commands" on page 28). Recall that the essence of user methods in VTK is that any class can invoke an event. If an observer is registered with the class that invokes the event, then an instance of vtkCommand is executed which is the implementation of the callback. There are a variety of events invoked by different VTK classes that come in handy when developing a user interface. A partial list of the more useful events is provided below.

All filters (subclasses of vtkProcessObject) invoke these events:

- StartEvent
- EndEvent
- ProgressEvent

Figure 13–1 GUI feedback as a result of invoking the StartEvent, ProgressEvent, and EndEvent as a filter executes.

The class vtkRenderWindow invokes these events (while rendering):

- AbortCheckEvent

The classes (and subclasses of) vtkActor, vtkVolume, and vtkPicker invoke these events while picking:

- PickEvent
- StartPickEvent (available to vtkPicker only)
- EndPickEvent (available to vtkPicker only)

The class vtkRenderWindowInteractor invokes these events:

- StartPickEvent — while picking
- EndPickEvent — while picking
- UserEvent — in response to "u" keypress in the render window
- ExitEvent — in response to the "e" keypress in the render window

And don't forget that you can define your own vtkInteractorStyle with its own set of special callbacks.

The StartEvent, EndEvent, and ProgressEvent invocations can be used to provide feedback to the user on what the application is doing and how much longer it will take. All filters invoke the StartEvent and EndEvent events if they have been defined. ProgressEvents are supported by imaging filters, some readers, and many (but not all) of the visualization filters. The AbortCheckEvent can be used to allow the user to interrupt a render that is taking too long (requires the use of vtkLODActors). The PickEvents and virtual methods can be used to override the default VTK interactor behavior so that you can create your own custom interaction style.

To help you get started, consider the following two examples that incorporate user methods. Both are written in Tcl but can be easily converted to other languages. The first defines a proc that catches the ProgressEvent to display the progress of the vtkImageShrink3D filter. It then catches the EndEvent to update the display to indicate the processing is complete (**Figure 13–1**).

```
# Halves the size of the image in the x, y and z dimensions.
package require vtk

# Image pipeline
vtkImageReader reader
    reader SetDataByteOrderToLittleEndian
    reader SetDataExtent 0 255 0 255 1 93
    reader SetFilePrefix $env(VTK DATA ROOT)/Data/headsq/quarter
    reader SetDataMask 0x7fff

vtkImageShrink3D shrink
    shrink SetInput [reader GetOutput]
    shrink SetShrinkFactors 2 2 2
    shrink AddObserver ProgressEvent {
      .text configure -text \
              "Completed [expr [shrink GetProgress]*100.0] percent"
      update
    }
    shrink AddObserver EndEvent {
     .text configure -text "Completed Processing"
     update
    }

button .run -text "Execute" -command{
    shrink Modified
    shrink Update
}
label .text -text "Waiting to Process"
pack .run .text
```

For pipelines consisting of multiple filters, each filter could provide an indication of its progress. You can also create generic Tcl procs (rather than define them in-line as here) and assign them to different filter.

Figure 13–2 Aborting the rendering process. This is used to improve overall interaction with VTK. Rendering can be aborted whenever an event is pending. Make sure that you are using immediate mode rendering.

The second example makes use of the AbortCheckEvent to interrupt a long render if a mouse event is pending. Most of the code is typical VTK code. The critical changes are that you must use instances of vtkLODActor, which is currently only supported under OpenGL, it is best if you turn on GlobalImmediateModeRendering() since the abort method cannot be invoked in the middle of display list processing, and finally you must add a few lines of code to process the abort check. In this example we define a simple procedure called TkCheckAbort which invokes the GetEventPending() method of vtkRenderWindow and then sets the AbortRender instance variable to 1 if an event is pending. The resolution of the mace model has been dramatically increased (**Figure 13–2**(left)) so that you can see the effects of using the AbortRender logic. Feel free to adjust the resolution of the sphere to suit your system. If everything is working properly then you should be able to quickly rotate and then zoom without waiting for the full resolution sphere to render in between the two actions (**Figure 13–2**(right)).

```
package require vtk
package require vtkinteraction
# this is a tcl version of the Mace example

# Create the RenderWindow, Renderer and both Actors
# vtkRenderer ren1
vtkRenderWindow renWin
    renWin AddRenderer ren1
vtkRenderWindowInteractor iren
    iren SetRenderWindow renWin

# create a sphere source and actor
vtkSphereSource sphere
    sphere SetThetaResolution 40
    sphere SetPhiResolution 40
vtkPolyDataMapper    sphereMapper
    sphereMapper SetInput [sphere GetOutput]
```

```
    sphereMapper GlobalImmediateModeRenderingOn
vtkLODActor sphereActor
    sphereActor SetMapper sphereMapper

# create the spikes using a cone source and the sphere source
#
  vtkConeSource cone
vtkGlyph3D glyph
    glyph SetInput [sphere GetOutput]
    glyph SetSource [cone GetOutput]
    glyph SetVectorModeToUseNormal
    glyph SetScaleModeToScaleByVector
    glyph SetScaleFactor 0.25
vtkPolyDataMapper spikeMapper
    spikeMapper SetInput [glyph GetOutput]
vtkLODActor spikeActor
    spikeActor SetMapper spikeMapper

# Add the actors to the renderer, set the background and size ren1 AddActor
sphereActor
ren1 AddActor spikeActor
ren1 SetBackground 0.1 0.2 0.4
renWin SetSize 300 300

# render the image
iren AddObserver UserEvent {wm deiconify .vtkInteract}

set cam1 [ren1 GetActiveCamera]
$cam1 Zoom 1.4
iren Initialize

proc TkCheckAbort {} {
   if {[renWin GetEventPending] != 0} {renWin SetAbortRender 1}
}
renWin AddObserver AbortCheckMethod TkCheckAbort

# prevent the tk window from appearing; start the event loop
wm withdraw .
```

13.3 X Windows, Xt, and Motif

Figure 13–3 Simple Motif application using VTK.

Most traditional UNIX based applications use either Xt or Motif as their widget set. Many of those that don't directly use Xt or Motif end up using Xt at a lower level. There are two common ways to integrate VTK into your Xt (or Motif) based application. These examples might be found in the VTK/Examples/GUI/Motif source directory. First we will look at an example where the VTK rendering window and the application UI are in separate windows (**Figure 13–3**). This helps avoid some problems that can occur if VTK and the UI do not use the same X visual. Both windows will use the same X event loop and the UI can own that loop as is typical. Consider the following example application. It draws a mace into a VTK render window and then creates a Motif push button and associated callback in a separate window.

```
// include OS specific include file to mix in X code
#include "vtkRenderWindow.h"
#include "vtkXRenderWindowInteractor.h"
#include "vtkSphereSource.h"
#include "vtkConeSource.h"
#include "vtkGlyph3D.h"
#include "vtkPolyDataMapper.h"
#include <Xm/PushB.h>
void quit_cb(Widget,XtPointer,XtPointer);
main (int argc, char *argv[])
{
  // X window stuff
  XtAppContext app;
  Widget toplevel, button;
  Display *display;
  // VTK stuff
  vtkRenderWindow *renWin;
  vtkRenderer *ren1;
  vtkActor *sphereActor1, *spikeActor1;
  vtkSphereSource *sphere;
  vtkConeSource *cone;
  vtkGlyph3D *glyph;
  vtkPolyDataMapper *sphereMapper, *spikeMapper;
  vtkXRenderWindowInteractor *iren;
```

The first section of code simply includes the required header files and prototypes a simple callback called quit_cb. Then we enter the main function and declare some standard X/ Motif variables. Then we declare the VTK objects we will need as before. The only significant change here is the use of the vtkXRenderWindowInteractor subclass instead of the typical vtkRenderWindowInteractor. This subclass allows us to access some additional methods specifically designed for X windows.

```
renWin = vtkXRenderWindow::New();
ren1 = vtkRenderer::New();
renWin->AddRenderer(ren1);

sphere = vtkSphereSource::New();
sphereMapper = vtkPolyDataMapper::New();
sphereMapper->SetInput(sphere->GetOutput());
sphereActor1 = vtkActor::New();
sphereActor1->SetMapper(sphereMapper);
cone = vtkConeSource::New();
glyph = vtkGlyph3D::New();
glyph->SetInput(sphere->GetOutput());
glyph->SetSource(cone->GetOutput());
glyph->SetVectorModeToUseNormal();
glyph->SetScaleModeToScaleByVector();
glyph->SetScaleFactor(0.25);
spikeMapper = vtkPolyDataMapper::New();
spikeMapper->SetInput(glyph->GetOutput());
spikeActor1 = vtkActor::New();
spikeActor1->SetMapper(spikeMapper);
ren1->AddActor(sphereActor1);
ren1->AddActor(spikeActor1);
ren1->SetBackground(0.4,0.1,0.2);
```

The above code is standard VTK code to create a mace.

```
// do the xwindow ui stuff
XtSetLanguageProc(NULL,NULL,NULL);
toplevel = XtVaAppInitialize(&app,"Sample",NULL,0,
                             &argc,argv,NULL, NULL);

// get the display connection and give it to the renderer
display = XtDisplay(toplevel);
renWin->SetDisplayId(display);

// we typecast to an X specific interactor
// Since we have decided to make this an X program
```

```
iren = vtkXRenderWindowInteractor::New();
iren->SetRenderWindow(renWin);
iren->Initialize(app);

button = XtVaCreateManagedWidget("Exit",
                                 xmPushButtonWidgetClass,
                                 toplevel,
                                 XmNwidth, 50,
                                 XmNheight, 50,NULL);

XtRealizeWidget(toplevel);
XtAddCallback(button,XmNactivateCallback,quit_cb,NULL);
XtAppMainLoop(app);
}
// simple quit callback
void quit_cb(Widget w,XtPointer client_data, XtPointer call_data)
{
  exit(0);
}
```

Finally we perform the standard Xt initialization and create our toplevel shell. The next few lines are very important. We obtain the X display id from the toplevel shell and tell the render window to use the same display id. Next we create the vtkXRenderWindowInteractor, set its render window and finally initialize it using the X application context from our earlier XtVaAppInitialize() call. Then we use standard Xt/Motif calls to create a push button, realize the toplevel shell, and assign a callback to the pushbutton. The last step is to start the XtAppMainLoop. The quit_cb is a simple callback that just exits the application. It is critical in this type of approach that the VTK render window interactor is initialized prior to creating the rest of your user interface. Otherwise some event may not be handled correctly.

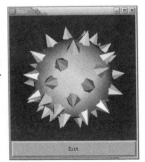

Figure 13–4 Simple Motif application with integrated VTK render window.

Now we will modify the proceeding example so that the rendering window is part of the user interface (**Figure 13–4**). This will require that we create a toplevel shell with a visual that VTK can use for rendering. Fortunately vtkXOpenGLRenderWindow includes some methods for helping you create an appropriate toplevel shell. Much of the code in the following example is the same as the previous example. The differences will be discussed shortly.

```
// include OS specific include file to mix in X code
#include "vtkXOpenGLRenderWindow.h"
#include "vtkXRenderWindowInteractor.h"
#include "vtkSphereSource.h"
#include "vtkConeSource.h"
#include "vtkGlyph3D.h"
#include "vtkPolyDataMapper.h"
#include <Xm/PushB.h>
#include <Xm/Form.h>
void quit_cb(Widget,XtPointer,XtPointer);
main (int argc, char *argv[])
{
  // X window stuff
  XtAppContext app;
  Widget toplevel, form, toplevel2, vtk;
  Widget button;
  int depth;
  Visual *vis;
  Display *display;
  Colormap col;

  // VTK stuff
  vtkXOpenGLRenderWindow *renWin;
  vtkRenderer *ren1;
  vtkActor *sphereActor1, *spikeActor1;
  vtkSphereSource *sphere;
  vtkConeSource *cone;
  vtkGlyph3D *glyph;
  vtkPolyDataMapper *sphereMapper, *spikeMapper;
  vtkXRenderWindowInteractor *iren;

  renWin = vtkXOpenGLRenderWindow::New();
  ren1 = vtkRenderer::New();
  renWin->AddRenderer(ren1);

  sphere = vtkSphereSource::New();
  sphereMapper = vtkPolyDataMapper::New();
  sphereMapper->SetInput(sphere->GetOutput());
  sphereActor1 = vtkActor::New();
  sphereActor1->SetMapper(sphereMapper);
  cone = vtkConeSource::New();
  glyph = vtkGlyph3D::New();
  glyph->SetInput(sphere->GetOutput());
  glyph->SetSource(cone->GetOutput());
  glyph->SetVectorModeToUseNormal();
  glyph->SetScaleModeToScaleByVector();
```

```
glyph->SetScaleFactor(0.25);
spikeMapper = vtkPolyDataMapper::New();
spikeMapper->SetInput(glyph->GetOutput());
spikeActor1 = vtkActor::New();
spikeActor1->SetMapper(spikeMapper);
ren1->AddActor(sphereActor1);
ren1->AddActor(spikeActor1);
ren1->SetBackground(0.4,0.1,0.2);
// do the xwindow ui stuff
XtSetLanguageProc(NULL,NULL,NULL);
toplevel = XtVaAppInitialize(&app,"Sample",NULL,0,
                             &argc,argv,NULL, NULL);
```

The initial code is relatively unchanged. In the beginning we have included an additional Motif header file to support the Motif form widget. In the main function we have added some additional variables to store some additional X properties.

```
// get the display connection and give it to the renderer
display = XtDisplay(toplevel);
renWin->SetDisplayId(display);
depth = renWin->GetDesiredDepth();
vis = renWin->GetDesiredVisual();
col = renWin->GetDesiredColormap();

toplevel2 = XtVaCreateWidget("top2",
      topLevelShellWidgetClass,toplevel,
      XmNdepth, depth,
      XmNvisual, vis,
      XmNcolormap, col,
      NULL);
```

Here is where the significant changes begin. We use the first toplevel shell widget to get an X display connection. We then set the render window to use that display connection and then query what X depth, visual, and colormap would be best for it to use. Then we create another toplevel shell widget this time explicitly specifying the depth, colormap, and visual. That way the second toplevel shell will be suitable for VTK rendering. All of the child widgets of this toplevel shell will have the same depth, colormap, and visual as toplevel2.

```
form    = XtVaCreateWidget("form",xmFormWidgetClass, toplevel2, NULL);
vtk     = XtVaCreateManagedWidget("vtk",
    xmPrimitiveWidgetClass, form,
    XmNwidth, 300, XmNheight, 300,
    XmNleftAttachment, XmATTACH_FORM,
```

```
        XmNrightAttachment, XmATTACH_FORM,
        XmNtopAttachment, XmATTACH_FORM,
        NULL);
  button        = XtVaCreateManagedWidget("Exit",
        xmPushButtonWidgetClass, form,
        XmNheight, 40,
        XmNbottomAttachment, XmATTACH_FORM,
        XmNtopAttachment, XmATTACH_WIDGET,
        XmNtopWidget, vtk,
        XmNleftAttachment, XmATTACH_FORM,
        XmNrightAttachment, XmATTACH_FORM,
        NULL);

  XtAddCallback(button,XmNactivateCallback,quit_cb,NULL);
  XtManageChild(form);
  XtRealizeWidget(toplevel2);
  XtMapWidget(toplevel2);

  // we typecast to an X specific interactor
  // Since we have decided to make this an X program
  iren = vtkXRenderWindowInteractor::New();
  iren->SetRenderWindow(renWin);
  iren->SetWidget(vtk);
  iren->Initialize(app);
  XtAppMainLoop(app);
}
/* quit when the arrow */
void quit_cb(Widget w,XtPointer client_data, XtPointer call_data)
{
  exit(0);
}
```

Finally we create a few Motif widgets including a xmPrimitiveWidgetClass which is what
VTK will render into. The form widget has been added simply to handle layout of the button and the rendering window. The SetWidget() call is used in this example to tell the
interactor (and hence the render window) what widget to use for rendering.

13.4 MS Windows / Microsoft Foundation Classes

The basics of integration of VTK within the Windows environment has been shown previously (see "Create An Application" on page 28). You can also develop MFC-based appli-

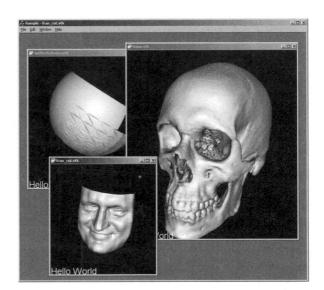

Figure 13–5 A sample application built with the Microsoft multi-document interface.

cations that make use of VTK in two different ways. The first way to use VTK within a MFC based application. Here, following the code from VTK/Examples/GUI/Win32/ SimpleCxx/Win32Cone.cxx, we create a vtkRenderWindow in the MFC application and if desired, parent it with a MFC-based window. The second way is to make use of the vtkMFCView, vtkMFCRenderView and vtkMFCDocument classes that are provided in the Examples/GUI/Win32/SampleMFC subdirectory. In fact, the Sample.exe application is a sample MFC-based application that demonstrates the use of these classes. This MDI application (Multi-Document Interface) shows how to open several VTK data files and interact with them through the GUI (**Figure 13–5**). You should be able to copy these classes into new MFC applications you develop. Refer to Chapter 3 to check how the Microsoft Visual Studio project file should be modified to compile this example.

13.5 Tcl/Tk

Integrating VTK with Tcl/Tk user interfaces is typically a fairly easy process thanks to classes such as vtkTkRenderWidget, vtkTkImageViewerWidget, and vtkTkImageWindowWidget. These classes can be used just like you would use any other Tk widget. Up-to-date informations and new examples might be found both in the VTK/Examples/GUI/Tcl and Wrapping/Tcl source directories. Consider the following example (**Figure 13–6**):

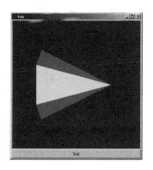

Figure 13–6 Tcl/Tk example.

```
package require vtk
package require vtkinteraction
# This script uses a vtkTkRenderWidget to create a
# Tk widget that is associated with a vtkRenderWindow.

# Create the GUI: two renderer widgets and a quit button
wm withdraw .
toplevel .top
frame .top.f1
vtkTkRenderWidget .top.f1.r1 -width 400 -height 400
button .top.btn  -text Quit -command exit
pack .top.f1.r1 -side left -padx 3 -pady 3 -fill both \
     -expand t
pack .top.f1  -fill both -expand t
pack .top.btn -fill x
# Get the render window associated with the widget.
set renWin [.top.f1.r1 GetRenderWindow]
vtkRenderer ren1
$renWin AddRenderer ren1

# bind the mouse events
BindTkRenderWidget .top.f1.r1

# create a Cone source and actor
vtkConeSource cone
vtkPolyDataMapper    coneMapper
    coneMapper SetInput [cone GetOutput]
    coneMapper GlobalImmediateModeRenderingOn
vtkLODActor coneActor
```

```
    coneActor SetMapper coneMapper
# Add the actors to the renderer, set the background and size
#
ren1 AddActor coneActor
ren1 SetBackground 0.1 0.2 0.4
```

The first line is the standard `package require vtk` command that is used to load the VTK Tcl package. It may also be used on UNIX if the VTK target has been built with shared libraries (but this is not required). The `vtkinteraction` package contains default bindings for handling mouse and keyboard events for a render widget. Specifically it defines the `BindTkRenderWidget` proc which sets up those bindings for a particular vtk-TkRenderWidget. Next we withdraw the default toplevel widget and create a new one called `.top`. On some systems you may need to create `.top` with the following line instead of the one given above:

```
toplevel .top -visual best
```

Next we create and pack the frame, vtkTkRenderWidget, and a button in the traditional Tk manner. The next line queries the vtkTkRenderWidget for the underlying render window that it is using. We store this in a variable called `renWin`. We then create a renderer, associate it with the render window, and then bind the mouse events to the vtkRenderWidget using the `BindTkRenderWidget` proc. Finally we create a cone and actor in the normal manner. If you wish the render window can be provided as an argument on the creation of the vtkTkRenderWidget as follows:

```
vtkRenderWindow renWin
vtkTkRenderWidget .top.f1.r1 \
    -width 400 -height 400 -rw renWin
```

Then simply use `renWin` instead of `$renWin` since it is now an instance, not a variable reference.

For your application development you will probably want to customize the event handling. The best way to do this is to make a copy of `TkInteractor.tcl` located in VTK/Wrapping/Tcl and then edit it to suit your preferences. The format of this file is fairly straight forward. The beginning of the file defines the `BindTkRenderWidget` proc which associates events with specific Tcl procedures. The remainder of the file defines these procedures. The same techniques used with vtkTkRenderWidget can be used with vtkTkImageViewerWidget and vtkTkImageWindowWidget for image processing. Instead of having a `-rw` option and GetRenderWindow() method, vtkTkImageViewerWidget supports `-iv` and GetImageViewer().

vtkTkImageWindowWidget supports -iw and GetImageWindow(). Likewise, there is a TkImageViewerInteractor.tcl file that provides some default event handling for the image viewer, which are loaded by the vtkinteraction package.

When using the vtkTkWidget classes you should not use the interactor classes such as vtkRenderWindowInteractor. While it may work, the behavior may be unstable. Normally you should use either an interactor or a vtkTkWidget but never both for a given window.

13.6 Java

The *Visualization Toolkit* includes a class specially designed to help you integrate VTK into your Java based application. This is a fairly tricky procedure since Java does not provide any "public" classes to support native code integration. It is made more difficult by the fact that Java is a multithreaded language and yet windowing systems such as X11R5 do not support multithreaded user interfaces. To help overcome these difficulties, we have provided a Java class called vtkPanel. This class works with Java to make a vtkRender-Window appear like a normal Java AWT Canvas. The App2.java example which can be found in the your java subdirectory makes use of the vtkPanel class. vtkPanel.java can be found in vtk.jar for executable distributions and in vtk/java/vtk for source code distributions.

Be aware that the vtkPanel class comes in two different varieties: Windows and UNIX. The code to support both operating systems is in the same file. If you experience difficulty you should take a look at your copy of vtkPanel.java and make sure the appropriate lines are commented out. Be aware that vtkPanel uses some classes that are not officially supported by Sun and may not be portable to other vendors' Java development environments. We of course don't like using these classes, but Sun makes the rules and they have made it fairly difficult to integrate user interface code into their language. But as long as you use the JDK you should be okay.

## Chapter 14

Coding Resources

This chapter provides information to make the job of building VTK applications and classes a little easier. Object diagrams are useful when you'd like an overview of the objects in the system, and are included here in symbolic form known as object modeling diagrams. The diagrams we use here are simplified to mainly show inheritance, but some associations between classes are shown as well. Succinct filter descriptions are provided to help you find the right filter to do the job at hand. This chapter also documents VTK file formats, which, along with the object diagrams, have changed since the release of vtk2.0 (and the release of the second edition of the *Visualization Toolkit* text.)

14.1 Object Diagrams

The following section contains abbreviated object diagrams using the OMT graphical language. The purpose of this section is to convey the essence of the software structure, particularly inheritance and object associations. Due to space limitation, not all objects are shown, particularly "leaf" (i.e., bottom of the inheritance tree) objects. Instead, we choose a single leaf object to represent other sibling objects. The organization of the objects follows that of the synopsis.

Foundation

The foundation object diagram is shown in **Figure 14–1**. These represent the core data objects, as well as other object manipulation classes.

Cells

The cell object diagram is shown in **Figure 14–2**. Currently, 14 concrete cell types are supported in VTK. The special class vtkGenericCell is used to represent any type of cell (i.e., supports the thread-safe vtkDataSet::GetCell() method). The class vtkEmptyCell is used to indicate the presence of a deleted or NULL cell.

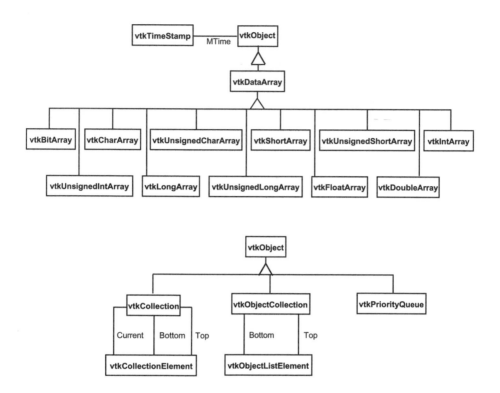

Figure 14–1 Foundation object diagram.

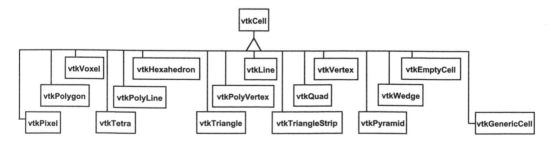

Figure 14–2 Cell object diagram.

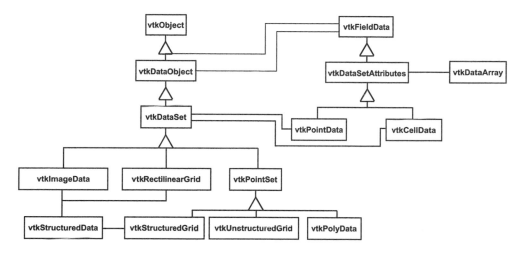

Figure 14–3 Dataset object diagram.

Datasets

The dataset object diagram is shown in **Figure 14–3**. Currently, five concrete dataset types are supported. Unstructured point data can be represented by any of the subclasses of vtkPointSet. Rectilinear grids are represented using vtkStructuredGrid. vtkImageData used to be vtkStructuredPoints, and represents 2D image and 3D volume data.

Pipeline

The pipeline object diagram is shown in **Figure 14–4**. These are the core objects to represent data.

Sources

The source object diagram is shown in **Figure 14–5**.

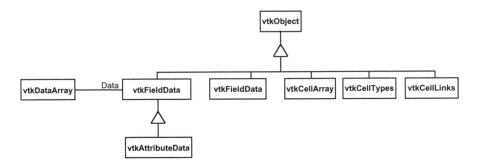

Figure 14–4 Pipeline object diagram.

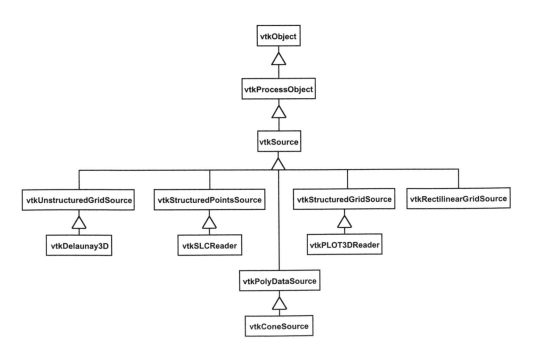

Figure 14–5 Source object diagram.

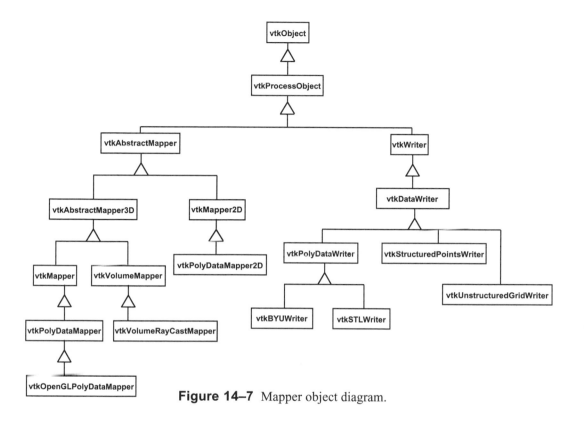

Figure 14–7 Mapper object diagram.

Filters

The filter object diagram is shown in **Figure 14–6**.

Mappers

The mapper object diagram is shown in **Figure 14–7**. There are basically two types: graphics mappers that map visualization data to the graphics system and writers that write data to output file (or other I/O device).

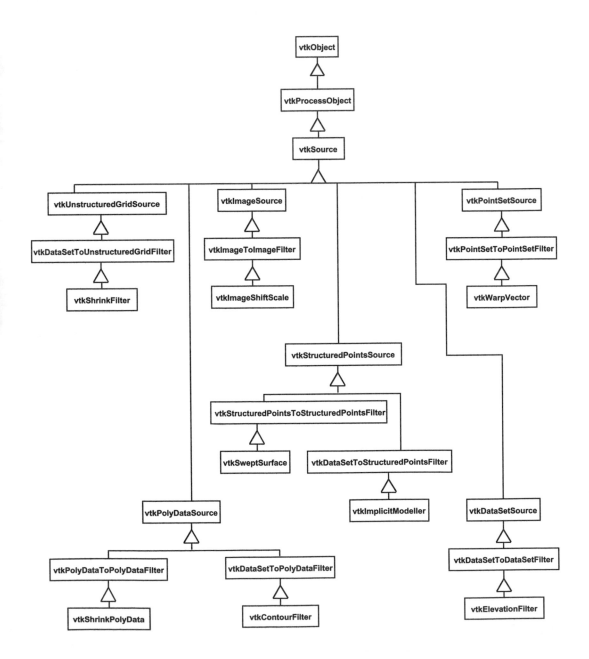

Figure 14–6 Filter object diagram.

Graphics

The graphics object diagram is shown in **Figure 14–8**. The diagram has been extended to include some associations with objects in the system. If you are unfamiliar with the object-oriented graphics notation see Rumbaugh et al., *Object-Oriented Modeling and Design*.

Volume Rendering

The volume rendering class hierarchy is shown in **Figure 14–9**. Note that volume rendering and surface rendering are integrated together via the renderer. The renderer maintains a list of both actors and volumes (in the vtkPropCollection) and handles compositing the image.

Imaging

The imaging object diagram is shown in **Figure 14–10**. Imaging integrates with the graphics pipeline via the structured points dataset. Also, it is possible to capture an image from the renderer via the vtkRendererSource object, and then feed the image into the imaging pipeline.

OpenGL Renderer

The OpenGL renderer object diagram is shown in **Figure 14–11**. Note that there are other rendering libraries in VTK. The OpenGL object diagram is representative of these other libraries.

Picking

The picking class hierarchy is shown in **Figure 14–12**. vtkPropPicker and vtkWorld-PointPicker are the fastest (use hardware) pickers. All pickers can return a global *x-y-z* from a selection point in the render window. vtkCellPicker uses software ray casting to return information about cells (cell id, parametric coordinate of intersection). vtkPoint-

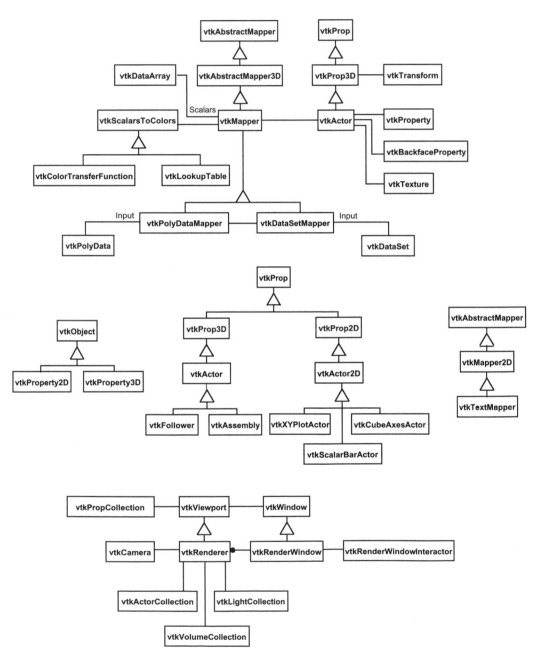

Figure 14–8 Graphics object diagram.

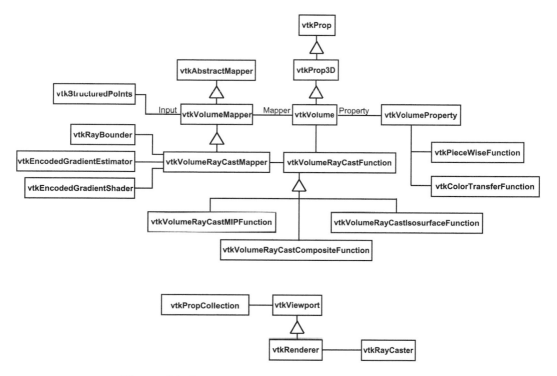

Figure 14–9 Volume rendering object diagram.

Picker returns a point id. vtkPropPicker indicates which instance of vtkProp was picked, as well as returning the pick coordinates.

Transformation Hierarchy

VTK provides an extensive, powerful transformation hierarchy. This hierarchy supports linear, non-linear, affine, and homogeneous transformations. The transformation object diagram is shown in **Figure 14–13**.

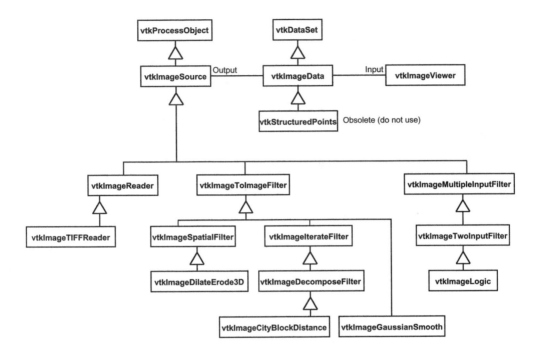

Figure 14–10 Imaging object diagram.

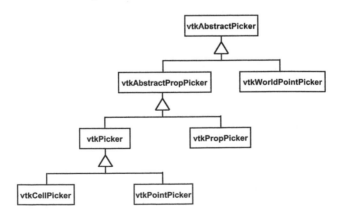

Figure 14–12 Picking class hierarchy

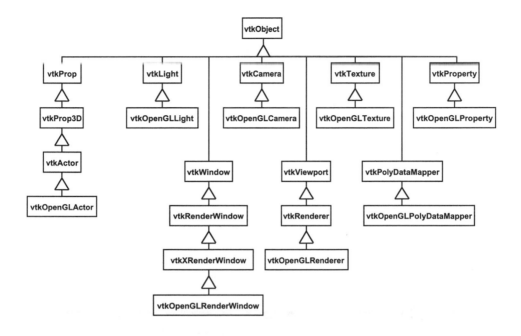

Figure 14–11 OpenGL / graphics interface object diagram.

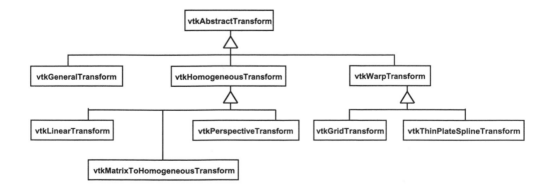

Figure 14–13 Transformation class hierarchy

14.2 Summary Of Filters

In this section we provide a brief summary of VTK filters. The section is divided into three parts: an overview of source objects, a description of visualization filters, and a list of imaging filters. Classes used to interface with data (i.e., readers, writers, importers, and exporters) are described in Chapter 8 "Data Interface & Miscellaneous" on page 185.

Source Objects

In this section we provide a brief description of source objects. Source objects initiate the visualization pipeline. Note that readers (source objects that read files) are not listed here. Instead, find them in Chapter 8 "Data Interface & Miscellaneous" on page 185. Each entry includes a brief description including the type of output they generate.

- vtkBooleanTexture — create a 2D texture map (structured points) based on combinations of inside, outside, and on implicit functions.
- vtkConeSource — generate a polygonal representation of a cone.
- vtkCubeSource — generate a polygonal representation of a cube.
- vtkCursor3D — generate a 3D cursor (represented as lines) given a bounding box and focal point.
- vtkCylinderSource — generate a polygonal representation of a cylinder.
- vtkDiskSource — generate a polygonal representation of a cone.
- vtkEarthSource — generate a polygonal representation of the earth.
- vtkImageCanvasSource2D — create an image by drawing into it with primitive shapes.
- vtkImageEllipsoidSource — create an image of a ellipsoid distribution.
- vtkImageGaussianSource — create an image of a Gaussian distribution.
- vtkImageMandelbrotSource — create an image of the Mandelbrot set.
- vtkImageNoiseSource — create an image filled with noise.
- vtkImageSinusoidSource — create an image of sinusoidal values.
- vtkLineSource — generate a polygonal representation of a cone.
- vtkOutlineSource — generate a polygonal representation of a cone.

- vtkPlaneSource — generate a polygonal representation of a cone.

- vtkPointLoad — generate a tensor field from a point load on a semi-infinite domain.

- vtkPointSetSource — create an image with sinusoidal image values.

- vtkPointSource — generate a polygonal representation of a cone.

- vtkProgrammableDataObjectSource — a filter that can be programmed at run-time to read or generate a vtkDataObject (i.e., a field).

- vtkProgrammableSource — a filter that can be programmed at run-time to read or generate any type of data.

- vtkRendererSource — an imaging filter that takes the renderer or render window into the imaging pipeline (great for screen capture).

- vtkSampleFunction — sample an implicit function unto a volume.

- vtkSphereSource — generate a polygonal representation of a cone.

- vtkSuperquadricSource — generates a polygonal representation of a superquadric.

- vtkTextSource — create text as a polygonal representation.

- vtkTexturedSphereSource — create a polygonal representation of a sphere with associated texture coordinates.

- vtkTriangularTexture — generate a triangular 2D texture map.

- vtkVectorText — create a polygonal representation of text.

- vtkVideoSource — grabs video signals as an image.

Imaging Filters

In this section we provide a brief summary of imaging filters. Note that descriptions of other visualization filters are found in "Visualization Filters" on page 337. Classes used to interface with data are described in Chapter 8 "Data Interface & Miscellaneous" on page 185.

All the filters described here take vtkImageData (or obsolete vtkStructuredPoints) as input, and produce the same type of output.

- vtkClipVolume — clip a volume with an implicit function to generate a tetrahedral mesh.

- vtkCompositeFilter — combine (composite) structured points into a single dataset.
- vtkDividingCubes — generate an isosurface as a cloud of points.
- vtkExtractVOI — extract a volume of interest and/or subsample the volume.
- vtkImageAccumulate — generate a histogram of the input image.
- vtkImageAnisotropicDiffusion2D — iteratively apply a 2D diffusion filter.
- vtkImageAnisotropicDiffusion3D — iteratively apply a 3D diffusion filter.
- vtkImageAppend — merge multiple input images into one output image.
- vtkImageAppendComponents — merge the components from two input images.
- vtkImageBlend — blend multiple images according to the alpha values and/or the opacity setting for each input.
- vtkImageButterworthHighPass — apply a frequency-domain high pass filter.
- vtkImageButterworthLowPass — apply a frequency-domain low pass filter.
- vtkImageCacheFilter — cache images for future use to avoid pipeline re-execution.
- vtkImageCanvasSource2D — basic image display / primitive drawing functionality.
- vtkImageCast — cast the input image to a specified output type.
- vtkImageCityBlockDistance — create a distance map using the city block metric.
- vtkImageClip — reduce the size of the input image.
- vtkImageComposite — composite multiple images using pixel and Z-buffer data.
- vtkImageConstantPad — pad the input image with a constant value.
- vtkImageContinuousDilate3D — evaluate the maximum value in an elipsoidal neighborhood.
- vtkImageContinuousErode3D — evaluate the minimum value in an elipsoidal neighborhood.
- vtkImageCorrelation — create a correlation image for two input images.
- vtkImageCursor3D — add a cursor to the input image.
- vtkImageDataStreamer — initiate streaming for image data.
- vtkImageDataToPolyDataFilter — convert an image to polygons.
- vtkImageDifference — generate a difference image / error value for two images.
- vtkImageDilateErode3D — perform dilation / erosion on a boundary.

- vtkImageDivergence — create a scalar field that represents the rate of change of the input vector field.

- vtkImageDotProduct — create a dot product image from two vector images.

- vtkImageEuclideanToPolar — convert 2D Euclidean coordinates to polar coordinates.

- vtkImageExtractComponents — extract a subset of the components of the input image.

- vtkImageFFT — perform a Fast Fourier Transform.

- vtkImageFlip — flip an image about a specified axis.

- vtkImageFourierCenter — shift the zero frequency from the origin to the center.

- vtkImageGaussianSmooth — perform 1D, 2D, or 3D Gaussian convolution.

- vtkImageGradient — compute the gradient vector of an image.

- vtkImageGradientMagnitude — compute the magnitude of the gradient vector.

- vtkImageHSVToRGB — convert HSV components to RGB.

- vtkImageHybridMedian2D — perform a median filter while preserving lines / corners.

- vtkImageIdealHighPass — perform a simple frequency domain high pass filter.

- vtkImageIdealLowPass — perform a simple frequency domain low pass filter.

- vtkImageIslandRemoval2D — remove small clusters from the image.

- vtkImageLaplacian — compute the Laplacian (divergence of the gradient).

- vtkImageLogarithmicScale — perform a log function on each pixel.

- vtkImageLogic — perform a logic operation: AND, OR, XOR, NAND, NOR, NOT.

- vtkImageLuminance — calculate luminance of an RGB image.

- vtkImageMagnify — magnify the image by an integer scale factor.

- vtkImageMagnitude — compute the magnitude of the components of an image.

- vtkImageMapToColors — map an image through a lookup table.

- vtkImageMarchingCubes — a streaming version of marching cubes.

- vtkImageMask — apply a mask to an image.

- vtkImageMaskBits — apply a bit-mask pattern to the image components.

- vtkImageMathematics — apply basic mathematical operations to one or two images.
- vtkImageMedian3D — compute a median filter in a rectangular neighborhood
- vtkImageMirrorPad — pad the input image with a mirror image.
- vtkImageNonMaximumSuppression — perform non-maximum suppression.
- vtkImageNormalize — normalize the scalar components of an image.
- vtkImageOpenClose3D — perform two dilate / erode operations.
- vtkImagePermute — permute the axes of an image.
- vtkImageQuantizeRGBToIndex — quantize an RGB image to an index image and a lookup table.
- vtkImageRange3D — compute the range (max - min) in an ellipsoidal neighborhood.
- vtkImageResample — resample an image to be larger or smaller.
- vtkImageRFFT — perform a Reverse Fast Fourier Transform.
- vtkImageRGBToHSV — convert RGB components to HSV.
- vtkImageReslice — reslice the volume along a specified axis.
- vtkImageSeedConnectivity — evaluate connectivity with user supplied seeds.
- vtkImageShiftScale — perform a shift and scale operation on the input image.
- vtkImageShrink3D — shrink an image by subsampling on a uniform grid.
- vtkImageSkeleton2D — perform a skeleton operation in 2D.
- vtkImageSobel2D — compute the vector field of an image using Sobel functions.
- vtkImageSobel3D — compute the vector field of a volume using Sobel functions.
- vtkImageThreshold — perform binary or continuous thresholding.
- vtkImageVariance3D — compute the variance within an ellipsoidal neighborhood.
- vtkImageWrapPad — pad an image using a mod operation on the pixel index.
- vtkLinkEdgels — link edgels together to form digital curves.
- vtkMarchingCubes — high-performance isocontouring algorithm.
- vtkMarchingSquares — high-performance isocontouring algorithm in 2D.
- vtkRecursiveDividingCubes — generate an isocontour as a cloud of points.

- vtkStructuredPointsGeometryFilter — extract geometry (points, lines, planes) as vtkPolyData.

- vtkSweptSurface — generate a swept surface of a moving part.

- vtkSynchronizedTemplates2D — high-performance isocontouring algorithm in 2D.

- vtkSynchronizedTemplates3D — high-performance isocontouring algorithm in 3D.

Visualization Filters

The classes listed below are organized to the type of data they input. Each class contains a brief description of what it does and any special notations regarding multiple inputs or outputs.

Input Type vtkDataSet. These filters will process any type of dataset (that is, subclasses of vtkDataSet).

- vtkAppendFilter — appends one or more datasets into a single unstructured grid.

- vtkAsynchronousBuffer — enables asynchronous pipeline execution.

- vtkAttributeDataToFieldDataFilter — transform attribute data (either point or cell) into field data.

- vtkBrownianPoints — assign random vectors to points.

- vtkCastToConcrete — cast a abstract type of input (e.g., vtkDataSet) to a concrete form (e.g., vtkPolyData).

- vtkCellCenters — generate points (vtkPolyData) marking cell centers.

- vtkCellDataToPointData — convert cell data to point data.

- vtkCellDerivatives — compute derivatives of scalar and vectors.

- vtkClipDataSet — clips arbitrary vtkDataSets with an implicit function.

- vtkConnectivityFilter — extract connected cells into an unstructured grid.

- vtkContourFilter — generate isosurface(s).

- vtkCutter — generate a *n-1* dimensional cut surface from a *n*-dimensional dataset.

- vtkDashedStreamLine — generate a streamline with dashes representing elapsed time.

- vtkDataSetToDataObjectFilter — converts a dataset into a general data object.

- vtkDicer — generate data values based on spatial (or other) segregation.
- vtkEdgePoints — generate points along edge that intersect an isosurface value.
- vtkElevationFilter — generate scalars according to projection along vector.
- vtkExtractEdges — extract the edges of a dataset as lines.
- vtkExtractGeometry — extract cells that lie either entirely inside or outside of an implicit function.
- vtkExtractTensorComponents — extract the components of a tensor as scalars, vectors, normals, or texture coordinates.
- vtkFieldDataToAttributeDataFilter — convert general field data into point or cell attribute data.
- vtkGaussianSplatter — generate a scalar field in a volume by splatting points with a Gaussian distribution.
- vtkGeometryFilter — extract surface geometry from a dataset; convert a dataset into vtkPolyData.
- vtkGlyph2D — a 2D specialization of vtkGlyph3D. Translation, rotations, and scaling is constrained to the x-y plane.
- vtkGlyph3D — copy a vtkPolyData (second input defines the glyph) to every point in the input.
- vtkGraphLayout — distribute undirected graph network into pleasing arrangement.
- vtkHedgeHog — generate scaled and oriented lines at each point from the associated vector field.
- vtkHyperStreamline — use tensor data to generate a streamtube; the tube cross section is warped according to eigenvectors.
- vtkIdFilter — generate integer id values (useful for plotting).
- vtkImplicitModeller — generate a distance field from the input geometry.
- vtkImplicitTextureCoords — create texture coordinates with an implicit function.
- vtkInterpolateDataSetAttributes — interpolate attribute data between two datasets (useful for animation).
- vtkMaskPoints — select a subset of input points.
- vtkMergeDataObjectFilter — merge a data object and dataset to form a new dataset (useful for separating geometry from solution files).

- vtkMergeFilter — merge pieces from different datasets into a single dataset.
- vtkOBBDicer — divide a dataset into pieces using oriented bounding boxes.
- vtkOutlineFilter — create an outline around the dataset
- vtkPointDataToCellData — convert point data to cell data.
- vtkProbeFilter — probe, or resample, one dataset with another.
- vtkProgrammableAttributeDataFilter — a run-time programmable filter that operates on data attributes.
- vtkProgrammableFilter — a run-time programmable filter.
- vtkProgrammableGlyphFilter — a run-time programmable filter that can generate glyphs that vary arbitrarily based on data value.
- vtkProjectedTexture — generate texture coordinates projected onto an arbitrary surface.
- vtkSelectVisiblePoints — select the subset of points that are visible; hidden points are culled.
- vtkShepardMethod — resample a set of points into a volume.
- vtkShrinkFilter — shrink the cells of a dataset.
- vtkSimpleElevationFilter — generate scalars based on z-coordinate value.
- vtkSpatialRepresentationFilter — create a polygonal representation of spatial search (i.e., locator) objects.
- vtkStreamer — abstract superclass performs vector field particle integration.
- vtkStreamLine — generate a streamline from a vector field.
- vtkStreamPoints — generate a set of points along a streamline from a vector field.
- vtkSurfaceReconstructionFilter — constructs a surface from unorganized points.
- vtkTensorGlyph — generate glyphs based on tensor values.
- vtkTextureMapToBox — generates 3-D texture coordinates.
- vtkTextureMapToCylinder — generate 2-D texture coordinates using cylindrical coordinates.
- vtkTextureMapToPlane — generate 2-D texture coordinates by projecting data onto a plane.

- vtkTextureMapToSphere — generate 2-D texture coordinates using spherical coordinates.

- vtkThreshold — extract cells whose scalar values lie below, above, or between a threshold range.

- vtkThresholdPoints — extract points whose scalar values lie below, above, or between a threshold range.

- vtkThresholdTextureCoords — compute texture coordinates based on satisfying threshold criterion.

- vtkTransformTextureCoords — transform (e.g., scale, etc.) texture coordinates.

- vtkVectorDot — compute scalars from dot product between vectors and normals.

- vtkVectorNorm — compute scalars from Euclidean norm of vectors.

- vtkVectorTopology — mark points where the vector field vanishes (i.e., singularities exist).

- vtkVoxelModeller — convert an arbitrary dataset into a voxel representation.

Input Type vtkPointSet. These filters will process datasets that are a subclass of vtkPointSet. (These classes explicitly represent their points with an instance of vtkPoints.)

- vtkDelaunay2D — create constrained and unconstrained Delaunay triangulations including alpha shapes.

- vtkDelaunay3D — create 3D Delaunay triangulation including alpha shapes.

- vtkTransformFilter — transform the points using a 4x4 transformation matrix.

- vtkWarpLens — transform points according to lens distortion.

- vtkWarpScalar — modify point coordinates by scaling according to scalar values.

- vtkWarpTo — modify point coordinates by warping towards a point.

- vtkWarpVector — modify point coordinates by scaling in the direction of the point vectors.

Input Type vtkPolyData. The input type must be vtkPolyData. Remember that filters that accept vtkDataSet and vtkPointSet will also process vtkPolyData.

- vtkAppendPolyData — append one or more vtkPolyData datasets into a single vtkPolyData.

- vtkApproximatingSubdivisionFilter — generate a subdivision surface using an approximating scheme.

- vtkArcPlotter — plot data along an arbitrary polyline.

- vtkButterflySubdivisionFilter — subdivide a triangular, polygonal surface using a butterfly subdivision scheme.

- vtkCleanPolyData — merge coincident points, remove degenerate primitives.

- vtkClipPolyData — clip a polygonal dataset with an implicit function (or scalar value).

- vtkDecimate — reduce the number of triangles in a triangle mesh (patented).

- vtkDecimatePro — reduce the number of triangles in a triangle mesh (non-patented).

- vtkDepthSortPolyData — Sort polygons based on depth, used for translucent rendering.

- vtkExtractPolyDataGeometry — extract polygonal cells that lie entirely inside or outside of an implicit function.

- vtkFeatureEdges — extract edges that meet certain conditions (feature, boundary, non-manifold edges).

- vtkHull — generate a convex hull from six or more independent planes.

- vtkLinearExtrusionFilter — generate polygonal data by extruding another vtkPolyData.

- vtkLinearSubdivisionFilter — subdivide a triangular, polygonal surface using a linear subdivision scheme.

- vtkLoopSubdivisionFilter — subdivide a triangular, polygonal surface using a loop subdivision scheme.

- vtkMaskPolyData — select pieces of polygonal data.

- vtkPolyDataConnectivityFilter — extract connected regions.

- vtkPolyDataNormals — generate surface normals.

- vtkQuadricClustering — a decimation algorithm for very large datasets.

- vtkQuadricDecimation — a decimation algorithm using the quadric error measure.

- vtkReverseSense — reverse the connectivity order or the direction of surface normals.

- vtkRibbonFilter — create oriented ribbons from lines.

- vtkRotationalExtrusionFilter — generate polygonal data by rotationally extruding another vtkPolyData.

- vtkRuledSurfaceFilter — construct a surface from two or more "parallel" lines. Typically used to create stream surfaces from a rake of streamlines.

- vtkSelectPolyData — select polygonal data by drawing a loop.

- vtkShrinkPolyData — shrink polygonal data by shrinking each cell towards its centroid.

- vtkSmoothPolyDataFilter — use Laplacian smoothing to improve the mesh.

- vtkStripper — generate triangle strips from input triangle mesh.

- vtkSubPixelPositionEdgels — adjust edgel (line) positions based on gradients.

- vtkThinPlateSplineMeshWarp — warp (or morph) polygonal meshes using landmarks.

- vtkTransformPolyDataFilter — transform the polygonal data according to a 4x4 transformation matrix.

- vtkTriangleFilter — generate triangles from polygons or triangle strips.

- vtkTriangularTCoords — generate 2D triangular texture map.

- vtkTubeFilter — wrap lines with tubes.

- vtkVoxelContoursToSurfaceFilter — convert line contours into a surface.

- vtkWindowedSincPolyDataFilter — smooths meshes using a windowed sinc function.

Input Type vtkStructuredGrid. The input type must be vtkStructuredGrid. Remember that filters that accept vtkDataSet and vtkPointSet will also process vtkStructuredGrid.

- vtkExtractGrid — extract a region of interest / subsample a vtkStructuredGrid.

- vtkGridSynchronizedTemplates3D — high-performance isocontouring algorithm.

- vtkStructuredGridGeometryFilter — extract portions of the grid as polygonal geometry (points, lines, surfaces)

- vtkStructuredGridOutlineFilter — generate a wire outline of the boundaries of the structured grid.

Input Type vtkUnstructuredGrid. These filters take vtkUnstructuredGrid as input. Remember that filters that accept vtkDataSet will also process vtkUnstructuredGrid's.

- vtkExtractUnstructuredGrid — extract a region of interest, points, or cells from an unstructured grid.

- vtkSubdivideTetra — subdivide a tetrahedral mesh into 12 tetrahedra for every original tetrahedron.

Input Type vtkRectilinearGrid. The input type must be vtkRectilinearGrid. Remember that filters that accept vtkDataSet will also process vtkRectilinearGrid.

- vtkRectilinearGridGeometryFilter — extract portions of the grid as polygonal geometry (points, lines, surfaces)

Mapper Objects

In this section we provide a brief description of mapper objects. mapper objects terminate the visualization pipeline. Note that writers (mapper objects that write files) are not listed here. Instead, find them in Chapter 8 "Data Interface & Miscellaneous" on page 185. Each entry includes a brief description including the type of input they require.

- vtkDataSetMapper — accept any type of dataset as input and map to the graphics system.

- vtkImageMapper — 2D image display.

- vtkLabeledDataMapper — generates 3D text labels for data.

- vtkPolyDataMapper — maps polygonal data to the graphics system.

- vtkPolyDataMapper2D — draw vtkPolyData onto the overlay plane.

- vtkTextMapper — generates 2D text annotation.

- vtkVolumeProMapper — maps volumes to an image via the VolumePro hardware.

- vtkVolumeRayCastMapper — maps volumes to an image via ray casting.

- vtkVolumeTextureMapper2D — maps volumes to an image via 2D textures.

Actor (Prop) Objects

The following is a brief description of the various types of vtkProp (e.g., vtkProp3D and vtkActor) available in the system.

- vtkActor2D — type of prop drawn in the overlay plane.
- vtkAssembly — an ordered grouping of vtkProp3D's with shared transformation matrix.
- vtkAxisActor2D — a single labeled axis drawn in the overlay plane.
- vtkCaptionActor2D — attach a text caption to an object.
- vtkCubeAxesActor2D — draw the x-y-z axes of a vtkProp.
- vtkFollower — a vtkProp3D that allows faces the camera.
- vtkImageActor — a special type of vtkProp that draws an image as a texture map on top of a single polygon.
- vtk Legend Box Actor — used by vtkXYPlotActor to draw curve legends; combines text, symbols, and lines into a curve legend.
- vtkLODActor — a simple level-of-detail scheme for rendering 3D geometry.
- vtkLODProp3D — level-of-detail method for vtkProp3D's.
- vtk Parallel Coordinates Actor — multivariate visualization technique.
- vtkPropAssembly — a group of vtkProps
- vtkProp3D — a transformable (i.e., has a matrix) type of vtkProp
- vtkScalarBar Actor — a labeled, colored bar that visually expresses the relationship between color and scalar value.
- vtkScaledTextActor — text that scales as the viewport changes size.
- vtkVolume — a vtkProp used for volume rendering.
- vtkXYPlotActor — draw an x-y plot of data.

14.3 VTK File Formats

The *Visualization Toolkit* provides a number of source and writer objects to read and write various data file formats. The *Visualization Toolkit* also provides some of its own file formats. The main reason for creating yet another data file format is to offer a consistent data representation scheme for a variety of dataset types, and to provide a simple method to communicate data between software. Whenever possible, we recommend that you use formats that are more widely used. But if this is not possible, the *Visualization Toolkit* formats described here can be used instead. Note, however, that these formats are not supported by many other tools.

The visualization file formats consist of five basic parts.

1. The first part is the file version and identifier. This part contains the single line: # vtk DataFile Version x.x. This line must be exactly as shown with the exception of the version number x.x, which will vary with different releases of VTK. (Note: the current version number is 3.0. Version 1.0 and 2.0 files are compatible with version 3.0 files.)

2. The second part is the header. The header consists of a character string terminated by end-of-line character \n. The header is 256 characters maximum. The header can be used to describe the data and include any other pertinent information.

3. The next part is the file format. The file format describes the type of file, either ASCII or binary. On this line the single word ASCII or BINARY must appear.

4. The fourth part is the dataset structure. The geometry part describes the geometry and topology of the dataset. This part begins with a line containing the keyword DATASET followed by a keyword describing the type of dataset. Then, depending upon the type of dataset, other keyword/data combinations define the actual data.

5. The final part describes the dataset attributes. This part begins with the keywords POINT_DATA or CELL_DATA, followed by an integer number specifying the number of points or cells, respectively. (It doesn't matter whether POINT_DATA or CELL_DATA comes first.) Other keyword/data combinations then define the actual dataset attribute values (i.e., scalars, vectors, tensors, normals, texture coordinates, or field data).

An overview of the file format is shown in **Figure 14–14**. The first three parts are mandatory, but the other two are optional. Thus you have the flexibility of mixing and matching dataset attributes and geometry, either by operating system file manipulation or using VTK filters to merge data. Keywords are case insensitive, and may be separated by whitespace.

Before describing the data file formats please note the following.

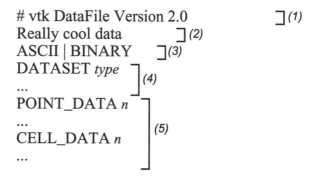

Part 1: Header

Part 2: Title (256 characters maximum, terminated with newline \n character)

Part 3: Data type, either ASCII or BINARY

Part 4: Geometry/topology. *Type* is one of:
```
STRUCTURED_POINTS
STRUCTURED_GRID
UNSTRUCTURED_GRID
POLYDATA
RECTILINEAR_GRID
FIELD
```

Part 5: Dataset attributes. The number of data items *n* of each type must match the number of points or cells in the dataset. (If *type* is FIELD, point and cell data should be omitted.

Figure 14–14 Overview of five parts of VTK data file format.

- *dataType* is one of the types bit, unsigned_char, char, unsigned_short, short, unsigned_int, int, unsigned_long, long, float, or double. These keywords are used to describe the form of the data, both for reading from file, as well as constructing the appropriate internal objects. Not all data types are supported for all classes.

- All keyword phrases are written in ASCII form whether the file is binary or ASCII. The binary section of the file (if in binary form) is the data proper; i.e., the numbers that define points coordinates, scalars, cell indices, and so forth.

- Indices are 0-offset. Thus the first point is point id 0.

- If both the data attribute and geometry/topology part are present in the file, then the number of data values defined in the data attribute part must exactly match the number of points or cells defined in the geometry/topology part.

- Cell types and indices are of type int.

- Binary data must be placed into the file immediately after the "newline" (\n) character from the previous ASCII keyword and parameter sequence.

- The geometry/topology description must occur prior to the data attribute description.

Binary Files

Binary files in VTK are portable across different computer systems as long as you observe two conditions. First, make sure that the byte ordering of the data is correct, and second, make sure that the length of each data type is consistent.

Most of the time VTK manages the byte ordering of binary files for you. When you write a binary file on one computer and read it in from another computer, the bytes representing the data will be automatically swapped as necessary. For example, binary files written on a Sun are stored in big endian order, while those on a PC are stored in little endian order. As a result, files written on a Sun workstation require byte swapping when read on a PC. (See the class vtkByteSwap for implementation details.) The VTK data files described here are written in big endian form.

Some file formats, however, do not explicitly define a byte ordering form. You will find that data read or written by external programs, or the classes vtkVolume16Reader, vtkMCubesReader, and vtkMCubesWriter may have a different byte order depending on the system of origin. In such cases, VTK allows you to specify the byte order by using the methods

```
SetDataByteOrderToBigEndian()
SetDataByteOrderToLittleEndian()
```

Another problem with binary files is that systems may use a different number of bytes to represent an integer or other native type. For example, some 64-bit systems will represent an integer with 8-bytes, while others represent an integer with 4-bytes. Currently, the *Visualization Toolkit* cannot handle transporting binary files across systems with incompatible data length. In this case, use ASCII file formats instead.

Dataset Format

The *Visualization Toolkit* supports five different dataset formats: structured points, structured grid, rectilinear grid, unstructured grid, and polygonal data. These formats are as follows.

- Structured Points
  The file format supports 1D, 2D, and 3D structured point datasets. The dimensions n_x, n_y, n_z must be greater than or equal to 1. The data spacing s_x, s_y, s_z must be greater than 0. (Note: in the version 1.0 data file, spacing was referred to as "aspect ratio". ASPECT_RATIO can still be used in version 2.0 data files, but is discouraged.)

```
DATASET STRUCTURED_POINTS
DIMENSIONS nx ny nz
ORIGIN x y z
SPACING sx sy sz
```

- Structured Grid
  The file format supports 1D, 2D, and 3D structured grid datasets. The dimensions n_x, n_y, n_z must be greater than or equal to 1. The point coordinates are defined by the data in the POINTS section. This consists of *x-y-z* data values for each point.

```
DATASET STRUCTURED_GRID
DIMENSIONS nx ny nz
POINTS n dataType
```
$p_{0x} \, p_{0y} \, p_{0z}$
$p_{1x} \, p_{1y} \, p_{1z}$
...
$p_{(n-1)x} \, p_{(n-1)y} \, p_{(n-1)z}$

- Rectilinear Grid
  A rectilinear grid defines a dataset with regular topology, and semi-regular geometry aligned along the *x-y-z* coordinate axes. The geometry is defined by three lists of monotonically increasing coordinate values, one list for each of the *x-y-z* coordinate axes. The topology is defined by specifying the grid dimensions, which must be greater than or equal to 1.

```
DATASET RECTILINEAR_GRID
```

```
DIMENSIONS nx ny nz
X_COORDINATES  nx dataType
```
$x_0 \, x_1 \ldots x_{(nx-1)}$
```
Y_COORDINATES  ny dataType
```
$y_0 \, y_1 \ldots y_{(ny-1)}$
```
Z_COORDINATES  nz dataType
```
$z_0 \, z_1 \ldots z_{(nz-1)}$

- Polygonal Data
  The polygonal dataset consists of arbitrary combinations of surface graphics primitives vertices (and polyvertices), lines (and polylines), polygons (of various types), and triangle strips. Polygonal data is defined by the POINTS VERTICES, LINES, POLYGONS, or TRIANGLE_STRIPS sections. The POINTS definition is the same as we saw for structured grid datasets. The VERTICES, LINES, POLYGONS, or TRIANGLE_STRIPS keywords define the polygonal dataset topology. Each of these keywords requires two parameters: the number of cells *n* and the size of the cell list *size*. The cell list size is the total number of integer values required to represent the list (i.e., sum of *numPoints* and connectivity indices over each cell). None of the keywords VERTICES, LINES, POLYGONS, or TRIANGLE_STRIPS is required.

```
DATASET POLYDATA
POINTS n dataType
```
$P_{0x} P_{0y} P_{0z}$
$P_{1x} P_{1y} P_{1z}$

...

$P_{(n-1)x} P_{(n-1)y} P_{(n-1)z}$

```
VERTICES n size
```
$numPoints_0, \, i_0, \, j_0, \, k_0, \, \ldots$
$numPoints_1, \, i_1, \, j_1, \, k_1, \, \ldots$

...

$numPoints_{n-1}, \, i_{n-1}, \, j_{n-1}, \, k_{n-1}, \, \ldots$

```
LINES n size
```
$numPoints_0, \, i_0, \, j_0, \, k_0, \, \ldots$
$numPoints_1, \, i_1, \, j_1, \, k_1, \, \ldots$

...

$numPoints_{n-1}, \, i_{n-1}, \, j_{n-1}, \, k_{n-1}, \, \ldots$

```
POLYGONS n size
```
$numPoints_0, i_0, j_0, k_0, ...$
$numPoints_1, i_1, j_1, k_1, ...$
...
$numPoints_{n-1}, i_{n-1}, j_{n-1}, k_{n-1}, ...$

```
TRIANGLE_STRIPS n size
```
$numPoints_0, i_0, j_0, k_0, ...$
$numPoints_1, i_1, j_1, k_1, ...$
...
$numPoints_{n-1}, i_{n-1}, j_{n-1}, k_{n-1}, ...$

- Unstructured Grid
  The unstructured grid dataset consists of arbitrary combinations of any possible cell type. Unstructured grids are defined by points, cells, and cell types. The CELLS keyword requires two parameters: the number of cells *n* and the size of the cell list *size*. The cell list size is the total number of integer values required to represent the list (i.e., sum of *numPoints* and connectivity indices over each cell). The CELL_TYPES keyword requires a single parameter: the number of cells *n*. This value should match the value specified by the CELLS keyword. The cell types data is a single integer value per cell that specified cell type (see vtkCell.h or **Figure 14–15**).

```
DATASET UNSTRUCTURED_GRID
POINTS n dataType
```
$P_{0x} P_{0y} P_{0z}$
$P_{1x} P_{1y} P_{1z}$
...
$P_{(n-1)x} P_{(n-1)y} P_{(n-1)z}$

```
CELLS n size
```
$numPoints_0, i, j, k, l, ...$
$numPoints_1, i, j, k, l, ...$
$numPoints_2, i, j, k, l, ...$
...
$numPoints_{n-1}, i, j, k, l, ...$

```
CELL_TYPES n
```

$type_0$

$type_1$

$type_2$

...

$type_{n-1}$

- Field
  Field data is a general format without topological and geometric structure, and without a particular dimensionality. Typically field data is associated with the points or cells of a dataset. However, if the FIELD *type* is specified as the dataset type (see **Figure 14–14**), then a general VTK data object is defined. Use the format described in the next section to define a field. Also see "Working With Field Data" on page 194 and the fourth example in this chapter "Examples" on page 354.

Dataset Attribute Format

The *Visualization Toolkit* supports the following dataset attributes: scalars (one to four components), vectors, normals, texture coordinates (1D, 2D, and 3D), 3×3 tensors, and field data. In addition, a lookup table using the RGBA color specification, associated with the scalar data, can be defined as well. Dataset attributes are supported for both points and cells.

Each type of attribute data has a *dataName* associated with it. This is a character string (without embedded whitespace) used to identify a particular data. The *dataName* is used by the VTK readers to extract data. As a result, more than one attribute data of the same type can be included in a file. For example, two different scalar fields defined on the dataset points, pressure and temperature, can be contained in the same file. (If the appropriate *dataName* is not specified in the VTK reader, then the first data of that type is extracted from the file.)

- Scalars
  Scalar definition includes specification of a lookup table. The definition of a lookup table is optional. If not specified, the default VTK table will be used (and *tableName* should be "default"). Also note that the *numComp* variable is optional—by default the number of components is equal to one. (The parameter *numComp* must range between (1,4) inclusive; in versions of VTK prior to vtk2.3 this parameter was not supported.)

SCALARS *dataName dataType numComp*
LOOKUP_TABLE *tableName*
s_0
s_1
...
s_{n-1}

The definition of color scalars (i.e., unsigned char values directly mapped to color) varies depending upon the number of values (*nValues*) per scalar. If the file format is ASCII, the color scalars are defined using *nValues* float values between (0,1). If the file format is BINARY, the stream of data consists of *nValues* unsigned char values per scalar value.

COLOR_SCALARS *dataName nValues*
$c_{00} \, c_{01} \cdots c_{0(nValues-1)}$
$c_{10} \, c_{11} \cdots c_{1(nValues-1)}$
...
$c_{(n-1)0} \, c_{(n-1)1} \cdots c_{(n-1)(nValues-1)}$

- Lookup Table
  The *tableName* field is a character string (without imbedded white space) used to identify the lookup table. This label is used by the VTK reader to extract a specific table.

  Each entry in the lookup table is a rgba[4] (*red-green-blue-alpha*) array (*alpha* is opacity where *alpha=0* is transparent). If the file format is ASCII, the lookup table values must be float values between (0,1). If the file format is BINARY, the stream of data must be four unsigned char values per table entry.

  LOOKUP_TABLE *tableName size*
  $r_0 \, g_0 \, b_0 \, a_0$
  $r_1 \, g_1 \, b_1 \, a_1$
  ...
  $r_{size-1} \, g_{size-1} \, b_{size-1} \, a_{size-1}$

- Vectors

VECTORS *dataName dataType*

$v_{0x}\ v_{0y}\ v_{0z}$
$v_{1x}\ v_{1y}\ v_{1z}$

...

$v_{(n-1)x}\ v_{(n-1)y}\ v_{(n-1)z}$

- Normals
  Normals are assumed normalized $|n| = 1$.

  NORMALS *dataName dataType*

  $n_{0x}\ n_{0y}\ n_{0z}$
  $n_{1x}\ n_{1y}\ n_{1z}$

  ...

  $n_{(n-1)x}\ n_{(n-1)y}\ n_{(n-1)z}$

- Texture Coordinates
  Texture coordinates of 1, 2, and 3 dimensions are supported.

  TEXTURE_COORDINATES *dataName dim dataType*

  $t_{00}\ t_{01}\ \cdots\ t_{0(dim-1)}$
  $t_{10}\ t_{11}\ \cdots\ t_{1(dim-1)}$

  ...

  $t_{(n-1)0}\ t_{(n-1)1}\ \cdots\ t_{(n-1)(dim-1)}$

- Tensors
  Currently only 3×3 real-valued, symmetric tensors are supported.

  TENSORS *dataName dataType*

  $t^0_{00}\ t^0_{01}\ t^0_{02}$
  $t^0_{10}\ t^0_{11}\ t^0_{12}$
  $t^0_{20}\ t^0_{21}\ t^0_{22}$

  $t^1_{00}\ t^1_{01}\ t^1_{02}$
  $t^1_{10}\ t^1_{11}\ t^1_{12}$
  $t^1_{20}\ t^1_{21}\ t^1_{22}$

  ...
  $t^{n-1}_{00}\ t^{n-1}_{01}\ t^{n-1}_{02}$

$$t^{n-1}_{10} \; t^{n-1}_{11} \; t^{n-1}_{12}$$
$$t^{n-1}_{20} \; t^{n-1}_{21} \; t^{n-1}_{22}$$

- Field Data

  Field data is essentially an array of data arrays. Defining field data means giving a name to the field and specifying the number of arrays it contains. Then, for each array, the name of the array *arrayName(i)*, the number of components of the array, *numComponents*, the number of tuples in the array, *numTuples*, and the data type, *dataType*, are defined.

  ```
  FIELD dataName numArrays
  ```
  arrayName0 numComponents numTuples dataType

  $f_{00} f_{01} \cdots f_{0(numComponents-1)}$
  $f_{10} f_{11} \cdots f_{1(numComponents-1)}$
  . . .
  $f_{(numTuples-1)0} f_{(numTuples-1)1} \cdots f_{(numTuples-1)(numComponents-1)}$

  arrayName1 numComponents numTuples dataType

  $f_{00} f_{01} \cdots f_{0(numComponents-1)}$
  $f_{10} f_{11} \cdots f_{1(numComponents-1)}$
  . . .
  $f_{(numTuples-1)0} f_{(numTuples-1)1} \cdots f_{(numTuples-1)(numComponents-1)}$

  . . .

  arrayName(numArrays-1) numComponents numTuples dataType

  $f_{00} f_{01} \cdots f_{0(numComponents-1)}$
  $f_{10} f_{11} \cdots f_{1(numComponents-1)}$
  . . .
  $f_{(numTuples-1)0} f_{(numTuples-1)1} \cdots f_{(numTuples-1)(numComponents-1)}$

Examples

The first example is a cube represented by six polygonal faces. We define a single-component scalar, normals, and field data on the six faces. There are scalar data associated with the eight vertices. A lookup table of eight colors, associated with the point scalars, is also defined.

```
# vtk DataFile Version 2.0
Cube example
ASCII
DATASET POLYDATA
POINTS 8 float
0.0 0.0 0.0
1.0 0.0 0.0
1.0 1.0 0.0
0.0 1.0 0.0
0.0 0.0 1.0
1.0 0.0 1.0
1.0 1.0 1.0
0.0 1.0 1.0
POLYGONS 6 30
4 0 1 2 3
4 4 5 6 7
4 0 1 5 4
4 2 3 7 6
4 0 4 7 3
4 1 2 6 5

CELL_DATA 6
SCALARS cell_scalars int 1
LOOKUP_TABLE default
0
1
2
3
4
5
NORMALS cell_normals float
0 0 -1
0 0 1
0 -1 0
0 1 0
-1 0 0
1 0 0
FIELD FieldData 2
cellIds 1 6 int
0 1 2 3 4 5
faceAttributes 2 6 float
0.0 1.0 1.0 2.0 2.0 3.0 3.0 4.0 4.0 5.0 5.0 6.0
```

```
POINT_DATA 8
SCALARS sample_scalars float 1
LOOKUP_TABLE my_table
0.0
1.0
2.0
3.0
4.0
5.0
6.0
7.0
LOOKUP_TABLE my_table 8
0.0 0.0 0.0 1.0
1.0 0.0 0.0 1.0
0.0 1.0 0.0 1.0
1.0 1.0 0.0 1.0
0.0 0.0 1.0 1.0
1.0 0.0 1.0 1.0
0.0 1.0 1.0 1.0
1.0 1.0 1.0 1.0
```

The next example is a volume of dimension $3 \times 4 \times 5$. Since no lookup table is defined, either the user must create one in VTK, or the default lookup table will be used.

```
# vtk DataFile Version 2.0
Volume example
ASCII
DATASET STRUCTURED_POINTS
DIMENSIONS 3 4 6
ASPECT_RATIO 1 1 1
ORIGIN 0 0 0
POINT_DATA 72
SCALARS volume_scalars char 1
LOOKUP_TABLE default
0 0 0 0 0 0 0 0 0 0 0 0
0 5 10 15 20 25 25 20 15 10 5 0
0 10 20 30 40 50 50 40 30 20 10 0
0 10 20 30 40 50 50 40 30 20 10 0
0 5 10 15 20 25 25 20 15 10 5 0
0 0 0 0 0 0 0 0 0 0 0 0
```

The third example is an unstructured grid containing 12 of the 14 VTK cell types. The file contains scalar and vector data.

```
# vtk DataFile version 2.0
Unstructured Grid Example
ASCII

DATASET UNSTRUCTURED_GRID
POINTS 27 float
0 0 0    1 0 0    2 0 0    0 1 0    1 1 0    2 1 0
0 0 1    1 0 1    2 0 1    0 1 1    1 1 1    2 1 1
0 1 2    1 1 2    2 1 2    0 1 3    1 1 3    2 1 3
0 1 4    1 1 4    2 1 4    0 1 5    1 1 5    2 1 5
0 1 6    1 1 6    2 1 6

CELLS 11 60
8 0 1 4 3 6 7 10 9
8 1 2 5 4 7 8 11 10
4 6 10 9 12
4 5 11 10 14
6 15 16 17 14 13 12
6 18 15 19 16 20 17
4 22 23 20 19
3 21 22 18
3 22 19 18
2 26 25
1 24

CELL_TYPES 11
12
12
10
10
7
6
9
5
5
3
1
```

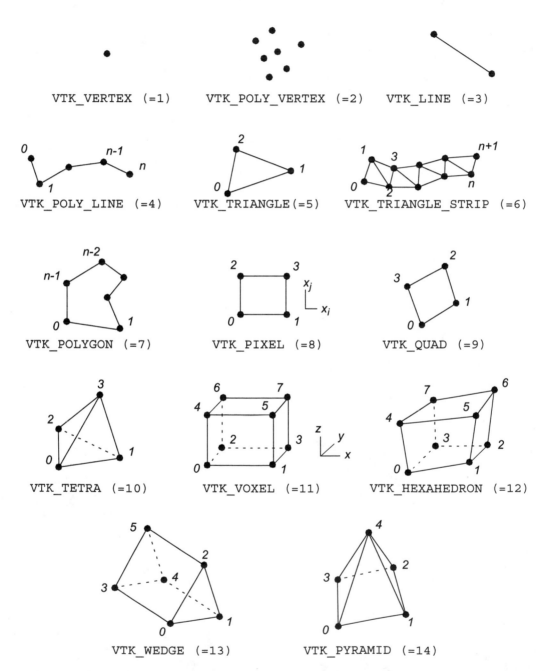

Figure 14–15 Cell type specification. Use the include file CellType.h to manipulate cell types.

```
POINT_DATA 27
SCALARS scalars float 1
LOOKUP_TABLE default
0.0    1.0    2.0    3.0    4.0    5.0
6.0    7.0    8.0    9.0    10.0    11.0
12.0    13.0    14.0    15.0    16.0    17.0
18.0    19.0    20.0    21.0    22.0    23.0
24.0    25.0    26.0
VECTORS vectors float
1 0 0    1 1 0    0 2 0    1 0 0    1 1 0    0 2 0
1 0 0    1 1 0    0 2 0    1 0 0    1 1 0    0 2 0
0 0 1    0 0 1    0 0 1    0 0 1    0 0 1    0 0 1
0 0 1    0 0 1    0 0 1    0 0 1    0 0 1    0 0 1
0 0 1    0 0 1    0 0 1
```

The fourth and final example is data represented as a field. You may also wish to see
"Working With Field Data" on page 194 to see how to manipulate this data. (The data file
shown below can be found in its entirety in $VTK_DATA_ROOT/Data/financial.vtk.)

```
# vtk DataFile Version 2.0
Financial data in vtk field format
ASCII
FIELD financialData 6
TIME_LATE 1 3188 float
 29.14    0.00    0.00 11.71    0.00    0.00    0.00    0.00
...(more stuff — 3188 total values)...

MONTHLY_PAYMENT 1 3188 float
  7.26    5.27    8.01 16.84    8.21 15.75 10.62 15.47
  ...(more stuff)...

UNPAID_PRINCIPLE 1 3188 float
 430.70   380.88   516.22 1351.23   629.66 1181.97   888.91 1437.83
 ...(more stuff)...

LOAN_AMOUNT 1 3188 float
 441.50   391.00   530.00 1400.00   650.00 1224.00   920.00 1496.00
 ...(more stuff)...

INTEREST_RATE 1 3188 float
  13.875 13.875 13.750 11.250 11.875 12.875 10.625 10.500
```

```
...(more stuff)...

MONTHLY_INCOME 1 3188 unsigned_short
 39   51   51   38   35   49   45   56
  ...(more stuff)...
```

In this example, a field is represented using six arrays. Each array has a single component and 3,188 tuples. Five of the six arrays are of type `float`, while the last array is of type `unsigned_short`.

Additional examples are available in the data directory.

## Chapter 15

CD-ROM

Along with this *User's Guide* you should find a CD-ROM. The CD-ROM contains source code, examples, data, documentation, and some applications. The following is a brief overview of the contents of the CD-ROM.

15.1 Source Code

The source code is located in two directories. For Windows users, the source code can be found in E:\vtk-src-windows (assuming that the CD drive is E:\). Unix users can find the source code in /cdrom/vtk-src-unix. Under this main directory, you will find several other subdirectories including Common, Rendering, Filtering, Graphics, Imaging, IO, Hybrid, and Patented. The directory Wrapping contains code related to the wrapping of VTK with Tcl, Python, and Java. These directories contains the .cxx/.h source code, and CMakeLists.txt that CMake uses during the build process.

15.2 Example Code

Along with the source code, you will find several hundred examples. The best place to look for examples is in the Examples/ directory. In addition, there are several hundred tests located in the source tree with the subdirectory names Testing/Tcl, Testing/Cxx, and Testing/Python. For example, in VTK/Graphics, you would find VTK/Graphics/Testing/Tcl, VTK/Graphics/Testing/Cxx, and VTK/Graphics/Testing/Python. These tests are not documented and are typically used to test the VTK distribution.

The Tcl, Python, and Java examples require that you have compiled the source code with Tcl support (Unix systems), or installed the appropriate PC binaries (Windows systems). The C++ examples will require you to set paths to include files and libraries as necessary.

15.3 Windows 9x/NT/ME/2000/XP Pre-Compiled Binaries

Pre-compiled binaries and libraries are available for Windows 9x/NT/ME/2000/XP systems. To install these binaries, run E:\setup.exe and follow the instructions as described in "Binary Installation" on page 8. (The actual installation executables are in the Windows-Binaries\ directory.)

15.4 Data

The data for the examples is located in VTKData/Data and the several subdirectories there. If you copy examples from the CD onto local disk, you may have to change paths in the example file to pick up the data on the CD. (Alternatively, the Tcl examples check the environment variable VTK_DATA_ROOT for the location of the data directory.)

15.5 Documentation

Documentation is available by browsing README.html found on this CD, and then clicking on the documentation link vtkhtml/html/classes.html. This is an alphabetized list of classes; clicking on a particular class gives you a description of methods and other information.

15.6 Regression Test Images

Also included in the CD is a directory of compressed regression test images (found in VTKData/Baseline). These images, which correspond to the examples in the various Testing/Tcl/, Testing/Cxx, and Testing/Python subdirectories, are used to validate the installation and execution of VTK.

15.7 Kitware Applications

On the CD in the Kitware/ directory you will find Windows9x/NT/ME/2000/XP binaries of Kitware commercial applications (e.g., *Acti*Viz, VolView and GoFly). These applications can be run on a trial basis for 30-days. At the end of this trial period, contact Kitware at kitware@kitware.com to purchase a license, or visit Kitware's on-line store at www.kitware.com to electronically purchase the license.

Index